EARTH'S MORNING:

OR,

THOUGHTS ON GENESIS.

Earth's Morning:

OR,

THOUGHTS ON GENESIS.

BY

HORATIUS BONAR, D.D.

NEW YORK:
ROBERT CARTER AND BROTHERS.
1875.

PREFACE.

WITHIN the last twenty years the book of Genesis has come very prominently into view, as the starting-point of numerous discussions. Science and history have combined to lead us back to it. The former has taken up its story of *creation;* the latter its *nationalities,* as contained in its genealogies and chronology.

The present volume does not enter into these discussions. It aims at exposition, not controversy. Its object is to investigate the meaning of each verse and word; that, having done so, the exact revelation of God in these may be brought out, and the spiritual truth evolved.

Here are the rudiments of all Scripture-truth. And in this book we have the first materials on which to construct a true theory of *development;*—development not simply of 'truth,' but of the purpose of God respecting man, and man's earth. The germs of true development are to be found here in their earliest stage. God here unfolds Himself and reveals His mind step by step; His truth expanding itself age after age, under divine superintendence, so as to prevent the consequences of mere human interpretations, or development according to the mind of man.

All Scripture connects itself with Genesis, and ought to be read in this connection; for it is not so much the later Scriptures that throw light on Genesis, as it is Genesis that throws light on the later Scriptures.

Genesis is not merely the first book of Scripture, but it is the fountainhead of revelation. It must be studied as such if we would understand it aright.

THE GRANGE, EDINBURGH,
November 1874.

CONTENTS.

GENESIS.

NOTES.

Thoughts on Genesis.

CHAPTER I.

IT is our 'faithful Creator' (1 Pet. iv. 19) who here speaks to us. He loves us too well to hide from us the great things which He has done. He would have us know how He made all things; and as He delighted in them, so He would have us delight in them.

When creation came forth, 'the morning stars sang together, and the sons of God shouted for joy' (Job xxxviii. 7); and when the different parts of the new creation come into being, there is likewise 'joy in heaven.' In both creations God is represented as taking divine delight (Prov. viii. 31); and in both cases 'He calls together His friends and neighbours, saying unto them, Rejoice with me' (Luke xv. 6).

'He has not left Himself without witness' (Acts xiv. 17): and in this first book of Scripture we have His testimony to Himself and to the work of His hands. Creation says 'God is love,' though on a lower key and with less distinctness than redemption. 'The invisible things of Him from the creation of the world are clearly seen, being understood by the things that are made' (Rom. i. 20).

And this creation bears testimony to the Son of God; for by 'Him He made the worlds' (Heb. i. 2). 'By Him were all things created that are in heaven and that are in earth, visible and invisible: all things were created by Him and for Him' (Col. i. 16). His connection with creation reveals to us His love. His love to man and man's world is no new thing. It did not begin when He was made flesh. Long before that we find that He 'rejoiced in the habitable parts of His earth, and that His delights were with the sons of men' (Prov. viii. 31).[1]

Nor less has the Holy Spirit His part in the mighty work. He 'moved' or 'brooded' over the face of the waters (Gen. i. 2). 'By His Spirit He hath garnished the heavens' (Job xxvi. 13). 'Thou sendest forth Thy Spirit, they are created' (Ps. civ. 30). In creation, as in redemption, Father, Son, and Spirit are spoken of as working. Creation belongs to each: and the love manifested in creation is the love of Father, Son, and Spirit. 'God is love:' and this, though in dimmer characters, is written on the heavens and earth, and shines out in sun, and moon, and stars. The Holy Spirit is

[1] Thus old Joseph Beaumont (1648) describes the manifestation of God and His love in creation, or rather in the purpose to create:—

'All things at first was God, who dwelt alone
Within His boundless self. But bounteous He
Conceived the form of the creation,
That other things by Him might happie be.
A way to ease its streams His goodness sought,
And at the last into a world burst out.'

love; and His love is in the sunshine of the first creation as truly as of the second.

Yet, though surrounded with the loving works of God each day, how little have we learned the lessons of heavenly love which creation teaches! How sadly do we misinterpret creation;—reading in it power, wisdom, majesty, and greatness; yet how seldom, LOVE!

HEAVEN and EARTH are the two places or regions whose history God, in His word, purposes to write.

Ver. 1. '*In the beginning God created the heaven* (or "*heavens*") *and the earth.*'

He who alone knows everything relating to these, secret or open, visible or invisible, physical or spiritual, undertakes to put on record for us, 'at sundry times and in divers manners,' some memorials of the varied wonders which have taken place within their bounds: to tell us something of what 'eye hath not seen, nor ear heard;' and what man, in the full sweep of his science, could not discover.

It is to 'heaven and earth' that He confines His information; and of things beyond these He says but little. Of what He intended them to be; of what He made them; of what they have been; and of what they yet shall be, when His great original purpose shall unfold itself in all its parts in the ages to come, He gives us His own account. Who but Himself could do this? Man may guess or fancy, God only can make known the things of God, in any part of His universe (1 Cor. ii. 11); the Architect alone can give us the eternal plan of His great structure, at least in outline, and tell us something of its carrying out, the process of erection, the hindrances, the successes, the failures.

The Bible is God's history of heaven and earth,—the only authentic history of them in existence. He is His own historian. He begins and ends His volume with these: and throughout it, they form the scene of His manifold plans and workings, the circle *over which* His divine love spreads itself in its manifestations of wisdom and power, and within which it gets vent to its eternal fulness, — a fulness which finds its way into all that which we call 'nature' (*i.e.* essential constitution of things, Rom. xi. 24), or 'creation' (*i.e.* things as coming from a Creator, Mark x. 6).[1]

He sets out with asserting His own prerogative as Creator, — His exclusive and undivided prerogative,— the originating One, the unbeginning One.[2] He tells us that the things we see are not self-produced, nor are they from eternity. They once were not. They once

[1] Both of these words are sanctioned by inspiration: the latter expressive of derivation from God, the former of the nature or essence of that which God has imparted to that which He has brought into being.

[2] 'Beginning' is sometimes used, as here, to mean former ages or times (Gen. x. 10; Isa. xlvi. 10); the corresponding Greek word (ἀρχή) is applied to Christ in reference to the *eternal past* (John i. 1; Prov. viii. 22). Hence His name, 'Him from *the beginning*' (1 John ii. 13), and 'the beginning' (or head) of the creation of God; and simply 'the beginning' (Col. i. 18). Hence He is named 'the beginning and the end' (Rev. i. 8, xxi. 6, xxii. 13); and we may notice that the words in which He is designated (Heb. xii. 2) 'author (or leader) and finisher' (bringer up of the rear), are derived from the above expressions of the Apocalypse.

began to be. It was He whose name is GOD (Elohim) that caused them to begin. He created them all, upper and lower, far off and near: thus giving the lie to the pretensions of every idol, and setting aside the gods of the heathen as *non-creators* (Ps. xcvi. 5; Jer. x. 11).

He gives us no *date* for His creation. In many places afterwards He *dates* His signs and wonders, as when He brought the deluge over earth, or led Israel out of Egypt. But He does not tell us *when* the heavens and earth began to be. He affirms that they had a beginning, but *when* that was He does not say. It might be six thousand or it might be sixty thousand years ago. At some time during that past period which He calls 'the beginning' (ἀρχή), before 'the ages' (αἰῶνες) commenced, (which we call *time*), He created the heavens and earth. His object here is to claim creation as His own direct and exclusive handiwork, and to declare that when it began to be, it did so not as the result of a certain pre-existing, eternal order of things or laws, but as the simple offspring of His creating power.

It seems strange that any other thought should have entered man's mind. Self-creation, how absurd! Chance creation, how irrational! Evolution by innate law, how unphilosophical! A palace self-built! A temple evolving itself from dead atoms! A city reared by chance! Life without a living One to originate it! How incredible!

The world declares its Creator (Ps. viii. 1). It has a voice which says beyond mistake, 'I did not create myself: He who created me is infinitely more glorious than I am' (Rom. i. 20). Even man's reason sees this;

yet it is *faith* that discerns it fully, and sees WHO it is that made all things. The God of the Bible is just such an one as we could suppose to be the Creator of the world. What 'nature' shows us of God is altogether in harmony with the Jehovah of Revelation. The jarring things in this fallen creation are only to be explained and reconciled at the cross. The gods of the heathen (taking the loftiest descriptions of these deities) could not have made the world. It is far too glorious a creation for Baal, or Buddha, or Jupiter to have produced, or even conceived. Look at this earth and these starry heavens, and say if the worship of such gods as these is not the height of unreason. But read what the Bible makes known of God, and you will say this is just such a God as could have planned and made such a world as this. Read what is written on these blue heavens above us, and you will say, 'He who made these heavens is just such a God as could have written this Book.'

He who made all things TO BE, must be the I AM, the Being of beings, the fountainhead of being. And who but He can give us the history of creation? Who but the Beginning and the Ending could speak from His own knowledge, and say thus with authoritative certainty, 'In the beginning God created the heaven and the earth.' Reason may speak of 'a God,' for the visible creation does declare an invisible Creator (Rom. i. 20); but when asked 'what is His name, and what is His Son's name, if thou canst tell' (Prov. xxx. 4), it is speechless. God Himself must be the revealer of the mighty secret. And He has revealed it. He has told us His name, and His

Son's name. Man cannot give a name to God: God Himself has done it; and the name is our refuge and our joy. 'The NAME of the Lord is a strong tower; the righteous runneth into it, and is safe.'

O folly of atheism! O folly of those who tell us that matter is God, and God is matter! A world without a Maker! A law without a Lawgiver! O misery of atheism! No glorious One, no perfect One, no blessed One. How sad! What a blank, if this were true! A sky without a star, a world without a sun!

What feebleness in reason! It cannot even name the name of God; and when it tries, as heathenism has done, to repeat the name first given, it does so with a stammering tongue. What could reason tell us of Jehovah? What can it reveal to us of that which is outside the creature? What can it say without a Bible? No voice of God heard or to be heard! Nothing but the dull, unmeaning clank of matter's dead machinery, as it moves round and on;—as it rises and falls;—as it grinds on its various axles,—self-impelled, or driven by fate! No heart, no soul; what we call conscience only a corporeal nerve; what we call affection, only a pulsation of the blood; what we call sorrow and joy, only the movements of a finer materialism,—the twitches of invisible nerves which science will soon be able to discover and control! No communication between Creator and creature! No message either of love or wisdom from One infinitely wise and loving! No Book of sure wisdom, whose teachings can be beyond dispute! Impossible. Surely this is the height, or rather the depth, of unreasoning credulity: sillier than the fables of heathendom, poorer than the dreams of pagan savage.

Ver. 2. '*And the earth was without form, and void; and darkness was upon the face of the deep.*'

Such was the state of this earth about the period when this history begins. It was a region of rayless darkness. Deepest night rested over it. It was without form, utterly shapeless in all its parts. It was *void*, that is, *unfilled up*. None of these things existed which make up its 'fulness' (Ps. xxiv. 1). In none of its parts was there any filling up. It was like the newly quarried block ere the sculptor's chisel has touched it. Evidently pointing back to this chaos, and using it as a figure, Job describes the grave as 'a land of darkness, and the shadow of death; a land of darkness; as darkness itself; of the shadow of death; without any order, and where the light is as darkness.' Jeremiah also describes the land of Israel, in the day of calamity, in language of the same kind (Jer. iv. 23), and Nahum predicts the ruin of Nineveh in words taken from this description of the original chaos (chap. ii. 10). Then further it is called 'deep,' or *abyss;* as if it presented one great mass of confused and turbid water.

How long this state of chaos might have existed, we know not. Not a word is said to intimate the time. It is not such a condition of things as might have been expected to come directly from the hand of God; for all that comes from Him is *perfect*, in its kind and in its degree. The infant is perfect in all its parts, though it is not a man; the seed is perfect, though it is not a flower or a tree. So that this chaos looks like the wreck of a former world, the ruins of some vast city or temple; it seems to be the result of the destruction of a previous state of things. It is not the infancy of a new creation that we behold, but the mangled and corrupting corpse of the old, which must be buried out of sight ere the new can be begun.

Ver. 2. '*And the Spirit of God moved upon the face of the waters.*'

How long or how brief the period of chaos was, it matters not. The appointed time was now come when these ruins were to undergo a change, and under the hand of the great Master Builder to rise into another temple. God's Spirit went forth to renew the face of creation.[1] Like a bird brooding over its eggs, and bringing life out of them by its vital heat, the Spirit brooded over the face of the deep or abyss. Immediately the quickening, renewing process began. In what way He wrought upon creation we know not, but His almighty

[1] The different senses of the word may be thus classified:—1. It means *wind* (Ex. x. 13), which is by a figure the spirit of the earth. 2. The spirit of a man (Prov. xviii. 4). 3. The spirit of the evil one (Judg. ix. 2, 3). 4. The Spirit of God (Isa. lxi. 1). In all of these there is *personality* implied, not mere vague influence. As when the spirit of a man is spoken of it is a *personality* that is referred to, not an *influence;* so when the Spirit of God is spoken of it is the same. It is of this personality in God, which comes out everywhere in Scripture, so vividly and so blessedly, that rationalism robs us; thereby snapping the firmest links that bind us, whose own personality is such a conscious thing, to Him who is infinitely personal, the three-one Jehovah.

touch produced some change, and vitality was diffused throughout creation (Job xxvi. 13; Ps. xxxiii. 6, civ. 30). And when the great restoring process is begun at the Lord's second coming, the Holy Spirit takes the same part in the work of restitution as at first; for it is when He 'is poured out from on high,' that 'the wilderness becomes a fruitful field' (Isa. xxxii. 15), thus identifying Him as at once the converter of the soul and the restorer of creation. He is the great agent in every process for restoring or perfecting or beautifying soul and body, nay the very earth itself. He is the author of all the loveliness that we see around us in herb, or shrub, or tree, or flower. All life, all beauty, all order, all perfection are from the Holy Spirit! How near should we feel Him to be, how gracious, how willing to quicken us, and to restore to us the lost beauty of our first creation!

Ver. 3. '*And God said, Let there be light, and there was light.*'

God put this question to Job, 'Where is the way where light dwelleth?' (chap. xxxviii. 19);[1] and this verse is an answer to this, as if God had said, 'The light dwelleth with me; for I issued the command, "Be light," and "light was."' Thus God claims light as His production,

[1] In Job xxxvii. 15 we read, 'Dost thou know when God disposed them, and *caused the light of His cloud to shine?*' As this seems to refer to the time of creation, are we not to understand that the light then made to shine was kindled by the 'cloud,' the same cloud which gave light to Israel in the desert, and is, in the latter day, to pour down its glorious brightness on Mount Zion? (Isa. iv. 5.) Is not the Shekinah the abode and fountainhead of light? 'who coverest Thyself with light as with a garment' (Ps. civ. 2).

as He had already claimed creation. The name of the Maker of light is *Elohim*,—God! 'I form the light' (Isa. xlv. 7). Of all light, both for soul and body, He is the Creator, nay the great central sun and source. 'I am the light of the world' (John viii. 12).[1]

God does not mean to teach us here that this was the first time that such a thing as light existed at all. There must have been light before, light with God, light with the angels, light in heaven, and, it may be, light shining on this very earth before its state of chaos began. It is a heathen or philosophic fable that darkness was the original and uncreated state of things.[2] Darkness is always associated with death in Scripture, just as light is with life. Nay, darkness is associated with 'him who has the power of death, even the devil;' he is 'the ruler of the darkness of this world;' and it is in connection with

[1] 'Hail, holy light! Offspring of heaven first-born,
Or of the Eternal co-eternal beam,
May I express thee unblamed? Since God is light,
And never but in unapproachèd light
Dwelt from eternity, dwelt then in thee
Bright effluence, of bright essence increate.
Or hear'st thou rather, pure ethereal stream,
Whose fountain who can tell? Before the sun,
Before the heavens thou wert, and at the voice
Of God as with a mantle didst invest
The rising world of waters dark and deep,
Won from the vast and formless infinite.'
—Milton's *Paradise Lost*, b. iii.

[2] We may notice that Christ adds here, 'He that followeth me shall not walk in darkness, *but shall have the light of life*,'—τὸ φῶς τῆς ζωῆς, 'the light of *the life*;' referring to chap. i. 4, 'the *life* was the *light* of men,' ἡ ζωὴ ἦν τὸ φῶς τῶν ἀνθρώπων. It is as the *living* One that He is the *light-giving* One.

the sin and doom both of him and his angels that darkness is spoken of (2 Pet. ii. 5; Jude 4).[1] Whatever may have been the origin of the darkness, we know that it covered the earth, thick and impenetrable in its gloom. But now the command went forth, and the darkness began to disappear. The sun did not at once show itself, but its light began to find its way dimly and faintly through the gloom, which from this time became less and less dense, so that there was now only partial darkness, such as there is in a dull misty morning. How this alteration was produced we know not. We know this, indeed, that a very slight change in the component parts or elements of our atmosphere, or in the proportions in which these elements are combined, would completely

[1] The question may arise here, What was the connection of Satan with this world before this time? Was it through him and his rebellion that the world was first wrecked and brought to the state of chaos and darkness mentioned in the second verse; was the restoration of light (third verse) an invasion of his domain? Was the fall a *partial* quenching of the light;—*partial*, for grace was to prevent its being total? Has not the state of the world ever since been one of darkness and subjection to the prince of darkness? Were not the words of Christ (Luke xxii. 53) an intimation of a crisis in the history of this darkness and of its ruler, as if it were for a time to succeed in its long-waged conflict with the light: *αὕτη ὑμῶν ἐστιν ἡ ὥρα, καὶ ἡ ἐξουσία τοῦ σκότους.* The expression, *ἐξουσία τοῦ σκότους*, is a very remarkable one, and full of solemn meaning. And had not the darkness on the cross a reference to the past history of the world, as the region of darkness and the kingdom of its prince? And does not the darkening of the sun and moon, just before the coming of the Lord, betoken that darkness had reached its destined crisis, both spiritually and morally, the earth being reduced to the state of chaos described by Moses; and therefore ready once more for the interposing power of Him who said at first, 'Let light be'?

disorganize it, and prevent its being the medium of light. Its transparency depends on combinations which require to be most nicely proportioned; so that as, on the one hand, an alteration in these could have produced the previous state of total darkness, so another change would, by restoring its lucidity, let in light upon the earth. Accordingly the command went forth which was to restore transparency to our atmosphere, which at this time was not only unfit to transmit, but even to bear, the dense humid vapours that loaded it. One word from Almighty lips effected the change, whatever it might be. He spake, and it was done! A word, no more! How easy with God! And He who lighted up the world, is the same as He that lights up the soul (2 Cor. iv. 6). He is the 'light of the world,' 'the morning star,' the sun of righteousness. His work in the soul is to fit it for receiving light, and then to pour it in. He restores transparency to the faculties of the soul, and then the light begins to find its way into each region and recess.

'On whom does not His light arise?' asks Bildad (Job xxv. 3). David says, in reference to the heavenly orbs, 'Their line is gone out through all the earth' (Ps. xix. 4); and our Lord says, 'He maketh His sun to rise on the evil and the good' (Matt. v. 45). What a declaration of grace does each day's light make to us! What a gospel does each sunbeam preach! He has not turned our earth into a region of 'outer darkness;' and this is grace. He still bids His sun go forth each morning to light our ways, sinners as we are; and this tells us of His willingness to give light to the darkest.

'Light is sown for the righteous!' Yes, it is *sown* in the fullest sense of that word; not merely *scattered abroad*, as commentators would have it, but *sown.* And this both naturally and spiritually. (1.) *Naturally.* This is not the time of light. A change has passed upon it by the fall. It has lost much of its purity and brightness. And the mere increase of its *intensity* would not serve unless its innocuous mildness were restored along with it. But there is a time predicted when 'the light of the moon shall be as the light of the sun, and the light of the sun shall be sevenfold, as the light of seven days' (Isa. xxx. 26).[1] Were the sun still to 'smite by day, and the moon by night' (Ps. cxxi. 6), this increase of light would be no blessing; but the 'restitution of all things' shall embrace in it a restitution of primeval mildness to the light; and who can tell how much of the removal of the curse upon the earth may be effected by this restoration of its genial, health-giving, fructifying properties to the light. But this is only the time of sowing. It doth not yet appear what it shall be. It is underground, or at most it is but in the blade or bud. And oh, if this its imperfect state be so very beautiful, what will not its perfection be in the

[1] There seems to be in reference to the *light*, just as in regard to all the various parts of creation, a time of crisis spoken of in those predictions, which point to the latter-day glory, and the previous signs of its arrival. The deterioration which took place at the fall, and which has been going on since, arrives at its *crisis* just at the coming of the Great Restorer. Everything is to be at its worst just when on the point of being renewed. Hence the darkness which is to be spread over the earth—'the day of darkness and gloominess,' etc.,—the darkening of the sun, and the withdrawal of the light of the moon, etc. (Matt. xxiv. 29).

coming harvest? if the bud be so fair and fragrant, what will be the expanded blossom in the new earth wherein dwelleth righteousness? The sowing time is one of tears, the shower and the sunshine mingled together; but the reaping time shall be glorious. (2.) *Spiritually.* This is the hour and the power of darkness. In one sense we have been brought into 'marvellous light' (1 Pet. ii.); 'Christ has given us light' (Eph. v.). But still we see through 'a glass darkly' (1 Cor. xiii.). Clouds fold themselves round us; sorrow and conflict, misgivings and faintings, beset us on each side. But sunshine shall yet burst on us. Light is *sown* for us; the light of an unsetting and an unsmiting sun; the light of Him who is light itself, and in whom is no darkness at all. Through this sowing time of darkness and sorrow we are passing to the reaping time of light and joy.

Ver. 4. *'And God saw the light, that it was good: and God divided the light from the darkness.'*

On the light that was now beginning to stream in upon the earth God fixed His eye. He *saw* the light; it did not steal in unobserved; it was not too trivial to attract His notice. It is minute, noiseless, unaccompanied with vast or terrible results. Yet He looked upon it, considered it, surveyed it fully. For each stray beam of light, each twinkle of the distant star, each undulation of the atmosphere, each faint ripple of the ocean, came under the notice of His eye. He sees them all. Such is the eye of Him with whom we have to do,—the eye that searches all things: yet the eye that delights to rest in love upon each part of the workmanship of His hand.

But God not only looked upon the light;—He tells us His opinion of it. It was *good.* Such is the divine verdict. He made it, He compounded it of its subtle elements, and therefore He knows it well. It was He who arranged its parts and proportions; it was He who twisted its sevenfold radiance; it was He who bade it shine forth in its beauty. Who, then, can speak of it as *He* can? And He calls it *good.* He approves of it, delights in it, sees it to be altogether suited to the end He had in view. It was 'good' in respect of its innate excellence, 'good' in respect of its beauty, 'good' in respect of its usefulness; one of the fairest, most needful, and most gladdening of all His handiworks; apparently feeble, yet working mightiest wonders; altogether noiseless, yet accomplishing each moment, by its silent, secret virtue, greater results than the lightning or the hurricane; calling forth little of man's wonder or praise, yet diffusing throughout earth a greater and more continuous amount of gladness than any other of the material elements; coming down each day upon us with reviving, refreshing, healing power. All God's creation is good, but light is especially excellent, the brightest and purest part of all. It is the only thing that cannot be soiled or stained. It corrupts not, it withers not. We may bend a sunbeam, or decompose a sunbeam, or shut it out of our dwelling, but we cannot soil it. It is the fairest, and freshest, and most heaven-like of all created things,—fittest emblem of Godhead, both of the Father and the Son.

The wise man says, 'Truly the light is sweet, and a pleasant thing it is for the eyes to behold the sun' (Eccles. xi. 7). Yes, it is even so; and what marvellous love does this betoken in our God!—love that was not dried up when sin entered, but only came out more largely in another form, that of *grace.* Though, doubtless, there has been some change in the light since the fall, some deterioration, yet still it is the most joyous thing in nature.[1] It might have been made so feeble as hardly to impart the needed warmth and light, or it might have been so intense (as it shall be when the fourth angel pours out his vial on the sun, Rev. xvi. 8) as to scorch the dwellers on the earth, but it has not been so. God has so attempered it to our condition that it suits us well. And in so suiting us sinners, it preaches to us the 'grace' of God. We might have been in the blackness of darkness, but we are not; and this is grace. We might have been in the everlasting burnings, but we are not; and this is grace.

And if light be so 'good' even now when shining through a sin-obscured atmosphere upon a cursed earth, what will it be hereafter when coming down through the new heavens upon the new earth, wherein dwelleth right-

[1] In that passage of the book of Esther which speaks of the deliverance of the Jews, we read that 'the Jews had *light,* and *gladness,* and *joy,* and honour' (Esth. viii. 16). And when referring to Israel's coming days of gladness, Isaiah says, 'Thy sun shall no more go down, neither shall thy moon withdraw itself; for the Lord shall be thine everlasting *light,* and the *days of thy mourning shall be ended*' (Isa. lx. 20). In both of these, as in other passages, the connection between light and joy on the one hand, and darkness and grief on the other, is strikingly brought out.

eousness? What will it be in the New Jerusalem, 'when the glory of God shall lighten it, and the Lamb shall be the light thereof.'

But next, God made a division between light and darkness. He then introduced the alternation between them which has continued ever since, the 'grateful vicissitude of day and night.' Now it was, perhaps, that the earth began again to revolve round its axis, God laying His finger on it and giving it the precise impulse needed. How simply is the division effected! No vast curtain alternately drawn and undrawn; no huge cloud wrapping the earth in its foldings, and again disappearing; no alternate kindling and quenching of the great source of light! God speaks, or stretches out His hand, or sends out one of those 'angels that excel in strength,' and the earth begins to revolve.[1] Thus the light and the darkness are sundered, or rather alternated.

[1] Milton speaks of *angels* as employed in altering the earth's position and motions:

'Some say He bid His angels turn askance
The poles of earth twice ten degrees and more
From the sun's axle; they with labour pushed
Oblique the centric globe.'

—*Paradise Lost*, Book x. line 668.

A commentator on the Apocalypse has thus finely caught up the thought: 'That angels do excel in strength we well know, from Ps. ciii., and other parts of Scripture. And when the proclamation, Who is able to open the book? was to be made throughout the region of the heaven and the earth and the deep, a strong angel was chosen to lift up the creation-filling voice. Whose is it to wheel the spheres in their courses, as if they were bowling balls? Whose strength is it that splits the solid rocks, that heaves the ocean from its oozy bed, that holdeth the winds, and anon letteth them fly amain? I believe these things are under the angels. God will not leave inanimate matter to

In the present state of our earth, and according to the present constitution of its inhabitants (both animate and inanimate—man, animals, and herbs), this alternation is absolutely needful. A world all light would be nearly as uninhabitable and unhealthy as a world all darkness! What wisdom and grace are displayed in this division! We sometimes say, What would become of us if it were always *night?* Have we ever thought what would become of us if it were always day? We need the change, and God has kindly thought on us and provided for it, in the surest, yet the simplest of all ways,—a way which, in producing this alternation, produces along with it a thousand other things, all pleasing and helpful. Let us

have the glory of these wonderful powers. He hath some intelligent ones, I make no doubt, who have the noble consciousness of working the will of God therein, and of rendering unto Him the homage which thence is due. This is the way in which these philosophists have dispeopled the world of intelligence, by supposing that, because they see not spiritual agencies in the mechanical and chemical regions of nature which they examine, therefore there are no such intelligences. But because we cannot see beings whose property it is to be invisible, are there therefore no such beings? Not to see them is the very condition of their being. If we could see them, they were not. But, for my part, I believe out of this text, that the strength, the main strength and force of things, consisteth in their subjection to mighty angels, who work the work under God, and so display the goodness—the creative goodness, and the riches of the providence of God. I reverence tradition; and I find herein the most venerable traditions of all men concurring, from the superstitions of my native land, which people the waters, and the earth, and the woods, and everything with invisible power and agencies, up to those of the remotest antiquity of which we have any record. In ascribing their strength unto the Lamb, therefore, I do think that these angels acknowledge all the powers which we are wont to call the powers of nature, the laws of the created world, to be due unto Him, and unto Him alone.'

praise Him for the revolving earth! Let us praise Him for the darkness as well as for the light, for the night as well as for the day![1]

Ver. 5. '*And God called the light Day, and the darkness He called Night.*'

God does not leave His works nameless. He who made them and knew their properties and uses, gave them their names; for names are the properties or features of a being or thing expressed to the ear or eye in words, so that He who hears or reads them may at once understand what the thing or being is, and wherein it differs from other things and beings. At the outset we see how God proclaimed His own name; now He names all His creatures in succession. Of the stars we read, 'He calleth them all by names' (Ps. cxlvii. 4). He tells us how to call His works. Let us not overlook this part of God's proceedings, nor forget Him as the *namer* of His works. When we speak of night or day, let us remember that He called them by these names. God does not count even the naming of His creatures beneath Him. He has named the heavens and the earth;

[1] Yet the darkness which God has so graciously given for repose and refreshment, and the quiet both of the vexed soul and the weary body, man has perverted and made a covering for his sin. Deeds which he fears to do in the light he reserves for the darkness. Hence the expression 'works of darkness,' 'children of night,' and such-like; and hence the use of the term darkness for 'sin;' and hence Satan is called 'ruler of this world's darkness;' and hence the difference between the world and God is spoken of as that between darkness and light: 'What communion hath light with darkness?' (2 Cor. vi. 14.)

He has named the changes of light and darkness. How closely and how lovingly must His eye have rested on our world! Is there anything, great or small, of which He was or is unmindful?

Ver. 5. '*And the evening and the morning were the first day.*'

Thus He sums up these wondrous statements by announcing the completion of a day,—of that period which embraces an evening and a morning. He begins now to number time. 'This is day the first.' Thus God *dates* His operations. He not only says, 'I did these things,' but He adds, 'I did them then and there, in such a place, and at such a time.' And throughout Scripture we may notice the same minute accuracy as to dates. In the prophets especially, God sets down the year, the month, the day when He spoke or did such and such things. How wonderful is it to see the Eternal One thus numbering the minutest sections of time! He is truly the God of order, and arrangement, and method, and accuracy, in all things great and small. It is the fool that takes no note of time. God takes note of it, and in so doing teaches us to prize it, and to 'number our days.' Though He 'inhabiteth eternity' (Isa. lvii. 16); though He calls Himself the 'Eternal God' (Deut. xxxiii. 27); though a 'thousand years are in His sight as yesterday' (Ps. xc. 4), yet He reckons up and names the smallest fragments of time. And He who says, 'Before the day was, I am He' (Isa. xliii. 13), is the same who records so carefully the date of His doings as Creator: 'It was evening and it was morning, day the first.'

What a marvellous day has this been! Order, light, motion, beauty, are all now begun. God has spoken the word! He has set His hand to the mighty work, and He will not rest till He has finished it, for He is the eternal Purposer, and all His purposes shall stand. There can be no defeat, no reversal. This earth is to be the sphere of His mightiest work; and in these first days' operations He is gathering together the stones for the foundation of His vastest and fairest temple, which, though delayed and obstructed for a season in its erection by Satan's craft and man's sin, shall not on that account suffer loss, but shall, by this temporary frustration, have its foundations laid broader and deeper, that its walls may rise the higher, and its compass stretch the wider, in the day of final restitution still in reserve for it. Scoffers may mock, and say, What! all this care for this little fragment of creation, this pebble on the shore of infinite space! Yes, even so. It is God's way, and shall be so to the last, alike in creation and redemption, 'for the stone which the builders rejected has become the head of the corner.'

Vers. 6–8. *And God said, Let there be a firmament* (or *expanse*) *in the midst of the waters, and let it divide the waters from the waters.* 7. *And God made the firmament, and divided the waters which were under the firmament from the waters which were above the firmament: and it was so.* 8. *And God called the firmament Heaven. And the evening and the morning were the second day.*

Up to this time the atmosphere had not been sufficiently dense to bear up the evaporating waters; for there had hitherto been two kinds of waters, the more solid waters of the abyss, and the evaporating waters rising from these. This evaporation would go on much more rapidly and incessantly if the atmosphere were *rarer* (or thinner), and yet it would not be borne up, but would rest over the immediate surface of the earth, so that there were these two bodies of water, the thicker and the thinner, the more solid and the rarer, in close conjunction with each other; the deep still throwing up its vapours, yet these vapours unable to rise, but mantling the earth with one vast watery shroud, allowing light to penetrate, yet not revealing the bright round disc of sun or moon, nor permitting the stars to show their sparkling lustre. The scene somewhat resembled the state of earth during those months when the waters of the deluge were descending; the waters above meeting the waters beneath, and wrapping the globe round with inexhaustible rain-clouds.

God again interposes. There is need for both kinds of waters in that world which He is preparing; but they must be separate, not intermingled. There can be no life either of man, or beast, or vegetable so long as they are thus mingled. Accordingly the word goes forth; the atmosphere is made to undergo a change by which it is enabled to bear up the vapours, and thus divide the two bodies of water, while the needful process of evaporation is still carried on. This atmosphere is made to stretch round the earth like a firmament or expanse, and bears up into its higher regions the ever-ascending waters of the lower, yet furnishing them also with the means of re-descent in the form of the gladdening shower. How simple the change! How vast and wonderful its results! Let us note the following passages in connection with all this:—Gen. vii. 11, 12; Job xxvi. 8, and xxxvii. 11, 18; Ps. cxlviii. 4; Prov. viii. 28; Jer. x. 10–13, li. 15, 16; Zech. xii. 1. Such are some of the references in Scripture to the two great bodies of water, upper and under, and such the way in which the division is ascribed to the *wisdom* of Jehovah; as if now His *wisdom* were specially coming forth, whereas hitherto it had been His *power* chiefly that had been seen.

God names and dates His handiwork. He calls the firmament, heaven or the lofty place; and this characteristic is in many ways and figures brought under our notice in Scripture (Job xi. 8; Ps. ciii. 21; Prov. xxv. 3; Isa. lv. 9). The love, the power, the majesty of God, His thoughts, His ways, His purposes, when compared with those of man, are set forth to us by the height of the heaven above the earth. And in this way He gives us some faint measure of these, some poor conception of His infinite glory and grace. This heaven or firmament shared the curse when man fell, either directly, by being in itself altered for the worse, or indirectly through the curse which took possession of the soil and exhaled into the mantling air. There is something in earth's atmosphere that blights and injures. It is not the same healthful, genial, joyous firmament that it was when God created it. And this deterioration has doubtless contributed to the decay of creation, to the propagation of disease, and to the curtailment of life; as if the seeds of death were in it after the fall as largely as were the elements of life before. After the deluge it became yet more deteriorated, and man's life became shortened,—gradually shortening in its dates till it reached the threescore years and ten. Since that time it has remained the same, and probably will do so during the short remaining period of earth's fallen state. We do indeed read of a period when the seventh angel is to pour out his vial into the air (Rev. xvi. 17) as if *its* crisis had come; so that having been brought into its worst condition, it was preparing to put on its best,—just as death is our way to resurrection-glory,—but how far this is connected with the curse or its removal we cannot say.[1] After this the firmament is made new; for just as there is a renewal of the earth, so there is a renewal of the encompassing atmosphere. This upper part of creation must partake in the deliverance from 'the bondage of corruption.' This renovation of the firmament will contribute to the superior brightness of sun and moon, which millennial days are to witness; and it will contribute to the restored longevity of man on earth when his days shall be 'as the days of a tree' (Isa. lxv. 22). How many of the groans of creation will this restoration, this healing of the firmament still! What health to the body, what vigour to the soul of man will it tend to impart, when the primeval blessing is renewed, which man's sin had so long restrained!

[1] The angel's pouring out his vial into the air may point both to the natural and spiritual crisis in the history of that part of creation, and indicate that the time is come when not only physical evils are to be purged out, but the spiritual wickedness in high places expelled.

What new strength, yet also what new gentleness of nature, will it bring to the animal creation! What new verdure to the leaf, what new beauty and fragrance to the flower will it impart! What a change in the blue of the heavens and in the green of the earth, when this long-poisoned air is at length disinfected by the healing touch of Him who has disease, with all its varied sources, seen and unseen, at His command; who, when on earth, showed Himself as the world's great Healer, and whose voice shall then be heard saying, 'Behold, I make all things new!'

It is in this old firmament, this defiled atmosphere of ours, that Satan has taken up his abode. How the darkness became his peculiar birthright we know not. How or when he was permitted to take up his abode in the air so as to become 'the prince of the power of the air,' and thence to wield the darkness, which is his heritage, we know not. We know simply that it is so. The encompassing air of earth is Satan's special residence and domain. From it he 'rains his plagues on men like dew.' In it he has set his throne, and from that throne he rules this world and its kingdoms, sending down his legions to scour the earth, to reinforce his citadels, to assail the Church, to form the bodyguard of Antichrist, to lead men captive at his will, till the day arrive when he shall be cast down from his seat and bound in the dark abyss for a thousand years, in preparation for the 'outer darkness' in which he is to dwell for ever. And who, believing these things, can look up into the fair yet wan azure without longing for the time when its sickliness shall be exchanged for the intensity of brightness? Who, remembering that it is the haunt of Satan and his angels, can gaze into its depths, either of midnight or of noon, without longing for the time when he shall be cast out, and these old haunts of his purified and filled with blessed angels carrying on their glad ministry both in the upper and lower regions of God's redeemed creation?

It is into the air that the saints are to be caught up to meet their reappearing Lord. In the progress of His descent to earth, He halts there with His angelic retinue; and pitching His pavilion on the confines of earth, He calls up His saints to meet Him; there to hear the final sentence of 'no condemnation' announced, to celebrate the completed union, to sit down at the marriage-supper, and to begin the long festivity of the bridal day.[1]

[1] These verses give us one of the first intimations of the distinction which Scripture preserves throughout, between 'the earthly' and 'the heavenly,' the upper and the lower chamber of the palace of the great King, this earth the lower, these skies (the floor of a more glorious heaven) the upper. At present it is full of ungodliness, it lies ἐν τῷ πονηρῷ; and the air is full of unclean spirits. But God's purpose must be fulfilled, and the day is coming when both shall be purged; when earth and heaven shall be reunited; when the ladder of communication between the upper and the lower region shall be set up (Gen. xxviii. 12; John i. 51); when, in the Jerusalem above, the risen saints shall dwell; and in the Jerusalem below, Israel shall abide; and over the whole blessed earth, now delivered from the curse, shall dwell the nations of the saved, rejoicing in the double splendour of the upper and the lower glory, filling the new firmament with the odour of their incense and the harmony of their songs. 'Change of air!' how common the expression, how little thought of what it implies!

Vers. 9, 10. '*And God said, Let the waters under the heaven be gathered together unto one place, and let the dry land appear: and it was so.* 10. *And God called the dry land Earth; and the gathering together of the waters called He Seas: and God saw that it was good.*

No change had as yet taken place upon the mighty mass of waters, which, like one vast and unbroken ocean, covered the whole earth. It was still in the condition referred to in the 104th Psalm, 'Thou coveredst it with the deep as with a garment: the waters stood above the mountains.' It was truly 'the melancholy main.' There was no life, no joy, no intercourse of happy being. If then the earth is to be the dwelling-place of life, there must be a change. These waters must, in part at least, be dried up. They are not wholly to pass off; for they are needful in many ways. They are needful for *beauty*, and God considers this in all His works. They are needful for supplying the atmosphere with vapours, and the earth with showers, as well as for filling the rivers which fertilize and gladden it. They are not indeed needful to the extent in which they now exist; and hence in the new earth they shall be largely curtailed, if not wholly done away (Rev. xxi. 1). But though in a measure needful, they must be changed, and their limits abridged. The land which they cover must rise above the surface, and become a fit habitation for man. *How* this was done we are not told. God said, 'Let it be, and it was so.' It is but a word, and all is done. This one word went, like lightning, through the deep foundations of earth, upheaving some parts into mountains, sinking others into valleys or deeper receptacles for the ocean. The process is alluded to in such passages as the following:—Job xxvi. 10, xxxviii. 8; Ps. xxxiii. 7, xcv. 5, cxxxvi. 6; Prov. viii. 29; Jer. v. 22; 2 Pet. iii. 5. Thus God refers to His operations, giving us indeed but little insight into the actual process, yet finely painting and spreading out before us its great features.

The two parts of the globe, thus formed, received their names from God, the dry land being called *earth*, and the gathering of the waters *seas*. God then looked upon His handiwork, surveying it in all its parts, and then pronounced it 'good.' The earth was 'good,' as it now spread itself out in all its inequalities of valley and mountain, of plain and precipice. A goodly earth! Fit to be the dwelling of creatures made in His own image; fit to be the material out of which the bodies of these creatures were to be fashioned; nay, fit to be the material out of which the body of His own Son was to be composed when He took flesh in the virgin's womb. A goodly sea! Goodly in its stretch of illimitable vastness, and in its transparent depths of unpolluted blue; goodly in the grandeur of its deafening storms, and in the still more wondrous grandeur of its majestic calms; goodly in all its moods whether of gloom or gladness, whether shadowed with the cloud, or spanned with the rainbow, or reflecting the sky's clear azure, or bathed in sunshine, or silvered with the moonbeam, or strewn with starlight; whether breaking in surges against the rock, or stealing in soft ripples over the glittering sand.[1]

If sea and earth be thus 'good,' according to God's own judgment, there can be no inherent evil in matter, as philosophy would teach. Matter is not in itself carnal. It is not the corrupter of spirit. It was created good, and it cannot corrupt itself. It is spirit that has done this. It is spirit, not matter, that is the fountainhead of evil.

What a world is this of ours for scenes, and associations, and remembrances! Earth and sea are full of them; evil and good, sorrowful and glad. What feet have trodden this earth, what eyes have gazed on that sea, since God brought them into being! Here holy men have lived; here the wicked have triumphed; here Abel's blood was shed; here Enoch walked with God; here angels have been visitors; here the Son of God abode; His footsteps were on the earth and on the sea. It is a small enough speck in the map of the universe, but it is the most wondrous of all. And though it has felt the curse for a season, it is to taste the blessing again. And when the mighty angel is seen descending to claim the heritage (Rev. x. 2), he sets his right foot on the sea, and his left upon the earth, in token of his having

[1] We may notice some things connected with this part of creation. (1.) God is very often spoken of as Maker of heaven and earth and sea, and as such to be praised (Ps. xcv. 4–6, cxxxvi. 6; Rev. xiv. 7). (2.) The wicked are compared to the troubled sea (Isa. lvii. 20). (3.) It is symbolically the place whence the four great beasts come up (Dan. vii. 3). (4.) It is the emblem of vastness (Job xi. 9). (5.) Of tumult (Ps. lxv. 7). (6.) Of instability (Jas. i. 6).

come to take possession of all things which God at first created.

The earth and sea are now the depositories of the dead. The bodies both of the holy and the unholy are resting there. But the day is near when out of that earth and that sea the trumpet shall call the dead. Neither shall be able to detain their victims when the life-giving voice shall be heard (John v. 28, 29; Rev. xx. 13). In the dust of earth, or deep beneath the roar of ocean, the saint sleeps soundly, as in a peaceful bed, till Jesus come. In that same dust, or beneath these same cold surges, the sinner lies, like the criminal in his cell, awaiting the summons of the Judge.

Vers. 11–13. *And God said, Let the earth bring forth grass,*[1] *the herb yielding seed, and the fruit tree yielding fruit after his kind, whose seed is in itself, upon the earth: and it was so.* 12. *And the earth brought forth grass, and herb yielding seed after his kind, and the tree yielding fruit, whose seed is in itself, after his kind: and God saw that it was good.* 13. *And the evening and the morning were the third day.*

The great work proceeds apace. We are made to trace its successive steps, rising the one above the other, in fair order. There was first *light*, followed by the division into day and night. Then there was the *atmosphere*, followed by the division of the upper and the under waters. Then the *earth*, with its division into sea and land, so that a soil was prepared, with all the needful accompaniments and appliances for making it productive. This having

[1] Literally, 'Let the earth sprout forth grass of green herbage (βοτάνην χόρτου, as the LXX. give it), seeding seed; tree of fruit, making fruit after its kind.'

been done, the word goes forth, and the clothing of the earth begins, with the two great divisions of grass and trees, the smaller and the larger orders of the vegetable creation. All these sprang up at once when the divine command went out.[1] And in this first generation there is contained provision for all future time, each class being so created as to be able to *reproduce itself.* They could not produce others of a different kind, or gradually pass up from a lower into a higher order; each could only bring forth his own. Each species was to be separate from the other, bringing forth seed 'after its kind.' There was to be no confusion, no intermingling of diverse kinds. Such was the law of the Creator, and in the carrying out of that law no mistakes occur, and no rebellion is ever seen. Man may mistake or resist the law, but into the lower parts of creation mistakes and self-willed resistances cannot come. All there is order, certainty, continuity, and regularity of the most perfect kind. There is a law woven into every fibre of their being,—a law from which no power or skill can force them to deviate. In that law we read the will of God Himself,—a will stamped upon all creation, and meeting us in every clod of the soil, and in every herb,

[1] Milton thus describes the scene:

> 'He scarce had said, when the bare earth, till then
> Desert and bare, unsightly, unadorned,
> Brought forth th' tender grass, whose verdure clad
> *Her universal face with pleasant green.'*—*Par. Lost,* Book vii. 313.

The description of Lucretius is so exact that we may cite it:

> 'Principio genus herbarum, viridemque nitorem,
> Terra dedit, circum colles, camposque per omnes
> Florida fulserunt viridanti prata colore.'
> —*De Rer. Nat* Book v. 781.

or flower, or tree. Why does this seed bring forth only grass, and that other only corn, and that other only the shrub or tree? Because God so willed it at first, and because He has left the stamp of that SOVEREIGN WILL upon the minutest seed that ripens under the autumn sun. Why do they never run into each other, and become mixed or confounded, but everywhere preserve the original diversity assigned to them six thousand years ago; so that when at any time man with all his skill fails to discriminate different seeds, he has but to appeal to these seeds themselves, by covering them with a little moist soil, and forthwith each seed declares itself without mistake or uncertainty? Because in each of these atoms of creation there is a force at work, far superior to man,—the will of Jehovah. Why does not the acorn sometimes through mistake produce the elm, or the fir-cone the chestnut, or the thistle-down the rose of Sharon? Why does not the fig-tree sometimes pass into the vine, or the branching cedar shoot up into naked stateliness, and put on the coronet of the palm? In all these myriads of seeds there is oftentimes abortion, but never a mistake. The seed may rot and die, so failing in its end, but otherwise it fails not. In a perfect world there would be no abortion or decay, but this world of ours is blighted, and therefore failure exists. But it is simply failure, not mistake. It is JEHOVAH'S WILL that they should often prove abortive, in order to be a witness to sin and the curse; but it is also His will that there should be no mistake or confusion, that it may be seen, even in the lowliest, that He is still the sovereign of creation. Thus has God engraven the insignia of His sovereignty upon all His handiworks, even the minutest. The form and colour of each seed, each leaf, each blossom; all these continuing to this day without mixture or confusion, are the badges of His sovereignty as well as the witnesses of His wisdom and love.

This day's work, which God pronounces good, and which He *dates*, as in other places, may be called either the clothing or the painting of creation. Figure, size, proportion, had all been given before, but still earth was a dark-brown mass of mingled soil and rock. But now the command goes out for its adornment. For God's purpose is to make it a world of beauty as well as of stability, seeing He is Himself the possessor and source of all that is beautiful. He chooses *blue* for the colour of sky and sea, but he chooses *green* for the hue of earth. His word spreads over its varied surface the green mantle which has from that day to this made it to be known as the 'green earth.'[1]

[1] Let us notice two special references to earth's greenness. In Song of Sol. vi. 11, the Spouse says, 'I went down into the garden of nuts to see the *greenness* of the valley,' for it is greenness, not fruit, that is signified by the word (see Job viii. 12); the *beauty* of the *green* valley is what is reterred to. In Rev. iv. 3, the rainbow round the throne was 'to look upon like an *emerald*.' As the emerald is green, so the symbolical rainbow, all tinctured with that hue, declares the connection of the scene mentioned in the chapter with the *green earth*. It seems like the reflected verdure of earth formed into a canopy above the throne, to show that He who sat upon the throne was earth's Redeemer and King. That emerald rainbow is God's covenant-pledge to creation that He remembers it, and will ere long restore to it its blighted verdure.

Vers. 14-19. '*And God said, Let there be lights in the firmament of the heaven to divide the day from the night* (*between the day and between the night*); *and let them be for signs, and for seasons* (*set times*), *and for days, and years:* 15. *And let them be for lights in the firmament of the heaven, to give light upon the earth: and it was so.* 16. *And God made two great lights; the greater light to rule the day, and the lesser light to rule the night: He made the stars also.* 17. *And God set them in the firmament of the heaven, to give light upon the earth,* 18. *And to rule over the day and over the night, and to divide the light from the darkness: and God saw that it was good.* 19. *And the evening and the morning were the fourth day.*

There had been *light*[1] before, but there are to be *lights;* the light hitherto had been dimly diffused over creation. Its *source* has not yet become visible. The firmament was still clouded, so that neither sun nor moon could be seen; and it was under this cloud that God sowed His seed, and planted His herbs and trees. But now the veil is to be brushed away, and the two great centres of radiance to become visible. They, with the stars, had been created at first, as parts of the heaven and earth spoken of in the first verse. But not till now are they unveiled; for now they are needed to nourish and mature the springing plants of herb and tree, which God had on the previous day been planting. The operations of the third day suited best the *shade*, but now something more is required,

[1] In Ps. lxxiv. 16, the distinction between the light and the source of light is marked, while both are ascribed to God: 'Thou hast prepared light and the sun.' The words of the 136th Psalm are a commentary on the whole passage, teaching us, moreover, the infinite love of God in this part of His creation, so that we cannot enjoy the brightness of sun, or moon, or star, without feeling that 'His mercy endureth for ever.' Everlasting mercy is written on these great lights of the firmament. And as truly as they tell His love, so truly do they 'declare His glory' (Ps. xix. 1).

and the sun bursts forth in its strength. But let us more particularly mark the uses here assigned to these luminaries.

1. The first use is to divide between the day and between the night. Here again the process of *division* comes in, the sun and moon being the instruments for effecting it. This division is not arbitrary or useless. Man's health and comfort require it. The wellbeing of all the various tribes of being, living or lifeless, requires this. Without it, the present condition of creation would be undermined, and creation ere long destroyed. Without it there could be no order, no regularity. When day and night are confounded, then man suffers; for no law of creation can be violated without suffering or evil following. But while man neglects this regularity of division at the call either of pleasure or business, God keeps up His silent protest in the heavens against him. He prevents that disorder from becoming general by the fixture of the heavenly orbs, whose inexorable law of revolution is always bringing back order and regularity, restraining the folly and disorderliness of man.

2. *To be for signs and for seasons, for days and for years.*—(1.) *Signs;* that is, tokens, by means of which God points to something not before the eye, past, present, or to come, as the rainbow after the flood, or as the Sabbath, which was to be a 'sign.' These heavenly bodies are specially to be used as 'signs' in the latter day (Luke xxi. 25; Acts ii. 19). (2.) *Seasons;* that is, set times, not only the seasons of the year, but festivals and solemn days; all the recurring periods of man's time, great or small (Isa.

lxvi. 23; 1 Chron. xxiii. 31; Ps. civ. 19). Thus God has committed the keeping of man's time to the unintelligent, nay, the inanimate creation. The sun and moon keep time for man; he cannot do it for himself; and the regularity of the world as to *time* must be entrusted to creatures without mind or life. Much as man can do, he cannot keep or measure his time without their aid. He can construct an instrument for this, or he can let the sun or moon do it for him; but without some such appliances he soon loses all count of time. Thus, at every turn man's helplessness comes out, and he is made to feel his littleness as well as his greatness; his dependence on the inanimate creation as well as his superiority to it.

3. *To give light.*—Several times over this is stated, as if it were their prime and special object, to which the others were subordinate. They are man's servants—his torch-bearers, appointed for this service by God.[1] They shine, not for themselves, but for Him. It is towards Him that each ray is bending, as if doing homage to its King. Yet man in his folly has worshipped the light as if it were God! The master has bowed down to the servant: Oh, folly and stupidity beyond conception! Man alone

[1] Is not this the special reference in the 8th Psalm, when David exclaims, 'What is man, that Thou art mindful?' etc. It is not merely to contrast the magnificence of the starry arch with the meanness of man, as is generally supposed. It is rather to ask, What is man, that Thou shouldst make such provision for his comfort and wellbeing as these skies do furnish? What is man, that Thou shouldst light up so many sparkling orbs to give light to him? In reference to the stars being man's servants, Theodoret has somewhere this idea, that they turn their back upon the heavens in order to give light to the earth —νῶτα διδόντας οὐρανῷ.

mistakes or forgets the end of his creation; other creatures, even the inanimate, fulfil their end!

4. *To rule the day and night.*[1]—Each has his royal throne assigned. They sit like monarchs in the firmament, determining the bounds of day and night; that the light may not encroach upon the darkness, nor the darkness on the light, but each have its allotted share of time. They sit also there as if to regulate the movements of man, prescribing to him what these movements are to be during the day, and during the night,—saying to man each morning, Arise, and go forth to thy labour; and each evening, Return and rest. Thus these 'powers that be (emblems of the princedoms of earth) are ordained of God.' It is His purpose that they are fulfilling; it is by His law that they are moving, and revolving, and radiating, carrying healing and gladness as well as light along with them,—being to man 'the ministers of God for good.'

In all this we see again the impress of Jehovah's *sovereign will.* It is that *will* that shines out in the day, or darkens in the night. It is that *will* that is to be traced in the hours, and days, and weeks, and months, and years, and cycles, that give to earth and its inhabitant man, a chronology and a history. To all this God sets His seal.

[1] As each of the six periods is measured from the evening to the morning, the *moon* must have appeared first. In that night when her face was first unveiled she began her less potent rule, and it was not till morning that the sun burst forth. So it is first the Church, 'fair as the moon,' shining in and ruling this world's deep midnight, till the morning wanes and the long-hidden Sun of Righteousness goes forth 'like a bridegroom out of his chamber,' to take His place in the firmament, and with His bride, the Church, to rule the endless day.

It was good. And again, He dates His work, 'The evening was, and the morning was, day the fourth.[1]

Vers. 20–25. '*And God said, Let the waters bring forth abundantly the moving creature that hath life* (lit. *let the waters make to creep the creeping thing, soul of life,* i.e. *that has life in it*), *and fowl that may fly above the earth on the open firmament of heaven* (lit. *and let fowl fly upon or above the earth on the face of the expanse of the heavens*). 21. *And God created great whales* (lit. *the great sea-monsters*), *and every living creature that moveth* (or *creepeth*), *which the waters brought forth abundantly, after their kind, and every winged fowl* (lit. *every fowl of wing*) *after his* (*its*) *kind: and God saw that it was good.* 22. *And God blessed them, saying, Be fruitful, and multiply, and fill the waters in the seas, and let the fowl multiply on the earth.* 23. *And the evening and the morning were the fifth day.* 24. *And God said, Let the earth bring forth the living creature* (lit. *the soul of life*) *after his kind, cattle, and creeping thing, and beast of the earth after his kind: and it was so.* 25. *And God made the beast of the earth after his kind, and cattle after their kind, and everything that creepeth upon the earth after his kind: and God saw that it was good.*'

We have seen the creation of vegetable life, we have now to mark that of animal life. We are now climbing upwards in the scale of being, yet each step is a distinct

[1] It is interesting to notice the many applications made in Scripture of the heavenly bodies as emblems of the spiritual. (1.) God is a sun and shield (Ps. lxxxiv. 11). (2.) Christ is the Sun of Righteousness (Mal. iv. 2); the light of the world (John viii. 12); the morning star (Rev. ii. 16); the dispeller of the darkness (2 Sam. xxiii. 4). (3.) The Church is fair as the moon (Song vi. 10); clear as the sun (Song vi. 10); the moon under her feet (Rev. xii. 1); crowned with stars (*ib.*); the saints are to shine as the stars (Dan. xii. 3); with different glories (1 Cor. xv. 41); as the sun in his might (Judg. v. 31); as the sun in the kingdom of their Father (Matt. xiii. 43). (4.) Christ's ministers are likened to stars (Rev. i. 16–20). (5.) Apostates are likened to wandering stars (Jude 13). (6.) It was a star that lighted the wise men (Matt. ii. 2). (7.) At the coming crisis of earth's history, all these heavenly orbs are to be shaken and darkened for a season (Mark xiii. 25).

one. There is no confusion nor intermingling with each other. The rock does not gradually become a vegetable, and the vegetable gradually pass into an animal. No. There is entire separation in each class, and at every step the fiat of the Creator must come in. They cannot, by any innate power, or intermixture of species or development of latent power or capacity, create or produce each other. The stone remains the stone, however rough, and the gem remains the gem, however precious. The tree remains the tree, neither passing downwards into something less, nor upwards into something higher. The flower abides the flower, neither casting off its petals and shrinking into a clod, nor expanding its blossoms into the plumage of the dove or the eagle. On each, God has imprinted the law of its kind, which it cannot pass nor annul.

God first *created*, then He *arranged*, then He *enlightened*, then He *divided*, then He *clothed*, then He *regulated time;* now He proceeds to *people* the earth. Up to this time it might be fair and goodly, but it was unpeopled. No life was to be found on it. Now it was to be peopled by what are called 'things having a soul of life,' or living soul. The inanimate creation had been completed, the animate must now be proceeded with. In this the order of procedure is, first, the creatures belonging to the sea; second, those belonging to the air; third, those belonging to the earth. This was the order in which these three parts or regions of creation were prepared, and so the same order is preserved when providing inhabitants for them.

1. *The creatures of the sea.*—These we know are the lowest in the scale of creation, so God begins with these. And all species which the sea contains He creates at once; from the great sea-monsters down to the meanest reptile. God Himself gives us in the book of Job (chap. xli.) a description of Leviathan as a specimen of these (see also Ps. civ. 26). How mighty in power and manifold in wisdom must their Creator be! On every element He has representatives of His might and majesty. In the rugged caves of ocean there are creatures to glorify Him, so that the 'dragons and all deeps' are called on to praise Him (Ps. cxlviii. 7). And from the depth of ocean there comes up a hallelujah to Him 'who alone doeth great wonders; for whatsoever the Lord pleased, that did He in heaven and in earth—*in the seas and all deep places*' (Ps. cxxxv. 6). Nay, the voice which John heard ascribing blessing to the Lamb for ever, was from 'such as are in the sea, and all that are in them' (Rev. v. 13).

2. *The creatures of the air.*—We take the marginal reading as the true one, 'let the fowl fly,' that is, let the fowl be created, and let them fly in the firmament, there taking up their abode. Of these two, God has given His own description (Job xxxix. 13–26, 27), singling out specially the peacock, the ostrich, the hawk, and the eagle. Thus the air is vocal. It has a hallelujah of its own. The 'flying fowl' praise Him (Ps. cxlviii. 10); whether it be 'the stork that knoweth her appointed time' (Jer. viii. 7), or the 'sparrow alone upon the house-top' (Ps. cii. 7), or 'the raven of the valley' (Prov. xxx. 17),

or the eagle 'stirring up her nest, and fluttering over her young' (Deut. xxxii. 11), or the turtle making its voice to be heard in the land (Song ii. 12), or the dove winging its way to the wilderness (Ps. lxv. 6). This is creation's harp (truer and sweeter than Memnon's), which each sunrise awakens, 'turning all the air to music.'

3. *The creatures of the earth.*—The beast, the cattle, the creeping thing; all that the earth now rears upon its bosom. Of these also God has given us His description (Job xxxix. 1–12, 19), proclaiming His wondrous works. Thus earth too has her hallelujah, for 'beasts and all cattle' (Ps. cxlviii. 10) are summoned to join in the chorus, that the diapason of creation may be complete.

Thus sea, air, earth, are peopled, the three regions referred to in Ps. viii., which is quoted by the apostle (Heb. ii.), as so specially containing man's charter, and setting forth God's purpose. The 'soul of life' has now been given; sentient beings have taken up their abode on earth; beings capable of suffering and rejoicing. It is in LIFE that God is now manifesting Himself. Hitherto it has been in order, in shape, in colour, in beauty; now it is in *life*,—that which is nearest to His own nature, likest to Himself. The manifestation which it is His purpose to make of Himself is becoming more and more complete.

He blesses them, and pronounces them 'good.' He pours into them all the blessing of which their nature is capable, and gives it to them in perpetuity. For when God blesses His creatures, He is looking forward into the far future, and securing to them all that that future stands in need of. And having blessed them, He bids them multiply, as if He would point out that the blessing which He gives is an active and communicative blessing, to be spread abroad. And here we learn that the propagative powers of creation are the direct impartation of God. They are not a mere natural property or physical law, but the special gift of God. His sovereign will, His authoritative command are here. Fruitfulness and barrenness, the power to increase, or the drying up of that power, are from His hand! (Ps. cxiii. 9.) Hence it is that David gives vent to his joyful confidence, 'O Jehovah, Thou preservest man and beast: how excellent is Thy loving-kindness, O God! therefore the children of men put their trust in the shadow of Thy wings' (Ps. xxxvi. 7). And hence also, after surveying the work of God's hands, he thus concludes: 'I will sing unto the Lord as long as I live; I will sing praise to my God while I have any being. My meditation of Him shall be sweet; I will be glad in the Lord' (Ps. civ. 33, 34).

Vers. 26-31. '*And God said, Let us make man in our image, after our likeness; and let them have dominion over the fish of the sea, and over the fowl of the air* (lit. *heaven*), *and over the cattle, and over all the earth, and over every creeping thing that creepeth upon the earth.* 27. *So* (lit. *and*) *God created man* (lit. *the man*) *in His own image: in the image of God created He him; male and female created He them.* 28. *And God blessed them: and God said unto them, Be fruitful, and multiply, and replenish* (*fill*) *the earth, and subdue it; and have dominion over the fish of the sea, and over the fowl of the air, and over every living thing that moveth* (lit. *creepeth*) *upon the earth.* 29. *And God said, Behold, I have given you every herb bearing seed* (lit. *all grass seeding seed*), *which is upon the face of all the earth, and every tree, in which is the fruit of a tree yielding seed* (lit. *seeding seed*) ; *to you it shall be for meat.*' 30. *And to every beast of the earth, and to every fowl of the air* (lit. *heavens*), *and to every thing that creepeth upon the earth, wherein there is life* (lit. *the soul of life*), *I have given every green herb for meat: and it was so.* 31. *And God saw every-thing that He had made, and, behold, it was very good. And the evening and the morning were the sixth day.*'

The great temple of creation has now been reared and roofed in. It is perfect in its kind,—a glorious manifestation of its glorious Maker. But it wants a worshipper. It is at best but splendid desolation—a silent though wondrous city of the dead.

There must be a living inhabitant, and a living worshipper. God cannot rest in His work till this is done. And, accordingly, the completion of the work proceeds. But it is the most important part, and must be planned with care. The great idea has been in the divine mind from eternity, and is now to be executed; but in a way which manifests the profound interest which God took in what He was about to do. Hitherto it has been but the swift forth-going of a command; now there is a consultation, as if God were solemnly deliberating upon the great design. Hitherto it had been, 'Let there be;' now it is, 'Let us make;'—it is not a command to the elements, to bring forth what they contain; it is a work, spoken of as specially God's own. The creature to be formed must come more directly from the divine hand than any other; and hence we often read elsewhere, 'He made us, and not we ourselves.'

And with whom is this consultation held? 'With whom took He counsel?' Not with angels surely. But with Himself—Father, Son, and Spirit. The peculiar form of expression is not made use of without a purpose. And this is the more to be noted, because afterwards, when each of the Three Persons had come out as it were into greater distinctness of manifestation, so that sometimes the Father speaks, and at other times the Son, and at other times the Spirit, this plural form of speech is not made use of. It is always I, not we. The same remarks apply to the use of the word *our* immediately after.

The being about whose formation this consultation was held, was he to whom the name of *man* was to be given, as we read, 'He called their name Adam (or man), in the day when they were created' (chap. v. 2). The word signifies red, or ruddy, referring to the colour of his flesh, either as it appears under the skin, or as it is seen shining through the skin, forming the bright complexion of health; the token of perfect and vigorous manhood and womanhood. And hence it is said of Christ, who in body as well as soul was the perfection of manhood, 'He that sat on it was to look upon like a jasper and a sardine stone' (Rev. iv. 3). It is the same word used in the following passages:—1 Sam. xvi. 12: 'He was *ruddy* and withal of a beautiful countenance;' Song v. 10: 'My beloved is white and *ruddy;*' Lam. iv. 7: 'Her Nazarites were purer than snow, they were whiter than milk, they were more *ruddy* in body than rubies; their polishing was of sapphire.'

This being is to be made 'in our image, after our likeness' (this is repeated in ver. 27). The use of both image and likeness is not a repetition. Its meaning is, 'Let us make man in our image,' in order that he may resemble us, and so be our representative, the reflector of our image to others. The two words are used in Ex. xx. 4, 'Thou shalt not make unto thee any graven image, or any likeness of anything,' that is, anything intended to resemble or represent anything whatever on earth. God's special characteristics may be summed up in these: intelligence, holiness, blessedness. Man therefore was to be an intelligent, holy, blessed being; in these great features differing from and rising above all that had hitherto been created (see 1 Cor. xi. 7; Eph. iv. 24; Col. iii. 10). The idea of some, that the image of God consisted in his having dominion, is one resting on no Scripture, and is disproved by the passage before us, in which the possession of dominion is described as the *result* of his having the image, and so could not be the image itself. Man was to be God's king, *because* he was fitted to be so by being made in the image of God.

Then the gift of dominion follows. This kingship was directly from God. It was unlimited in so far as earth was concerned. All things were put under him, setting before us at the outset the great truth that it was God's purpose to rule the earth by a king, and that king not an angel, but a man (Heb. ii. 6). The further exercise of this dominion is afterwards expressed by 'subduing the earth,' bringing everything into submission to his royal will, and into conformity with God's plan and purpose. Not as if there was to be *resistance* to man in any part of creation, requiring coercion, but merely such a kind of resistance as he was to have in cultivating Eden; such a kind of resistance as implied that creation stood waiting for the utterance of his will, and the forth-putting of his power.

Then there comes the blessing (ver. 28). God blessed them, that is, He poured into them all the goodness, and the life, and the joy that they could contain, and declared that such as they were just now, such they were to be in time to come. This is the filling of the vessel, according to its measure, with the fulness of God. In virtue of this blessing, they were to be fruitful, and multiply, and fill the earth. And here, as we noticed formerly, is the true source of all power of propagation in man or beast, in herb or flower. The earth at first was 'void,' or empty, but now it was to be 'filled' (Ps. xxiv. 1).

Then food is granted. All that the earth brings forth of herb and tree. It would seem by the statement of the 30th verse, that the beasts and fowl were restricted to the herb of the field, while to man was specially assigned the fruit of the tree. That man was restricted to the latter cannot be said; but the special food befitting his higher nature was the fruit of the tree. No *life* was then taken for food; life did not need to be supported by death. Death was not then a necessary prerequisite to any creatures obtaining food for the body. The lion did eat straw like the ox, as it did even afterwards, in the ark, during the year of confinement there. Such was the divine law, and such was the true condition of creation ere sin had disordered the earth.

Then, when all is finished, God looked round upon His handiwork, surveying all its parts. He gives His verdict

—'very good.' He is well pleased, and He tells us this. Such is His estimate of creation. It is all perfect, all according to His plan and mind, each of its parts exhibiting the idea which He designed. And again He dates His work: 'The evening was, and the morning was, day the sixth.'

And is this the six days' work that we see around us? Yes; but how changed! It is not wholly ruined, for God has interrupted it in its fall, so that by its midway position it should point forward to restitution while it proclaims decay. But still it is not what God made it, and man is its destroyer! It is man that has made creation groan. It is man that is the undoer of what the great Maker had done.

And man himself, what is he now? The image of Elohim, where is it? Marred, faded, gone! A few fragments still remaining, a few torn leaves to show what has been the flower! We cannot recognise him as the same being. Man, 'thou hast destroyed thyself!' Compare thy present and thy former self, and be ashamed. Let the contrast between the first Adam and thyself humble thee profoundly; and let the contrast between the second Adam and thyself humble thee more profoundly still. The contrast, how sad! The ruin, how awful! And *you* did it!

Retrace your steps, get back the lost image; get it back in God's way. Thy connection with the first Adam is thy undoing; nothing but connection with the Second can be thy salvation. 'Put on Christ;' let every lineament of the earthly Adam be erased; let each feature of the heavenly Adam be engraven upon thee. Aim high; yet not in pride, as man did, and fell. To have the image of God is one thing, and it is right and blessed; to 'be as God' is another, and it is awfully presumptuous,—it is self-deification, and has been the ruin of the race. The day of perfection, and restoration, and dominion is coming; but it has not yet arrived. Live looking for it; live as men who believe it; walk worthy of it. It will then be seen what a God of glory our God is, and what blessedness there is in being knit to the second Adam, who shall then be manifested as the head of creation and the King of Glory.

CHAPTER II.

Ver. 1. '*Thus* (or *and*) *the heavens and the earth were finished, and all the host of them.*'

GOD now proclaims the completion of His creation-work.[1] It was no mere sketch or outline: it was no half-finished plan: it was a 'finished' work. A goodly and glorious work! Not merely on account of what we see and touch in it, but on account of what we cannot see or touch. For creation is full of secrets. Science, in these last days, has extracted not a few, but how many remain secrets still! What a multitude of *hidden* wonders does each part of creation contain! Outwardly, how marvellous for the order, beauty, utility of all its parts; inwardly, how much more marvellous for the secret springs of life, motion, order, health, fruitfulness, and power! Each part, how wondrous in itself, as perfect in its kind; yet no less wondrous, as wrapping up within

[1] It may be well to notice that the word 'finished' here is the same as is used in such passages as the following: Ex. xl. 33, 'So Moses *finished* the work;' 2 Chron. vii. 11, 'Thus Solomon *finished* the house.' And as of these types of redemption, the tabernacle and temple, it is said they were 'finished,' so of redemption itself it is said, 'It is finished' (John xx. 30). And as the *old* creation is thus spoken of as being 'finished,' so is the *new;* for after He that sat on the throne had said, 'Behold, I make all things new,' it is added, 'it is done'—it is finished (Rev. xxi. 5, 6).

itself the seeds of ten thousand other creations, as perfect, hereafter to spring from them! God proclaims the perfection of His works, not as man does, in vainglory, but that He may fix our eye on their excellency, and let us know that He, the Former of them, is fully satisfied, and that His work is now ready for its various functions and uses. The great machine is completed, and now about to begin its operations.[1]

Vers. 2, 3. '*And on the seventh day God ended (had finished, completed)*[2] *His work which He had made; and He rested on the seventh day from all His work which He had made.* 3. *And God blessed the seventh day, and sanctified it; because that in it He had rested from all His work which God created and made.*'

By the close of the sixth day God had finished His work, so that, as that day's sun set, announcing the seventh day begun, all was completed. God stands here on the line that separates these two days; He looks back on the past, and forward to the future. He sees and

[1] *The Host.* Such passages as Deut. iv. 19 and Isa. xxxiv. 4 show that this expression is used in reference to sun, moon, and stars; Josh. v. 14, that it means God's *living* army, probably referring to Israel, not to angels. (See Ex. xii. 41: 'The hosts of Jehovah went out from the land of Egypt.') It is used of angels, 1 Kings xxii. 19; Ps. ciii. 21, cxlviii. 2. In Luke ii. 13 we read of 'the heavenly host,' στρατιᾶς οὐρανίου referring to angels; and in Matt. xxiv. 29, δυνάμεις τῶν οὐρανῶν, the powers of heaven, referring to stars, etc. God's special name, Jehovah Sabaoth, Lord of hosts, is not used in the earlier books of Scripture. It does not occur till 1 Sam. i. 3; but after that it occurs about 300 times in the Old Testament; only twice in the new, Rom. ix. 29, Jas. v. 4.

[2] The Hebrew word here is the same as in the preceding verse, though our translation gives it as if it were different. Moses' meaning is, that God 'on the seventh day *had completed* His work.'

surveys a finished work, and He 'returns to His place'—He 'rests.' His rest is soon disturbed, as we shall see, by man's sin, so that He is compelled to begin anew His work (the far more laborious work of *renewing* a world); but meanwhile He 'rests;' and His purpose is to make all creatures partakers of this rest. He rests, not because weary, but because His work is done; and yet, no doubt, that word 'rest' was intended to declare to us the profounder tranquillity that there is, even to the Creator, in rest than in labour.

The day of this completion and this rest must be made memorable for ever.[1] From that moment, each seventh day must be marked off as a day of remembrance, a day to be kept differently from other days, even had man never fallen. For as man, being a dweller on earth, has many *common* duties to perform, which are no less needful than those which are directly spiritual, so God has appointed six days during which these common duties are to be sanctified, and one day during which they are to be wholly set aside. They that confound these two things,

[1] Calvin, in his *Commentary on Genesis*, points out this. He shows that God blessed and sanctified the Sabbath, 'ut seculis omnibus inter homines sancta foret;' and that its observance was not to be confined 'to one age or people, but is common to the whole human race.' He then shows that Judaism introduced certain peculiarities into the observance of the Sabbath. These were done away in Christ, but the Sabbath itself remained. Nay, in so far as the Sabbath prefigured the spiritual rest which Christ brought, it might be said to have passed into its antitype. But, in so far as it was a day set apart from the beginning for the service of God, it was to remain, *ad mundi finem usque durare oportet.* Such were Calvin's ideas of the 'abrogation' of the Sabbath, of which so much has been said!

and profess to make every day a Sabbath, are making void the original purpose of God. God's purpose never was to make every day a Sabbath, and it is mock-sanctity to say so. They who would raise every day to the level of a Sabbath are quite as far from the aim of the divine institution as they who drag down the Sabbath to the level of a common day. During the six days man was to show how he could serve and glorify God *in* the common duties of life; on the Sabbath, he was to show how God was to be served and glorified by acts of direct and unmingled worship. This is the *principle* of the great Sabbath-institute,—a principle which runs through all ages, more so than ever in these last days, when men are either denying religion altogether, or endeavouring to eject it from everyday life, and confine it to a peculiar region of its own.

This seventh day God 'blest.' He uttered His mind concerning it, calling it a day of blessing; and in so doing, communicated to it (as it were) the power to impart blessing—that is, He made it the day in which He would specially give blessing.[1] This is then the primary meaning and object of the Sabbath. It is the day on which

[1] In this sense it is that inanimate things are often spoken of as being *blessed* by God: Ex. xxiii. 25, 'He shall *bless* thy bread and thy water;' Ps. lxv. 10, 'Thou *blessest* the springing therof;' cxxxv. 15, 'I will abundantly *bless* her provision;' Prov. iii. 33, 'He *blesseth* the habitation of the just.' M. Stuart paraphrases it, 'God declared this day to be worthy of peculiar distinction, honour, and observance' (*Hebrew Chrestomathy*, p. 123). In the Greek it is εὐλόγησε, 'He spake well of the day.' We 'bless' God when we speak well of Him, that is, *tell* of His goodness. He blesses us when He speaks well of us, and *imparts* His goodness.

God specially blesses man. But more than this. It is added, He 'sanctified it.' He marked it off from all other days, as the tabernacle was marked off from all the tents of Israel. He drew a fence around it, which was not to be broken through. He set it apart for *Himself*, just as He set the six days apart for man. It was to be *His* day, not *man's;* just as the altar was *His* altar, the laver *His* laver, not man's.[1] And when, or where, or how has God's claim to a Sabbath been renounced? When has His setting apart been done away? Men speak and act as if this 'blessing,' this 'sanctification' of the day were a yoke not to be borne; as if the Sabbath were a curse, not a blessing; as if the gospel had at length broken fetters forged in Eden by God for man! But, no. The Sabbath was set up by God, and by Him only can be taken down. It was set up (1) as a memorial of past labour; (2) as a pillar of testimony to God as Creator; (3) as a proclamation of rest; (4) as a type and earnest of coming rest. These four points in particular contain God's reasons for the institution of this day. All these are still in force; nor has the gospel blunted the edge of any of them, least of all *the last.* Till the antitype come, the type must remain. Till that glorious rest

[1] This use of the word *sanctify* is so common, that we need only refer to such passages as the following in proof: Ex. xxix. 37, 44; Josh. xx. 7; Neh. iii. 1. The literal *seventh* was of no consequence. It could not be the same day over all the world. A *seventh* of days was all that was implied. In Heb. iv. 3, 4, the apostle's object is to state that there was a rest,—a rest which began on the finishing of the works, which was therefore *past*, not *future;* so that it could not be this rest into which faith is to introduce, and from which unbelief shuts us out. It is a future rest to which faith looks forward.

arrive,—better than creation-rest, better than Canaan-rest (Heb. iv.),—its type must remain. Nor is it easy to understand the reason why some, calling themselves expectants of this coming rest, should be so anxious to set aside the type of it. It is strange also that now, when the resurrection of Christ has added another to the many reasons for observing a day like this, we should be asked to abolish it.[1]

Vers. 4, 5. '*These are the generations of the heavens and of the earth when they were created, in the day that the Lord God made the earth and the heavens,* 5. *And every plant of the field before it was in the earth, and every herb of the field before it grew: for the Lord God had not caused it to rain upon the earth, and there was not a man to till the ground.*'

This fourth verse should commence a new chapter,

[1] No doubt God's rest was broken by man's sin. But this made it only the more needful to keep up the Sabbath as a memorial of that rest which man had broken, and an earnest of that rest which is in reserve for us. Let us not forget that the Sabbath was not a Judaical ordinance; and to prevent such an idea, the fourth commandment commences with REMEMBER, calling on Israel to keep in mind an old commandment which had been in the world from the beginning. The word Sabbath (signifying *rest*) does not only refer to *our* resting, but to *God's* resting. Man's sin marred God's rest-day, by compelling Him (we speak after the manner of men) to begin working anew. This new creation-work is still going on; and to this our Lord refers (John v. 17), 'My Father worketh hitherto, and I work'—that is, our Sabbath is not yet begun, and therefore I cannot be charged with breaking the Sabbath in working miracles. When this new creation-work has been finished (the old creation took six days, the new creation 6000 years), then the interrupted Sabbath shall be resumed, at the point where it was broken in upon; only on a higher and heavenlier scale, with Eden restored, Satan expelled, all things made new, the second Adam and the second Eve having dominion over all things;

and is connected with what follows.[1] The first three verses should be thrown back into the previous chapter. A new section of creation-history now begins, and the fourth verse is the title or heading: 'The following are the details of what took place when God created heaven and earth.' The fifth is intended to state that all that was done was entirely *God's doing*, without the help of second causes, without the refreshment of rain, without the aid of man. There had been no power in action hitherto but God's alone. His hand, directly and alone, had done all that was done, in making plants and herbs to grow. The soil was not *of itself* productive; no previous seed existed; there was no former growth to spring up again. All was the finger of God. He is the sole Creator. Second causes, as they are called, are His creations: they owe their being, their influence, to Him. The operations of nature, as men speak, are but the actings of the invisible God. God is in everything. Not as the Pantheist would have it, a part of

God resting from His work, and rejoicing in His Sabbath,—the *Sabbatism* which the apostle speaks of as remaining for the people of God (Heb. iv. 9).

[1] Generations. תּוֹלְדוֹת. The LXX. render it *αὕτη ἡ βίβλος γενέσεως*, as in Matt. i. 1. Literally it is *births*, things brought forth. Here and in chap. vi. 9, xi. 27, xxxvii. 2, it signifies accounts of the origin of—generations, descents, genealogical notices. After quoting this fourth verse, Pearson remarks, 'So the creation or production of anything, by which it is, and before was not, is a kind of *generation*, and consequently the creator or producer of it a kind of *father*: "Hath the rain a father, or who hath begotten the drops of dew?" (Job xxxviii. 28); by which words Job signifies, that as there is no other cause assignable of the rain but God, so may He, as the cause, be called the *Father* of it.'—*On the Creed, Art. I.*

everything, so that nature is God; but a personal Being, in everything, yet distinct from everything; filling, quickening, guiding creation in all its parts, yet no more the same with it than the pilot is with the vessel he steers, or the painter with the canvas on which he flings all the hues of earth and heaven. Let us beware of this subtle delusion of the evil one, the confounding of the creature with the Creator; of God, 'the King eternal, immortal, and invisible,' with the hills, and plains, and forests, and flowers which He has made. To deify nature seems one of the special errors of the last days. And no wonder; for if nature be deified, then man is deified too. Man becomes God, and nature is the throne on which he sits. Let us not lose sight of God in nature. Let not that which is the manifestation of His glory be turned by us into an obscuration of Himself. Let us look straight to the living God. Not nature, but God; not providence, but God; not the law, but the Lawgiver; not the voice, but the Speaker; not the instrument and its wide melodies, but the Master who formed the lyre, and whose hands are drawing the music out of its wondrous chords![1]

[1] Schiller's poetry is perhaps the saddest yet most fascinating exemplification of the spirit referred to above. His very beauties are often the most painful parts of his works. His poem on *The Gods of Greece* is one of his worst, much admired as it has been.

> 'Man gifted nature with divinity,
>   To lift and link her to the breast of love!
> Cold, from the north, has gone
>   Over the flowers, the blast that killed their May;
> And, to enrich the worship of the One,
>   A universe of gods must pass away!'

All this, and much more, from one of the lords of modern thought!

Ver. 6. '*But there went up a mist from the earth, and watered the whole face of the ground.*'

To supply the want of rain, God called up a mist which watered the ground, so that herb and plant were now refreshed. Ere He brings man into the midst of His works, He burnishes them, and makes them resplendent with freshest green. It is of this 'mist' that Job speaks (xxxvi. 27): 'He maketh small the drops of water; they pour down rain according to the vapour thereof;' Jeremiah also: 'He causeth the vapours to ascend from the ends of the earth' (x. 13); thus directly ascribing to Jehovah as much the continuance as the creation of this watering mist. He makes it! He who built the hills, and lighted up the stars,—He is the Creator of the thin airy vapour which disappears in a moment. And in all these parts of His infinitely varied handiwork He has taught us to read solemn lessons. In the ocean, the breadth of eternity; in the mountains, the stability of the covenant; in the vapour, the shortness of our mortal life (Jas. iv. 14).

Was Satan ever more beautifully disguised as an angel of light than in such a man? Is not German poetry, German metaphysics, German theology, making havoc among us? Is it not the combined action of the three that is producing that school which, with such supercilious dislike of Evangelical truth, is setting itself to make war against what it so childishly calls Bibliolatry? Under covert of this evil name, thus, after no brave or manly fashion, fastened on their opponents, they hope to advance to their great work of undermining and overthrowing the verbal inspiration of the Word of God.

All nature teems with truth, concerning the past, the present, and the future. And this God, who created the vapour, and made that vapour a figure of man's life, is the God who careth for us, the God who wants to give us the life that is no vapour, — the heritage that cannot pass away! And the mist that waters and revives the summer flower is not more free than the eternal life which He gives us in His Son.

Ver. 7. '*And the Lord God formed man of the dust of the ground, and breathed into his nostrils the breath of life; and man became a living soul.*'

In the fifth verse we were specially reminded that 'there was not a man to till the ground;' now this want is to be removed; and from this way of noticing man's creation we are taught that, just as the ground was made for man, so man was made for the ground. He has a claim on it, and it has a claim on him. Accordingly it is to the peculiar link between him and the ground that our attention is now turned. He is closely connected with the ground, for out of it he was made. Hitherto we have been merely told of man being created by God; but not a word has been said of *how*, or out of *what*, he was formed. Now we are told, it was of 'the dust of the ground;' of the finer and more elemental parts of this material earth. He was formed 'dust of the ground,' for so the words run literally. This refers, of course, to his body, teaching us that *it* was made first; and then, after that, God breathed into his nostrils the breath of life (or lives), and he became a living soul.[1] As we know that the stoppage of the breath causes the cessation of life, so the impartation of the breath was the production of life, as if the breath were the link between the soul and body, so that, in breaking it, the soul and body fall asunder. Here is the potter and the clay! Man bears no part in his own creation. His flesh is taken out of the dust beneath him; his soul comes down straight from God above, made out of we know not what; called, perhaps, directly out of nothing. That which is material may come out of a mass of previously existing matter; but who will say that the immaterial is brought out of a mass of previously existing spirit? No. The soul comes at once from Him of whom it is said, 'In Him was life, and the life was the light of men' (John i. 4). It is the Son, the second person of the Godhead, that is 'the Life'—the living and life-giving One. It was He who with one hand, as it were, taking up a body out of the dust, and with the other creating a soul by the word of His power, brought

[1] נֶפֶשׁ חַיָּה, literally, a soul of life, a living animated being,—εἰς ψυχὴν ζῶσαν, Sept. It is to this the apostle refers in 1 Cor. xv. 45, in which he uses the very words of the Septuagint, above quoted, preserving even the Hebrew idiom. The 'breath of lives' seems to be that breath by which the *lives* (animal and rational) are kept in play, as well as linked to the body. It is to this expression that the apostle seems to refer in Acts xvii. 25: 'He giveth to all, life and breath,'—ζωὴν καὶ πνοήν. On this whole subject the reader may consult Howe's *Principles of the Oracles of God*, Lect. 16, 17, 18, 19, 20; Flavel's *Treatise on the Soul;* and Christopher Ness' quaint work, *The History and Mystery of the Old and New Testament*, chap. iv. See also Tertullian's curious treatise, *De Anima.*

them together, and then cemented them together with the 'breath of lives,' which He breathed into the nostrils. Thus the threefold cord which is not quickly broken (the corporeal life, the animal life, and the intellectual life) was thrown around this new piece of creation, and the soul and body married together in a union which only sin could dissolve.

Such are the two extremes of man's nature, body and soul. Such are the sources of both; the one low, the other lofty. And possessed of this twofold being,—thus strangely compounded of the low and the high, of the material and the immaterial,—is he not taught on the one hand to be profoundly humble, and on the other to soar upwards to Jehovah with a noble ambition, resting satisfied nowhere but in the bosom of his God?

Of our original dust we are often reminded by God. He recurs frequently to the term, as a figure for such things as the following:—It is the emblem of frailty (Ps. ciii. 14); can we then be self-confident, or ever cherish 'the pride of life'? It is the emblem of *nothingness* (Gen. xviii. 27); and can we boast of our sufficiency, or deem ourselves aught when compared with the All-sufficient One? It is the emblem of *defilement* (Isa. lii. 2); and shall we vaunt of purity? It is the emblem of *humiliation* (Lam. iii. 29; Job xlii. 6); and shall we be puffed up, we who are but dust and ashes? It is the emblem of *mourning* (Josh. vii. 6); and shall we exult, as if no tribulation could reach us, or say with Babylon, 'I shall see no sorrow'? It is the emblem of *mortality* (Eccles. iii. 20, xii. 7); and shall we trust in our dying life, as if death could not invade us? O man, thou art dust! Canst thou be proud or high-minded? Canst thou put thy confidence in anything into which the element of dust enters?

Yet, let us remember, there is nothing sinful in this dust out of which we are framed. Ours is indeed a lowly origin, but not an unholy one. There is nothing sinful in the soil of earth. The curse is on it and in it, for man's sin. But the soil itself contains no defilement. Out of this very dust was fashioned the body of Him who took our flesh. The Son of the Highest has taken into His person this very dust of ours, thereby showing us that there is nothing in it really vile; nay, thereby putting wondrous honour upon it, and elevating it to a seat upon the very throne of God. Out of this dust our resurrection bodies are to be formed; so that when this corruptible shall put on incorruption, we shall not the less be possessors of a body derived from the 'dust of the ground.' This body of ours is yet to sit upon the throne of the universe. We have borne the image of the earthly, we shall also bear the image of the heavenly.

But we have souls as well as bodies; and these souls are specially God's handiwork. He made them what they are. We got them directly from Him at first, and 'in Him we live, and move, and have our being' (Job xii. 10, xxvii. 3, iii. 4, xxxiv. 14; Eccles. xii. 7). This is the highest and noblest kind of creation. Man cannot make, but he can unmake; he cannot create, but he can ruin; for he can introduce into the soul that which is its ruin,—SIN. God only can either make it out of nothing, or re-make after it is ruined. Both are the acts of Him who is 'the Life.' The first life came from Him, much more the new life; and His act when creating the first life corresponds strikingly to that of which it is said, 'He *breathed on them*, and said, Receive ye the Holy Ghost.' The second life is indeed produced in the way of *birth* (a birth of God, a birth from above), so that the whole mature soul is not imparted at once, but still the source of the life is the same,—the life-giving fountain is the same, only it communicates a higher kind of life (1 Cor. xv. 45). 'The first man Adam was made a living soul; the last Adam was made a quickening spirit.' It is more abundant life (John x. 10). 'I am come that they might have life, and that they might have it more abundantly.' Our whole new being is to be after a higher model, and cast in a far finer mould (1 Cor. xv. 49). 'As we have borne the image of the earthly, we shall also bear the image of the heavenly.'

Ver. 8. '*And the Lord God planted a garden, eastward, in Eden* (Heb. *in Eden from the East*), *and there He put the man whom He had formed.*'

We now learn in what region, and in what part of that region, man was placed. It was in the eastern extremity of a region named Eden; a region whose locality was, it would seem, well known in the days of Moses, but now only to be guessed at. *When* it took the name of 'Eden,' whether so named at first by God, or afterwards by Adam, or not till later ages, we know not. It signifies 'delight,' being so named from its surpassing beauty and fruitfulness. It was a land, the like of which has not since been seen on earth; fairer and richer than that which flowed with milk and honey; a land of broad rivers and streams; a land of sunshine and gladness; a land of flowers and gems; a land of the myrtle, and the olive, and the palm, and the vine; a land which was the glory of all lands; which has left its name behind it to all ages, as a name of fruitfulness, and fragrance, and beauty.

In the eastern corner of this 'delightsome land,' this more than Beulah, God planted a garden with His own hand, a garden which afterwards, from an Eastern term, took the name of Paradise, and is often alluded to in Scripture as the 'garden of the Lord,' the 'garden of God' (Gen. xiii. 10; Isa. li. 3; Ezek. xxviii. 13, xxxi. 8, 9, xxxvi. 35; Joel ii. 3).[1] This peculiar spot of earth, this inner circle, was to be man's residence. There he was to dwell. There he was to meet with God, there to walk with God, there, as in creation's palace, to take up his abode as creation's king; and from his throne there to exercise his kingly dominion over an undefiled and happy earth.[2]

[1] The paradise mentioned in Luke xxiii. 43, 2 Cor. xii. 4, Rev. ii. 7, is the heavenly counterpart to the earthly paradise; for no doubt the latter was 'after the pattern of heavenly things.'

[2] Paradise was the inner circle; Eden, around it, the outer; the whole earth around, the outermost; corresponding to the three divisions in the tabernacle, the most holy, the holy, and the outer court; and corresponding to the three great divisions in millennial

Ver. 9. '*And out of the ground made the Lord God to grow* (or *spring*) *every tree that is pleasant to the sight, and good for food; the tree of life also* (Heb. *and the tree of the life, or lives*) *in the midst of the garden, and the tree of the knowledge of good and evil.*'

The garden was nobly stored. It was a princely orchard. Its fruitful soil gave growth to every various tree and shrub. Nothing was awanting to make it altogether suitable for its dwellers. Every tree which the eye loves to look upon, or which is good for food, was there. No sense remained ungratified. But two special trees were there, the tree of life, and the tree of the knowledge of good and evil.[1]

1. *The tree of life.*—This was a real tree, as real as

days,—the heavenly Jerusalem, and the Church its dweller; the earthly Jerusalem, with Israel its dweller; and the earth at large, with the Gentile nations inhabiting it.

[1] It is interesting to notice the references to the trees of Eden. Not only is Eden itself used as a figure for a region of excellent beauty (Isa. li. 3; Ezek. xxxvi. 35; Joel ii. 3), but the *trees* of Eden are referred to three times by Ezekiel in a most striking way, 'cedars,' 'fir-trees,' and 'chestnut-trees' being specified (xxxi. 8). The Assyrian is compared to the trees of Eden, and it is said of him, 'that no tree in the garden of God was like unto him in his beauty,' nay, 'all the trees of Eden that were in the garden of God envied him.' Ezekiel's references to Eden cannot fail to strike the reader. It was in the Edenic region that he dwelt in his captivity, on the banks of Hiddekel, as in the case of Daniel (x. 4); and just as David's psalms bear witness to the deserts and hills where he was hunted, so Ezekiel's prophecies show us that before his eyes visions of Eden were brought, called up by the scene around and the histories or traditions connected with the scene. Ezekiel and John are the two prophets that abound in references to Eden and Paradise, with its trees and precious stones. Now Ezekiel's is the *Jewish* apocalypse, and John's the *Christian*. The former is the apocalypse of the 'earthly things,' the latter of the 'heavenly things.'

any of the rest, and evidently placed there for like purposes with the rest. The only difference was, that it had peculiar virtues which the others had not. It was a life-giving or life-sustaining tree,—a tree of which, so long as man should continue to eat, he should never die. Not that *one* eating of it could confer immortality; but the continuous use of it was intended for this. Not that man was made mortal as he now is; the use of means does not necessarily denote some such innate defect. Man had to eat of food even when unfallen, yet this did not prove him to have been originally a dying creature. Nay, Christ had to partake of food, but this did not argue any defect in Him. So did not the existence of the tree of life, and man's need to eat thereof, argue any original defect in man. The link between soul and body was to be maintained by this tree. So long as he partook of this, that tie could not be broken.[1]

2. *The tree of the knowledge of good and evil.*—Why may we not take this in the same literality of meaning as the former? Why may it not mean a tree, the fruit of which

[1] This is the natural meaning of the expression 'tree of life,' namely a life-imparting tree, just as 'the bread of life' means life-imparting bread, and as the 'water of life' means life-imparting water. Of course the expression itself does not prove it to be a literal tree, just as these others are not literal bread nor literal water. But then the tree having been proved to be a literal tree from the context, we may use these parallel forms of speech to illustrate its meaning. 'The very denomination "tree of life" would signify to us that there was in it a faculty of either giving or preserving life.'—Burton's *View of the Creation of the World*, p. 209. The son of Sirach calls it δένδρον ἀθανασίας, the tree of immortality. Lord Barrington, in his *Essay on*

was fitted to nourish man's intellectual and moral nature? *How* it did this I do not attempt to say. But we know so little of the actings of the body or the soul, that we cannot affirm it impossible. Nay, we see so much of the effects of the body upon the soul, both in sharpening and blunting the edge alike of intellect and conscience, that we may pronounce it not at all unlikely. We are only beginning to be aware of the exceeding delicacy of our mental and moral mechanism, and how easily that mechanism is injured or improved by the things which affect the body. A healthy body tends greatly to produce not only a healthy intellect, but a healthy *conscience.* I know that only one thing can really pacify the conscience,—the all-cleansing blood; but this I also know, that a diseased or enfeebled body operates oftentimes so sadly on the conscience as to prevent the healthy realization by it of that wondrous blood, thereby beclouding the whole soul; and there is nothing which Satan seems so completely to get hold of, and by means of it to rule the inner man, as a nervously-diseased body. Cowper's expression, 'A mind *well lodged*, and *masculine of course*,'

the Dispensations, says, 'The tree of life is a tree that could preserve life.' He then gives eight reasons for this. *Works*, vol. ii. pp. 408–412. He is more successful in these than when in a subsequent paragraph he endeavours to prove that the tree of knowledge was a poisonous tree producing death. Venema takes the same view of the tree of life: 'Nothing remains but that we consider the name given to it as meaning that it did possess a certain power, communicated to it by God, of preserving, prolonging, and gladdening the life of man on earth.'—*System of Theology*, chap. 26. Also his *Eccles. Hist.* vol. i. p. 26.

has in it more meaning than we have commonly attached to it.[1]

Vers. 10–14. '*And a river went out of Eden to water the garden; and from thence it was parted, and became into four heads.* 11. *The name of the first is Pison: that is it which compasseth the whole land of Havilah, where there is gold;* 12. *And the gold of that land is good: there is bdellium and the onyx-stone.* 13. *And the name of the second river is Gihon: the same is that which compasseth the whole land of Ethiopia* (Heb. *Cush*). 14. *And the name of the third river is Hiddekel: that is it which goeth towards the east of Assyria. And the fourth river is Euphrates.*'[2]

For this fair region a river was provided,—a noble river,—fit counterpart of that 'river of bliss' which

'Thro' midst of heaven,
Rolls o'er Elysian flowers her amber stream.'

Where this mighty river rose is not said. It found its way into Eden from the lofty mountains which encircled

[1] If our translation of Isa. vii. 15 (and the Vulgate) be correct ('Butter and honey shall he eat, that he may know to refuse the evil, and choose the good'), there would be a striking instance of the truth referred to above. But as the passage may as well run, '*when* he shall know,' etc., I do not press it. Jonathan's eyes were enlightened by the tasting of the honey (1 Sam. xiv. 27).

[2] Both in the writings of the Fathers and in the old Latin hymns, these four streams are spiritualized into the four evangelists. 'Paradisi hæc fluenta,' says one hymnist, and another enlarges on this with some beauty,—

'Paradisus his rigatur
Viret, floret, fœcundatur,
His abundat, his lætatur
Quatuor fluminibus.
Fons est Christus, hi sunt rivi,
Fons est altus, hi proclivi,
Ut saporem fontis vivi,
Ministrent fidelibus.'
—Daniel, *Thes. Hymnol.* vol. ii. p. 85.

that glorious region. Then passing through Eden, it glided onwards into Paradise, and there might be seen 'winding at its own sweet will,' till it reached the other extremity of the garden. There it was subdivided into four heads.[1] These were: (1) *Pison*,[2] compassing the

[1] Heads, רָאשִׁים, or beginnings, that is, 'four lesser rivers into which a larger spreads itself.' Ezek. xvi. 25, 'Every head of the way,' that is, the beginning, the place where ways branch off. That 'rivers' or 'beginnings of rivers' is meant, is evident from what follows.

[2] *Pison.* Robertson gives as the meaning of this, *magna aquæ diffusio;* Gesenius, 'water poured forth, overflowing.' The latter thinks it to be the *Indus;* Josephus, the *Ganges;* Reland and Rosenmüller, the *Phasis* or *Araxes.* In none of these is there aught of certainty, and we mention them only to show the difficulty of coming to a conclusion on this point. The land of Havilah, Gesenius makes to be India. But with no certainty. Ham had a descendant of that name (Gen. x. 7). Shem also had (Gen. x. 29); but from which of these the land took its name we cannot say. Only, it is remarkable that next to Havilah, among the posterity of Shem, stands *Ophir*, who, in all likelihood, gave his name to the land of Ophir; which conjunction of the persons, Havilah and Ophir, would lead us to infer a juxtaposition of the lands. In a paper read by Colonel Rawlinson at a meeting of the Royal Geographical Society some time ago, 'On the identification of the Biblical cities of Assyria, and on the geography of the lower Tigris,' it was shown 'that below the confluence of the Tigris and Euphrates, four cities had been successively built, as the sea had retired before the deposit of alluvium, to serve as commercial emporia. These cities were the *Havilah* of Genesis, Beth Yakina of the Assyrian inscriptions, Teredon of Nebuchadnezzar, and Obillah of the Sassanians.' This may lead us to place Havilah much nearer the Tigris and Euphrates than Gesenius would do. There is uncertainty also as to the meaning of *bdellium.* Most seem to understand it as the pearl. See Rosenmüller, Gesenius, and Robertson, the last of whom throws out *crystal* also as perhaps its meaning. It is curious that the LXX. should have rendered it ἄνθραξ, a burning coal or fiery stone, such as the carbuncle or ruby. Is there any connection between this and the 'stones of fire' mentioned in Ezekiel as the gems of Eden?

land of Havilah, in which land there is the fine gold, with bdellium and the onyx stone, showing us what a land of wealth it must have been, its soil fruitful, and its very rocks veined with gems and gold. To that land Job refers when he says, 'The stones of it are the place of sapphires; and it hath dust of gold' (Job xxviii. 6). To it also Ezekiel points when, speaking to the Prince of Tyre, he says, 'Thou hast been in Eden, the garden of God; every precious stone was thy covering, the sardius, topaz, and the diamond, the beryl, the onyx, and the jasper, the sapphire, the emerald, and the carbuncle, and gold.'[1] (2) *Gihon.*[2] It flowed round Ethiopia or Cush, and signifies a breaking forth of waters. More than this we cannot say of it. (3) *Hiddekel.*[3] It is said to go to

There is the same difficulty as to the word translated onyx. The Sept. give it ὁ λίθος ὁ πράσινος, the emerald. It is more generally rendered *onyx* or *sardonyx*, on account of its supposed resemblance to the human nail; though Robertson derives it from a word signifying, 'igneo ardore præditus,' and says it means, 'lapis coruscis micans ignibus.'

[1] It is remarkable that *fire* should be referred to in both the above passages. In Job it is, 'Under it is turned up as it were *fire.*' In Ezekiel it is, 'Thou hast walked up and down in the midst of the stone of *fire.*' Had not fire-worship its seat in these regions?

[2] *Gihon.* It was the opinion of Josephus and of most ancient writers, that the Nile is meant. Gesenius makes it to be the Ethiopic Nile. There is little likelihood in these conjectures.

[3] *Hiddekel.* It signifies lightness or swiftness, something active, vehement, rapid, as does the word Tiger from which Tigris is derived. The *Euphrates* is said to derive its name from the sweetness of its taste. These two latter rivers are well ascertained; the two former are, we believe, not now in existence, and cannot be ascertained. We say this, not only because no writer has ever been able to identify them; but because the whole four rivers had one common head, which is nowhere now the case; and also because it is an ascertained fact

the east of Assyria, and is certainly the *Tigris.* (4) The *Euphrates.* This was too well known to require minute description. It is spoken of elsewhere as 'the river' (1 Kings iv. 21; Ps. lxxii. 8), the 'great river' (Deut. i. 7), the 'flood' (Josh. xxiv. 2). It was the Euphrates that was to form one of the boundaries of Abraham's land: 'Unto thy seed have I given this land, from the river of Egypt (Nile) to the great river, the river Euphrates' (Gen. xv. 18). It was towards this river that

that the Tigris has more than once been divided into *two* streams, perhaps more. If so, or if the Euphrates were so divided, we have the four rivers on the spot. Colonel Rawlinson thus states the point: 'After describing the ruins of Sekherieh, which, on various grounds, he identified with the Mesene of the Greeks, he went on to notice the bifurcation of the Tigris. This curious natural feature had been very accurately described both by Pliny and Stephen, and the Arab writers enabled us to connect those ancient notices with the modern geography of the country. The Cauchian plains of Pliny were shown to be the Coche of the Syrians and Jukha of the Arabs, while the Delos of Stephen was still preserved in the name of Dieleh (quite distinct from Dijleh), which the Bedouins of the present day apply to the dry bed of the Tigris, running by the ruins of Wasit. The Tigris had changed its course several times. At the period of the Christian era it was divided into two streams. Under the Sassanians, the left hand or eastern branch was alone navigable. In the seventh year of the Hegira the right hand or western branch was reopened, while in the fifteenth century of our era the river took the form which it retains to the present day. The tract of country between the two arms, owing to its natural depression, had been always more or less subject to inundations, and boats had passed from Wasit to the Euphrates, along tracts artificially formed for them in the marshes. The character of the country was the same at the present day, and the Tigris from the tomb of Abdullah Ibn Ali to Kurna now ran in a channel which was formerly named the Abul Assad Canal, and which had been cleared out under the Caliph Mansur for the purpose of navigation.'

Israel was commanded to turn their steps (Deut. i. 7). It was on the banks of this river that Israel sat down and wept, remembering Zion (Ps. cxxxvii. 1). It was in a hole of one of the rocks that skirt Euphrates that Jeremiah was to hide his girdle (Jer. xiii. 4). It was into Euphrates that Jeremiah was to cast the book containing Babylon's burden, with the stone bound to it, as the type of Babylon's more terrible plunge (Jer. li. 63). It was in the Euphrates that the Apocalyptic angels were bound, and on it that the sixth angel poured out his vial, drying up its waters, and preparing the way for the kings of the East (Rev. ix. 16, xvi. 12). Babylon stood upon Euphrates,—Babylon, the great enemy of Jehovah and His people, as well as the representative of their great enemy through all ages. Hard by Paradise, it may be on the very spot, was Satan permitted to rear his mighty citadel. He had driven man from that happy seat; he had blighted its beauty, and now, as if in defiance of God and man, he rears his city upon the faded flowers of Eden. One has asked,—

> 'Having waste ground enough,
> Shall we desire to raze the sanctuary,
> And pitch our evils there?'

So was it with Satan, whether we regard Babylon as actually reared on the site of Paradise, or merely in some corner of the wider circle of Eden.[1] God's garden and

[1] There are several passages which seem to show some connection between Eden and the district around Babylon, as if the name of Eden had been retained in some parts (Isa. xxxvii. 12; Ezek. xxvii. 23).

Satan's city, close by each other, as if the latter were triumphing over the former! The emblem of the heavenly paradise and the symbol of the great city, 'Mother of harlots,' city of Antichrist, side by side with each other! The earthly pattern of heavenly things passing away, and replaced by the abode of darkness, the cage of unclean beasts, the counterpart of Satan's own dark dwelling below!

But what care and love God has shown towards man! What pains and cost to make him happy and comfortable! It is a father providing for his child, his first-born. God's desire was to bless. And that desire remains unchanged and undiminished. Our sin might have been expected to quench this desire, and to turn the blessing into a curse, the love into hate. It did so in the case of angels. It has not done so to us. He loves us still. He blesses, and curses not. Paradise with all its beauty and abundance was but a faint expression of God's love when compared with His unspeakable gift, or with the more glorious paradise yet in reserve. The earthly tree of life is as nothing compared with the heavenly original which shall ere long be ours, when, as the 'overcoming' ones, we shall eat of the 'tree of life which is in the midst of the paradise of God' (Rev. ii. 7, xxii. 2, 14).

Ver. 15. '*And the Lord God took the man, and put him into* (Heb. *placed, or set him in*) *the garden of Eden, to dress it* (Heb. *to till it*), *and to keep it.*'

Having prepared the garden, the Lord God took the man and placed him in it, that he might till it and keep it. It was made for him, and he for it, as the body is made for the soul, and the soul for the body.[1] It was fruitful beyond anything we now know of, yet it was not *so* fruitful as to make any kind of care or cultivation needless. It was so fruitful as to occasion no toil nor weariness to the cultivator, yet not so fruitful as not to afford occasion to man's skill and watchfulness. No amount of skill or toil now can call up beauty, or verdure, or fruit, beyond a certain narrow limit; for man has to do with a rugged soil. But in Adam's case the ground easily and gladly yielded its substance without limit to the most gentle toil. Nay, it was not *toil;* it was simple, pleasant occupation. No doubt the *amount* and kind of its actual fruit-bearing was to depend upon himself; he was to regulate this according to his wants and tastes; but still the fruit-bearing source was in the soil, imparted directly by the hand of God,—that all-quickening, all-fertilizing Spirit that brooded over the face of the deep. Afterwards that Spirit was grieved away from the soil by man's sin; but at first His power was most signally manifested in its fruitful richness. Man was lord of the soil, and of all that trod it or grew on it, and his daily employments were to manifest his dominion,—not dominion over

[1] There is evidently a meaning in so much being spoken of and to the *man* alone, before the creation of the woman. He was to be the head and representative of the *race*, of the female as well as the male, which he would not so properly have been had Eve been created at the same time, or directly out of the ground, instead of out of the man. 'Naturam igitur humanam in Adæ persona condidit, atque inde formavit Hevam, ut fœmina tantum portio esset totius generis.'—Calvin, *in loc.*

a rebellious earth, needing to be curbed or scourged into obedience, but a dominion over a willing world, that stood eagerly awaiting his commands. All creation was, like a well-tuned instrument, ready made to his hand; and all that was needed on his part was simply the amount of happy effort needful to set its strings in motion, and bring out of them all the rich compass of their music. And if such was creation under the first Adam, what will it be under the second? Then truly shall the wilderness and the solitary place be glad, the desert shall rejoice and blossom as the rose.[1]

Vers. 16, 17. '*And the Lord God commanded the man, saying, Of every tree of the garden thou mayest* (or *shalt*) *freely eat* (Heb. *eating thou shalt eat, that is, thou shalt go on eating unhindered*); 17. *But of the tree of knowledge of good and evil, thou shalt not eat of it: for in the day that thou eatest thereof thou shalt surely die* (Heb. *dying thou shalt die, that is, thou shalt begin to die, and go on dying*).'

We now come to the constitution under which God placed man. It was given in the form of a commandment,—'thou shalt,' and 'thou shalt not,'—an injunction, and a prohibition. 'The Lord God COMMANDED the man.' There was, as it were, a moral *necessity* laid upon

[1] Adam's tillage of the ground was of course not *toil;* but since the fall it has been hard and unceasing toil. Man has had to carry on a continual warfare with barrenness,—wringing from the soil its unwilling produce. In this process we notice that he keeps up the same *two circles* as before the fall, an outer and an inner,—Eden and Paradise,—seeking in general to fertilize and beautify the soil, yet always selecting some nook on which he bestows more special pains, converting it into a *garden* or paradise. In Sir Thomas Brown's *Treatise on the Garden of Cyrus*, the reader may get an idea of these efforts.

him to obey. This utterance of God's *will* imposed this necessity. It was not the mere declaration of certain consequences to arise from obedience or disobedience. It was such a declaration of *will* on the part of Jehovah as hedged him in on every side with the most overwhelming of all moral necessities. It was not indeed a necessity that left him without a free choice, but it was a necessity which gave a most preponderating bias to that free choice in the direction of obedience, even apart from consequences. Under a similar necessity has God in His announcement of grace placed fallen man. He has not simply left to us a choice of the evil or the good. He has given utterance to His will. 'This is His COMMANDMENT, that we believe in the name of His Son Jesus Christ.' A necessity is laid upon us. It is not a mere question as to our own woe or weal; it is a question of obedience or disobedience. Hence the inquiry so often made by those who have begun to learn what it is to be lost, but who as yet only dimly see how they may be saved,—'Am I at liberty to believe and to come to Christ as I am?' is one of the strangest that could be made. What should we have thought of Adam, had he asked, 'Am I at liberty to obey God's commands?' What are we to think of the sinner who asks, 'Am I at liberty to come to Christ?' At liberty to come! You *dare not* do otherwise, except you are prepared to defy God and disobey His commandment. At liberty to come! You are not at liberty to refuse. A necessity lies on you to come,—even that most solemn of all necessities, which springs from the declaration of the *will* of God. You can only be lost by acting all your life long in deliberate disobedience to the plainest of all commandments that ever came from the lips of God.

But let us consider the two points of this law given to Adam,—'Thou shalt,' and 'Thou shalt not.'

1. *The injunction.*—'Of every tree of the garden, eating thou shalt eat.' It is not 'mayest eat,' as our translation has it, but 'shalt eat.' As a sovereign's wishes are commands, so is it here. It is not a mere permission or invitation, but a command. And it is a peculiar form of speech,—the positive injunction that most truly comports with the authoritative dignity of a sovereign Jehovah, as well as suits best the condition of the responsible creature, by leaving no room for any doubt on his part as to what is the sovereign will of Him to whom all obedience is due.

2. *The prohibition.*— One tree is forbidden, only one, —the tree of the knowledge of good and evil; and this with the added threatening of death for any breach of this solemn prohibition. What might be God's ultimate purpose regarding this tree, we cannot say. Nor can we fully comprehend the reasons for setting it in Paradise, within sight and reach of man. It was both in appearance and in its properties the most attractive of all the trees (Gen. iii. 6), the one which appealed most directly to man's intelligent nature. And had the prohibition been permanent and irreversible, had God meant that a tree possessing such qualities should never, throughout man's whole future existence, be partaken of by him, it is not easy to see the reason either of the planting or the

prohibiting of the tree. But take the prohibition as a temporary one, intended to prove man; suppose that after a certain time of obedience free access to the tree was to be allowed, then the difficulty lessens, if it does not wholly disappear.[1] Man was, ultimately, to eat freely of it, and to obtain all its singular benefits. By means of it he would rise in the scale of being, and obtain, in so far as a finite nature can, a participation of the divine knowledge of good and evil, without having to pass through that sore and long experience through which alone we now reach it. The eating of that tree would have done for him, through physical means, in some measure at least, what our participation of Christ, our eating of His body, does for us now, and will do yet more abundantly hereafter. Had man waited God's time, —had he exercised faith,—he would have gotten all that

[1] We cannot help thinking that this tree gets its name from the *physical* properties of its fruit. Venema and others, who strongly insist that the *tree of life* gets its name from its physical properties, yet reject the idea that the tree of knowledge has its name from a like cause, simply because they cannot conceive how the body can so act upon the mind as that the latter shall be invigorated or elevated by means of the former. This, however, is no argument, as we have seen. To make it derive its name from the consequences of a *disobedient* eating of it, is surely a perversion of the words of the prohibition; it might have better been called in that case the 'tree of death,' as, indeed, some have insisted on naming it. Kennicott would paraphrase the name thus, 'the tree which is the test of good and evil;' that is, the tree by which God tried them to see whether they would choose good or evil, but this will not do (see his ingenious *Dissertation on the Tree of Life*, p. 25). It surely means some particular tree whose fruit had certain properties, so operative upon the soul of man as to make him grow in the knowledge or discernment of good and evil.

the tree could give him ere long, and that in the way of obedience. 'Believing' in God, he would not have 'made haste.' But he believed not; and made haste, as if resolved to have, whether through obedience or disobedience, all that the tree could yield him. It was to be proved whether he could trust God, and whether he loved God's will better than his own. Concerning this prohibition, we may note, (1) *It was a needful prohibition.* Man must be kept in remembrance that he is not an absolute sovereign,—that he is but a vicegerent. He must be made to feel that there is another will in the universe besides his own, greater than his own, independent of his own, an absolutely sovereign will. (2) *It was but one prohibition.* There was but one point in which his will and God's could come into collision. In great loving-kindness God had made it so. Man was not burdened, or fretted, or perplexed with many points of this kind. *Only one!* How gracious! How considerate, as if God sought to make man's trial the least possible, so as to leave him without excuse if he should disobey. (3) *It was a simple prohibition.* It had nothing intricate or dark about it. There was nothing mysterious about it, nothing in which man could mistake, nothing which could leave room for the question, Am I obeying or not? It was distinct beyond the possibility of mistake. (4) *It was a visible prohibition.* It was connected with something both visible and tangible. It was not inward, but outward. It was not a thing of faith, but of sight. Everything about it was palpable and open—the tree, the fruit, the place, the threat, the consequences. (5) *It was an easy prohibition.* Man could not say it was hard to keep. He was only to refrain from eating one fruit. Being a negative, not a positive requirement, it reduced obedience to its lowest form and easiest terms. Hence man's sin was the greater. He was wholly inexcusable. (6) *It was enforced by a most solemn penalty.* It began with a declaration of God's *will*, and it ended with the proclamation of the penalty,—*death.* How much this expression includes has been often disputed. There is no need of this. In the day that man ate of the tree he came under condemnation; he became a death-doomed man; the sentence went forth against him.[1] Grace came in afterwards, and suspended the full execution of the sentence; but still the sentence went out—'dying thou shalt die.' That *temporal* death, as it is called,—the dissolution of soul and body,—was the *first* thing contained in this sentence, there can be little doubt. Not as if the sentence rested there. Temporal death was but the entrance into that gloomy region of condemnation

[1] 'Tunc morti addictus fuit Adam, et mors regnum suum in eo inchoavit.'—CALVIN. 'Sinners are actually on the road to death and destruction from that moment, and a separation takes place between them and life.'—NITZSCH's *System of Christian Doctrine*, pt. ii. sec. 2. From the moment that man sinned he came under the curse; he was under doom. He commenced dying. This corresponds exactly to the way in which the repeal of the curse is declared, 'He that believeth *hath* everlasting life.' From the moment he believes he gets possession of this life, though the *full* life is reserved for another state; and as the first stroke of the sentence inflicted on Adam was *condemnation*, so the first part of its removal in believing is 'no condemnation:' and as the close and seal of the curse, in Adam's case, was bodily death, so the consummation of it, in the case of the saint, is resurrection.

within which all things terrible await the sinner. Temporal death was to be, not then only, but ever after, the *visible pledge or mark* of the sentence. Hence it is that we read, 'It is appointed unto men once to die;' in which words the apostle refers to the primeval sentence, —*man's once dying*,—and shows how this sentence was fulfilled in the *once dying* of the Substitute (Heb. ix. 28). This death brought with it all manner of infinite ills and woes. It brought with it, or included in it, condemnation, wrath, misery, separation from God; all endless; all immediate; all irreversible, had not free love come in; had 'grace not reigned through righteousness, unto eternal life, through Jesus Christ our Lord.' The sentence was, 'The soul that sinneth, it shall die.' But 'where sin abounded, grace did much more abound.'

Ver. 18. '*And the Lord God said, It is not good that the man should be alone; I will make him an help meet for him.*'

The previous verses have described the preparation of man's dwelling; the eighteenth and those that follow contain a minute detail of the formation of his help meet. In the case of the animal creation, male and female were created together. Not so with man. There must be an interval between his creation and that of the woman, just as there was to be an interval between the incarnation and the ingathering of the Church. In all things pertaining to man there must be something more special than in other beings. The work must be done more deliberately, step by step, that each thing done may be seen *in itself* before it is seen in its connection with other parts of creation. Man is created *alone* at first, that he may stand forth as the great model of God's workmanship, and that our eye may be fixed on him as the representative of our nature. He is the great head of humanity; its root; its fountain. In him, thus placed before us alone, we have the intimation of God's purpose regarding man's nature, and man's rule over the earth. Besides, he is thus made to feel his loneliness, his need of another like himself. He feels as if one half of his nature were awanting. He stood, indeed, amid a glorious world,—a world bursting with fresh, glad beauty on every side, and teeming with boundless life; but he stood alone! There was no one like himself—no soul to meet his soul, in all its buoyant outgoings. He stood

> 'An exile amid splendid desolation,
> A prisoner with infinity surrounded.'[1]

He had, it is true, God for his companion; but this was not all that was needed, as God Himself here testifies. There must be one like himself, in whom there will be more of equality and sympathy and nearness; one neither too high nor too low for him. 'I will make' (says God) 'an help meet for him.' God only understands his case, and can satisfy the cravings of his spirit for the intercourse of a spirit like his own. I will make for him an helper, corresponding to him; another self; his counterpart; the very being to fill up the void within him.[2]

[1] Montgomery's *Pelican Island.*

[2] עֵזֶר כְּנֶגְדּוֹ, literally, 'a helper as over against him'—corresponding to him. The Sept. has it βοηθὸν κατ' αὐτὸν in this verse, but at

Vers. 19, 20. '*And* (or *now*) *out of the ground the Lord God formed* (or *had formed*) *every beast of the field, and every fowl of the air* (Heb. *heaven*), *and brought them unto Adam* (or *to the man*), *to see what he would call them: and whatsoever Adam* (or *the man*) *called every living creature, that was the name thereof.* 20. *And Adam gave names to all* (*the*) *cattle, and to the fowls of the air* (the *heaven*), *and to every beast of the field.*'

God now proceeds to show man the exact point where the void lay. Adam had been made to feel that void, but God's object is to place him in circumstances such as shall lead him step by step to the seat of the unsatisfied longing within. Accordingly, God brings before him all the creatures which He had made, that Adam, in his choice, may have the whole range of creation. Adam surveys them all. He sees by instinctive wisdom the nature and properties of each, so that he can affix names to all in turn. His knowledge is large and full; it has come direct from God, just as his own being had come. It is not discovery, it is not learning, it is not

ver. 20, where the words are the same, it has *ὅμοιος αὐτῷ*. The Vulgate makes it 'adjutorium simile sibi,' which Isidore Clarius, in his amended edition of the Vulgate (1542), turns into 'adjutorium opportunum.' Coverdale renders it 'an helpe to bear him company.' The Hebrew expression seems to denote the correspondency or fitting in of the one nature to the other; the perfect *adaptation* of the woman to the man. Milton has brought out part of this idea in the fourth book of *Paradise Lost*:—

'Tho' both,
Not equal, as their sex not equal seemed;
For contemplation he and valour formed,
For softness she and sweet attractive grace
He for God only, she for God in him.'

And a writer of the last generation puts it thus: 'Is not man himself (humanity) split into two parts, man for condescending love, woman for reverent love?'

experience, it is not memory, it is intuition. By intuition he knew what the wisest king in after ages only knew by searching.[1] Solomon, we read, 'spake of trees, from the cedar tree that is in Lebanon even unto the hyssop that springeth out of the wall: he spake also of beasts, and of fowl, and of creeping things, and of fishes' (1 Kings iv. 33). But Adam's knowledge went far beyond this. In the case both of Adam and of Solomon, we see what man shall yet attain to; what widespread knowledge shall be theirs who are one with that second Adam, in whom are hid all the treasures of wisdom and knowledge. From these instances we see, not merely the folly, but the sin of those who depreciate science, as if it were the handmaid of ungodliness, and the result of the fall. Sorely misused has science been; sadly has it oftentimes risen up between the soul and God; between sinful man and the incarnate Son; between the intellect of the learned and the gospel of the grace of God. Fearfully has it wrought, as a deadly poison to the human spirit, through the workings of pride and self-sufficiency, and idolatry of the reason. But notwithstanding all these results, let us hold fast the truth which Adam's wondrous attainments teach us, that such knowledge is, in itself, most truly and surely good;—not evil.

[1] Some have asserted that man *rose* by the *fall;* that is, that he gained in intellect what he lost in spiritual character. There is no proof in Scripture for such a statement. The results of the fall were unmingled loss, both intellectually and morally.

Ver. 20. '*But for Adam there was not found an help meet for him.*'

No counterpart,—no being to fill up the void within him, was to be found in all these. There was no response from any one of them to the deep feelings of his breast. They were too far asunder from him; their nature was not in harmony or sympathy with his. The two extremities of being had thus been presented to Adam,—God Himself on the one hand, and the animal creation on the other. In neither of these can a help meet be found. The one is too far above him, the other too much beneath him. A being must be found liker and nearer himself. The whole creation, perfect as it was, yet contained nothing for true and loving companionship. Men may speak of fellowship with nature, in its various forms and orders of life,—of finding sympathies in the breeze, the cloud, the wave, the rock, the flower; but all this is but the exaggeration of sentiment or poetry. In all creation, animate or inanimate, there is no fellow, no companion for man.

Vers. 21–24. '*And the Lord God caused a deep sleep to fall upon Adam, and he slept: and he took one of his ribs, and closed up the flesh instead thereof.* 22. *And the rib, which the Lord God had taken from man, made He a woman, and brought her unto the man.* 23. *And Adam said, This is now bone of my bones, and flesh of my flesh: she shall be called Woman, because she was taken out of man.* 24. *Therefore shall a man leave his father and his mother, and shall cleave to his wife; and they shall be one flesh.*'

God now proceeds to supply the void, but in such a way as shall make man feel God's design and meaning. The peculiar process adopted by the Creator in forming the help meet was to intimate to man the nature of the companion presented to him, and the closeness of the tie between them. Adam was thrown into a deep sleep, which made him insensible to pain, though, perhaps, not unconscious of what was passing. When in this state, God took one of his ribs, and fashioned out of it a woman, healing the wound at once. Then God brought her to Adam, revealing at the same time to him the history of her formation. Adam recognises Jehovah's gracious purpose in this; he feels the void supplied; he acknowledges the oneness between himself and her; he gives her a name expressive of this. Her name is to be woman, *Isha*, derived from his own, *Ish*, man. Then follows the historian's statement regarding the oneness of the two, and man's duty to make this tie paramount. The conjugal relationship is closer than the filial. All other bonds must yield to this, however sacred and tender they may be. The words of the twenty-fourth verse are evidently not the words of Adam himself, but the comment of Moses upon the words of Adam. And a greater than Moses has enlarged this comment:—'From the beginning of the creation God made them a male and a female. For this cause shall a man leave his father and mother, and cleave to his wife; and they twain shall be one flesh; so then they are no more twain, but one flesh. What therefore God hath joined together, let not man put asunder' (Mark x. 6).

With one or two further remarks, we leave this passage.

1. *As to Adam's sleep.*—It was a heavy, or deep sleep. It was a sleep sent directly from God. It was a sleep

for a special end. In the case of Abraham and Daniel we see the same thing (Gen. xv. 12; Dan. viii. 18, x. 9). A deep sleep from God fell on both these, when God designed to communicate visions to them. In their case, God caused them to sleep that He might show them what was to be done; in the case of Adam, that He might actually do the thing. In both instances the individuals were rendered unconscious to outward things by that which we call sleep, and in that state God took possession of them; in Abraham's and Daniel's case, of the soul; in Adam's, of the body. It would seem to be intimated, that not until Adam had been brought into that state which approaches nearest to death could God accomplish his design. There must be sleep in the first Adam ere God can take out of him the ordained spouse; and there must be death in the second Adam ere God can take out of Him the chosen Bride. In this way there might be something prefigurative in Adam's sleep.[1]

2. *As to the taking of woman out of man.*—As it was God that caused Adam to sleep, so it was God Himself that took the rib out of him. Thus God shows Him-

[1] This subject was, of course, likely to be a favourite one with the Fathers. Their allusions to it are without number. Thus Augustine, 'Quando dormivit in cruce implebat quod significatum erat in Adam, quia cum dormiret Adam, costa illi detracta est et Eva facta est.'—*On Ps.* cxxvii. And Gotschalc, the Augustine or Calvin of the ninth century, writes, 'Eva de Adam, sic Ecclesia de Christo; et sicut Adamo dormiente inde formata est Ecclesia, sic Christo dormiente in cruce, inde formata est Ecclesia.'—*Sermon on the Nativity.* Tertullian thus writes, 'Somnus Adæ mors erat Christi dormituri in mortem et de injuria perinde lateris ejus, vera mater viventium figuraretur Ecclesia.'—*De Anima*, chap. xliii.

self to us as at once the great Purposer and the great Doer of all things. 'Second causes,' as we speak, are but the mysterious tools or instruments which He makes use of in carrying out His designs. He lays us to sleep each night, and He awakens us each morning with His own loving hand. He is the God of our nights and of our days. It was from Adam that God took the substance which He meant to fashion into woman, indicating that, as man was formed first, and as woman sprang from man, so man is to be her head. He from the dust, she from him. *He* directly from the Former's hand, *she* indirectly, and through *him*. 'Adam,' says the apostle, 'was first formed, then Eve' (1 Tim. ii. 13); therefore, says he, she is 'not to teach nor to usurp authority over the man, but to be in silence.' Thus, again, he states the gradation: (1) the head of the woman is the man, (2) the head of the man is Christ, (3) the head of Christ is God (1 Cor. xi. 3). Further, he adds that 'the woman is the glory (or ornament) of the man;' for, says he, 'the man is not of the woman, but the woman of the man; neither was the man created for the woman, but the woman for the man'[1] (1 Cor.

[1] We may notice here how all the different conditions of womanhood are made use of by God as setting forth some peculiar aspect of His Church:—(1.) *Virgin.* 2 Cor. xi. 2; Rev. xiv. 4. (2.) *Betrothed.* Hos. ii. 19; 2 Cor. xi. 2. (3.) *Wife.* Rev. xix. 7, xxi. 9. (4.) *Travailing.* Rev. xi. 2. (5.) *Desolate and forsaken.* Gal. iv. 27. (6.) *Mother.* Gal. iv. 26. (7.) *Barren.* Isa. liv. 1. (8.) *Widow.* Luke xviii. 3; Isa. liv. 4. And thus one of the Fathers illustrates the idea: '*Sponsa* est (ecclesia) quia inhæret Christo; *Mater* est, qui fœcundatur a Christo; *Virgo,* quia incorrupta perseverat in Christo.'—*Fulgentius,* Epist.

xi. 8, 9). Such is God's order of things; such His assignment of place and rank to the creatures which He has made. We may be sure that there is a reason for this gradation, not merely a *typical,* but a *natural* one, whether we fully understand it or not. We cannot alter this law, and be blameless. We cannot reverse it, and not suffer loss. The construction of our world's fabric is far too delicate and complex for man to attempt the slightest change without dislocating the whole. One star displaced, one planet thrown off its orbit, will confound the harmonies of space, and strew the firmament with the wrecks of the universe; so one law lost sight of or set at nought, will mar the happy order of God's living world below. In one age or nation man treads down woman as a slave; in another he idolizes her, and sings of her as of a goddess; in both cases inflicting a social wrong upon the race; in the latter case as truly as in the former; and who can say how deep an injury, both spiritual and social, has been wrought, and how fatal an influence has been sent forth, by that fond sentimentalism which, impregnating our poetry, and, coursing like fever through the veins of youth, not only 'costs the fresh blood dear,' but saps the whole social system, nay, propagates a principle of subtle ungodliness and creature-worship, in its praise of woman's beauty, and idolatry of woman's love.

3. *As to the taking of woman from the side of man.*— From neither extremity of Adam's body did God take the woman, signifying that she was neither to be man's lord, nor man's drudge, but his fellow, only with this

inferiority, that she was taken out of him, and therefore he was to be her head. From that part which lies nearest his heart did woman come. She was not so much to partake of man's intellectual as of his loving nature. It was not from man's thinking forehead or sinewy arm that she sprang, but from those parts where it may be said there is the least of *man* to be found. From the region where the warm blood flows, and the heart throbs, and the pulses take their rise, and the fountain of life wells up, did woman come. From that quarter of man's being where, in all ages, affection has been conceived to make its home, where joy and sorrow have their flowings and reflowings, where fear and hope are each hour sinking and swelling, did woman come. The fragrant plumage of the turtle tells us out of what spice-grove she has come. So does woman's tender nature of itself declare that it is from the region of the kindly and the gentle that she has been brought forth. As it was out of the bosom of the Father that the Eternal Son came down to us laden with the Father's love; as it was out of the bosom of the Son that the Church came forth, at once the object and the reflection of His mighty love; so it was out of man's side,—man's bosom,—that she came forth who was to be at once the embodiment of his gentler affections, and the being round whom these affections were to cling. And as it was on the high priest's breast,—his place of love,—that the names of Israel rested, in jewelled splendour, so is it on man's breast that woman is to rest;—ay, and so is it hereafter, on the breast of the eternal Bridegroom that the Church is to repose, in more than earthly glory, in that day when His 'left hand shall be under her head, and His right hand shall embrace' her; when she shall be 'set as a seal upon His heart, as a seal upon His arm' for ever.

4. *As to the making of woman from a rib of man.*—One of those protecting circles which prevents the sinking in of the flesh upon the heart, and which gives the heart full room to play, was to be taken out entire, that out of it woman might be formed. The bone and the flesh were both taken,—the softer and more solid parts of man's body,—that it might be seen how truly she was of man's very nature, though in some respects differing. Not a separate being formed out of the dust, in which man could not recognise a part of himself, but a being thoroughly identified with him; not merely like him, but one with him, so that her absence would be the absence of a part of himself,—a blank, a void, without whom he would be incomplete. This taking out a *rib* in order to form the woman, suggests very much the idea that would have been called up had a cedar plank, or a piece of gold, been taken out of the 'holiest of all' in the temple, to fashion into one of the vessels of the sanctuary. A vessel formed in such a way would be very different in the eyes of Israel from one formed of cedar direct from Lebanon, or gold direct from Ophir. It could not fail to remind them of the sacred place from which its materials were taken, and it would be for ever associated in their minds with all that 'the holy of holies' suggested to an Israelite. Thus

woman, taken from the very shrine of man's corporeal sanctuary (for the apostle teaches us to call our bodies temples, 1 Cor. vi. 19), is linked with all the sacred or tender associations that are called up by that well-known but mysterious word,—the heart!

5. *As to the making of the woman.*—The expression is a very peculiar one. It is neither of the two former that have been already employed,—'created' or 'made.' It is, literally, 'builded.' The word is a very common one, occurring about four hundred times, but here only in so peculiar a sense. It is the word used in reference to the building of a city, a house, a family, a temple, a throne, an altar, and such like. And there is surely some signification in applying such a word to the formation of woman. Of man it is said he was *made*, of woman she was *builded.* Now man was the type of Christ; and of the latter, in reference to His human nature, it might be said simply He was 'made,'—formed at once. But the woman signifies the Church, taken out of the wounded side of her dying Lord. And of the Church it is often said she is 'builded;' 'in whom,' says the apostle, 'all the *building*, fitly framed together, groweth unto an holy *temple* in the Lord; in whom ye also are *builded together* for an *habitation* of God, through the Spirit' (Eph. ii. 21, 22); and again, 'for the edifying'—literally, the *building*—'of the body of Christ' (Eph. iv. 12). By the term 'building,' applied to the formation of Eve, God has thought fit to shadow forth to us the process by which, age after age, the Church (which is the second Eve) was to be fashioned into a help

meet or counterpart for Christ, the second Adam; yet as the second Adam was far more glorious than the first, so does the second Eve, taken out of His pierced breast, far transcend the first, God in all respects bestowing more cost and pains upon the new creation than upon the old. For redemption has brought in, not simply a new order of things, but one far higher than that which it is designed to replace: the one being earthly, the other heavenly; the one fleshly, the other spiritual; the one human, the other divine. And thus the Church, Christ's chosen Bride, springing from his smitten side, is 'builded;'—builded by the same Almighty hands that built the wondrous heavens; builded, as was the temple of old, without sound of axe or hammer; builded, at once as the *City* of the Lamb's special habitation, and the *Companion* for His dearest fellowship, without whom this goodly universe would have been incomplete to Him; for even in it, though renewed and glorified, it would have been found that it was 'not good for Him to be alone.' For Him no help meet could have been found, had not the Father provided this 'glorious Church,' and had not He Himself, in the greatness of His longing for that help meet, consented to sleep the deep sleep of death upon the cross, that thus *she* might be taken out of Him, whose beauty, as seen pictured in the Father's purpose, had already 'ravished His heart' (Song iv. 9); whose presence could alone make even the better paradise complete; and union to whom, throughout eternity, was what His heart desired (John xv. 9, xvii. 23–26).

6. *As to the closing up of the flesh instead of what was taken out.*—Adam was not to be the loser in any way or sense, but the gainer. All deficiency was replaced, all loss supplied. God would teach him the nature of woman and the object of her creation (wrapping up in this also a type of things to come), but He would teach it in a way that would not leave man the sufferer. Jacob's lesson was to be learned by 'halting on his thigh' all his life after; but Adam's was to be learned by looking at his help meet, and then while remembering how she had been 'builded,' to feel that she had cost him nothing beyond the sleep into which he had been so mysteriously thrown. A sleep, but nothing more,—this was all the price for a boon so precious! No abiding pain, or loss, or weakness. He was still the same Adam as when he came from the hands of his Maker. Neither has the second Adam suffered loss for us. It did indeed cost him much to redeem us. It cost Him a darker, sadder, and more troubled sleep than Adam's. But it is all over now! He retains nothing of the weakness, or sorrow, or darkness of His low estate. He is not less the King of glory because He was once the humbled Jesus. He does indeed appear in heaven a Lamb 'as it had been slain;' He may, perhaps, retain the wounds of the cross; but more than this He does not. All other traces of His humiliation are erased. He has lost nothing by the Bride that He has gained. Nay, He has won much; for His weakness, sorrow, shame, when here, have bought for Him new strength, and gladness, and glory. Hence the song

of angels, 'Worthy is THE LAMB THAT WAS SLAIN to receive power, and riches, and wisdom, and strength, and honour, and glory, and blessing' (Rev. v. 12).

7. *As to the woman's introduction to the man.*—'He brought her unto the man.' God Himself, as if standing in a father's room, and acting the father's part, brings the bride to the bridegroom. As a beloved daughter He presents her to her future husband. He joined their hands and pronounced over them the marriage-blessing (chap. i. 28), 'Be fruitful, and multiply, and replenish the earth.'[1] A stranger, and yet no stranger,—a part of himself, the filling up of his being, she was brought before him, and knit to him in inseparable bonds. And it is thus that the true Eve speaks of herself in the Song, 'The King hath *brought* me into His chambers' (chap. i. 4); and again, 'He *brought* me to the banqueting-house' (chap. ii. 4). Of her also it is written, 'She shall be *brought* unto the King in raiment of needlework' (Ps. xlv. 14), and again, that she is 'prepared as a bride adorned for her husband' (Rev. xxi. 2). One of her special characteristics is, that she is 'given' of the Father to the Son; and in that day when He comes in His glory she shall be caught up to meet Him in

[1] Marriage was thus instituted *before* the fall; yet it remains *after* the fall, a standing ordinance. No precept concerning it was given afterwards till the time of Moses, yet it remained in force, and Christ appeals to this marriage transaction in the unfallen state as *the* basis of the law of marriage. The same with the Sabbath. It was given to unfallen man, yet the law remains in force after the fall, though there is no precept regarding it till Moses. And when that precept comes, it points back at once to the first institution of the rest-day. Our Lord does the same,—'The Sabbath was made for man.'

the air, and be brought into His presence by the Father, there to have the marriage service celebrated, and as a 'chaste virgin' (2 Cor. xi. 2), to be presented to Him to whom she has been so long betrothed. Then shall that song be sung to which all the new creation shall echo, 'Let us be glad and rejoice, and give honour to Him; for the marriage of the Lamb is come, and His wife hath made herself ready; and to her was granted that she should be arrayed in fine linen, clean and white, for the fine linen is the righteousness of saints' (Rev. xix. 7, 8).

8. *As to Adam's recognition of her.*[1]—Whether by revelation or consciousness we know not; but Adam knows the woman thus brought to him, and calls her woman, as being a part of man. This is his response to God's introduction of her. He acknowledges the oneness, and receives her as himself. We have God's consent in bringing, the woman's consent in coming, and now we have Adam's consent in receiving. Thus is the marriage completed by the full concurrence of all. And so is it with the second Adam too. He re-

[1] The words in the original are peculiar. It is not simply 'this is *now* bone of my bones;' the word translated *now* means 'this time' or 'this turn,' as if he had said, 'God has brought the animals to me one by one, and I have not found a counterpart to me,—but *this time* I have,—the being that He has brought to me *this time* is just such an one as I needed.' Bishop Kidder's explanation will not stand, 'for this once, as she should be otherwise produced afterwards.'—*Commentary on the Books of Moses*, vol. i. p. 11. Rungius comes nearer it when he translates it *nunc tandem*, now at length, and adds that it is the voice of one exulting and giving thanks to God for the boon conferred (p. 144).

ceives and owns His Bride. He welcomes her as indeed part of Himself, one with Himself. 'Both He that sanctifieth and they who are sanctified are all of one, for which cause He is not ashamed to call them brethren' (Heb. ii. 11). And again it is written, 'We are members of His body, of His flesh, and of His bones' (Eph. v. 30).[1] And thus recognising the mysterious oneness between Himself and His Bride, He expresses His admiration of her beauty, as the 'fairest among women' (Song i. 8), 'all glorious within' (Ps. xlv. 13); whilst she with joy responds and speaks of Him as 'fairer than the children of men' (Ps. xlv. 2). 'Behold, thou art fair, my love; thou art all fair; there is no spot in thee' (Song iv. 7), is the utterance of His admiring love of her; while she replies, 'My beloved is white and ruddy, the chiefest among ten thousand. His head is as the most fine gold; His locks are bushy, and black as a raven: His countenance is as Lebanon, excellent as the cedars: His mouth is most sweet; yea, He is altogether lovely' (Song v. 16). And in the happy consciousness of possessing Him and His love, she gives

[1] Theodoret, commenting on the verse in Ephesians, applies it thus: 'As Eve was formed (επλασθη) out of Adam, so are we out of the Lord Christ; for we are buried with Him in baptism, and rise again with Him; and we eat His body and we drink His blood.' And then, referring to a man's leaving his father, etc., he applies it thus: 'He (Christ) leaving His Father above (τὸν ἄνω πατέρα), was joined to the Church' (τῇ ἐκκλησίᾳ συνήφθη). We may notice here, that while in the passage before us it is the *man* that is said to leave his father's house, not the *wife*, yet this latter is evidently understood; for if the man must do it, much more the wife. Our readers also will remember in the 45th Psalm, it is the *bride* that is exhorted to forget her father's house.

vent to the deep feeling of her satisfied soul, 'My beloved is mine, and I am His; He feedeth among the lilies until the day break and the shadows flee away' (Song ii. 16).

All this transaction took place in silence; without noise and without violence. In the silence of deep sleep[1] (it might be midnight too) the Lord wrought His work. It might seem a deed of pain and violence to man. But no. There was the unconscious opening of the side, the gentle abstraction of the needed part, the tender and unfelt healing of the wound! How strange the work, yet how silent the doing! And how like the noiseless building of the temple on Moriah, on which no sound of axes or hammers was ever heard. How like the process that is now going on in this world for the building of the 'living Temple! The work advances in silence. No uproar, no shouting, no Babel-clamour of discordant tongues. From day to day it moves on noiselessly. Stone after stone is cut from the rude rock, hewn and polished, ready to be fitted into the glorious fabric. Member after member is gathered in, and added to the mystic body,

[1] May we not be allowed to suppose that man was created early on the sixth day;—during the day he reviewed and named the creatures, —then as it drew towards evening he fell into the deep trance-like sleep, and on awakening on the Sabbath morning, he saw and welcomed his mysterious help meet? On that Sabbath dawn it was that 'the morning stars sang together, and all the sons of God shouted for joy,'—chanting the bridal song;—and on the world's great Sabbath dawn shall that song be sung over paradise regained, as the Bride is seen descending, 'Behold, the tabernacle of God is with men, and He will dwell with them, and they shall be His people, and God Himself shall be with them, and be their God' (Rev. xxi. 3).

—the Bride, the Lamb's wife! All by an invisible hand, and by a process of which the world knows nothing! And when this midnight is over, and the world's great Sabbath dawns, then in a moment, in the twinkling of an eye, shall this prepared Bride, in full maturity of being, and bloom of resurrection beauty, stand forth to view, when the Bridegroom's voice shall be heard, 'Rise up, my love, my fair one, and come away; for lo! the winter is past, the rain is over and gone; the flowers appear on the earth; the time of the singing of birds is come, and the voice of the turtle is heard in our land' (Song ii. 10).

Ver. 25. '*And they were both naked, the man and his wife, and were not ashamed.*'

There they stood, just as they came from the hands of God. They did not need to blush; they felt no shame. It is sin that has connected nakedness and shame together. No sin, no shame. There is no blush upon an angel's brow. Unfallen man had the unashamed nakedness of innocence; but with the fall this has passed away, not to be returned to, even under redemption, but to be replaced by something higher, the glorious raiment of a righteousness that is unfading and divine. Unfallen man needed no covering, and asked for none; but fallen man, under the bitter consciousness of the unworthy and unseemly condition to which sin has reduced him, as unfit for God, or angels, or man to look upon, cries out for covering,—covering such as will hide his shame even from the eye of God. Hence He who undertook to provide this covering, must bear the shame. And He has borne it,—all the shame of hanging naked on the cross; the shame of a sinner; the shame of being made the song of the drunkard; the shame of being despised and rejected of men; the shame of being treated as an outcast, one unfit for either God or man to look upon,—unfit not only to live, but even to die within the gates of the holy city (Heb. xiii. 11, 12). All that shame has He borne for us, that we might inherit His glory. He stooped to the place of shame below, that we might obtain the place of honour in the better paradise above.

Thus walked our first parents amid the groves of a paradise that had not then been lost. Thus dwelt they in its bowers as a home, and worshipped in it as a sanctuary.[1] For with them the family mansion was the temple of their God. These were one, ere man had sinned. The entrance of sin divided these. Nor did grace, though coming in so largely and so swiftly, unite them again. From that day onward they have been separate. But the time is at hand when they shall be again united as in paradise; and in the new Jerusalem, the Church shall find at once her temple and her home.

[1] The long preserved traditions of paradise led men in after ages to worship in *groves* and under trees, and even to construct their temples in imitation of these. A Gothic cathedral is just a petrified forest-shrine,—the pillared trees shooting up on each side, and the interwoven branches embracing overhead and forming the roof. God seems to have taken special care to suppress this idea, both on account of the heathen abominations done in groves, and also because *His* times for a return to Eden worship was not yet come. Hence both the tabernacle and temple have nothing of the kind about them, save a few engravings of palm-trees on the walls.

Even now we anticipate this blessed reunion; for faith brings us into the holy of holies, there to worship and to dwell. We pitch our tents beside the mercy-seat, and under the shadow of the glory. In the innermost shrine of the temple is the Church's proper home. And when we pass from the visions of faith into the realities of possession and enjoyment, we shall find the same happy union of the home and the temple. In the Jerusalem beneath, the separation may be still kept up, but in the Jerusalem above, the palace and the temple are one; for as it is the Lord God Almighty that is to be the temple there, so it is in the Lord God Almighty and the Lamb that we are to abide, we in Him and He in us. It is the bosom of the Father that is to be our dwelling for ever.

That promised inheritance of the saints was prefigured by Adam's paradise, with this difference, that as the second Adam far transcends the first, so shall the paradise of the second Adam far excel and outshine the paradise of the first. The glory of the terrestrial is one, but the glory of the celestial is another. The glory of unfallen creation is one, but the glory of restored creation is another. The glory of earth standing *alone* in its beauty is one; but the glory of earth and heaven united,—of earth and heaven reflecting and augmenting each other's splendour,—is another. Yet still the earthly and the heavenly have their common features, by which the one is known to be a copy of the other, just as the tabernacle was a copy of heavenly things shown to Moses on the mount. In the Apocalyptic picture of the 'inheritance of the saints in light,' we can trace the likeness between the two in the main aspect of the outline, though the filling up may somewhat differ. This *unlikeness* certainly we notice, that in the one there was no building whatsoever, in the other there is a magnificent city. Yet this city is embosomed in a gorgeous paradise; and it is built of the various gems for which the ancient paradise was noted; as if God had for these many ages hedged in and veiled the sacred spot, that He might enlarge and beautify it after a fashion which eye had not seen; nay, that He might rear within its bowers and out of its rich mines a city worthy of Himself and of that Son who was to be its Lord, and of that company, redeemed by blood, who were to inhabit it; so that when at last the fence is taken down, and the covering removed, there stands forth to view, not the ancient paradise, for the dwelling of 'the man and his wife,' but the 'many mansions' (John xiv. 2), the 'prepared city' (Heb. xi. 16); the city of gems and gold, for the habitation of the nobler heirs, the great multitude that no man can number.

In the midst of the street of this city there reappears the tree of life; just as the former tree of life had been 'in the midst of the garden,' and just as the pot of manna (sole memorial for ages of the tree of life) was in the midst of the ark (Heb. ix. 4). Of the tree of knowledge no trace is to be found, as if no memorial of man's sin were to remain; or as if, the interdict being removed, there was no longer any need to specify it; or as if it had been entirely superseded by Him in whom are hid all the treasures of wisdom and knowledge; or as if knowledge and life, once separated, had now become so entirely one, that the tree of life might represent both; for 'this is *life* eternal, that they might *know* Thee the only true God, and Jesus Christ whom Thou hast sent.'[1] Adam in paradise had the tree of life; Israel in the wilderness had the manna (angels' food, Ps. lxxviii. 25, as temporary supply till the true bread should come down); but the Church, in the New Jerusalem, is to have the more glorious tree, of which the former was but a terrestrial shadow. Beyond 'the mountain of myrrh,' and the 'hill of frankincense,' when the day has broken and the shadows fled; beyond Lebanon, and Amana, and Shenir, and Hermon; beyond 'the lions' dens' and the 'mountains of the leopards' (Song iv. 6, 8), she shall sit down in the garden of her God, under the fair branches of the

[1] The spiritual reference to the tree of life may be seen in such passages as the following :—'She (wisdom) is a tree of life to them that lay hold of her' (Prov. iii. 18), and 'the fruit of the righteous one is a tree of life' (Prov. xi. 30)—that is, the fruit which the righteous one produces (words and deeds) is like a tree of life to all around; as in Jas. iii. 18, 'The fruit of righteousness is sown in peace of them that make peace'—that is, the fruit of righteousness, or righteous fruit, is sown by the peaceful walk and character of those who seek and make peace. The root of holiness is peace. Again we have, 'When the desire cometh (when the thing desired is obtained), it is a tree of life' (Prov. xiii. 12); deferred hope sickens, fulfilled hope revives and invigorates. Again, 'A wholesome tongue is a tree of life' (Prov. xv. 4); the healing of the tongue is like planting a tree of life. It diffuses life and health. Christ speaks of Himself as the 'Bread of life;' as if He were not merely fruit, but fruit specially prepared as the soul's food, ready to be partaken of, sent down from heaven, prepared by the Father's hands,—'The bread of God which came down from heaven, of which if a man eat he shall never hunger and never die.'

'Plant of renown,' partaking of Him who is her life, in a way such as she has never done on earth, and feeling that thus she has a life which Adam had not, which angels have not,—a life that flows out of the deepest well of life, the bosom of Him who is in the bosom of the Father.

CHAPTER III.

WE have been looking at a perfect world. We have seen it to be such as God could call 'good;' not a cloud in its sky, not a ruffle on its ocean-breadth, not a tinge upon its verdure; not a pang, or sigh, or groan, or tear, all over its bright plains. It is the dwelling of the unfallen, the outer chamber of heaven, the land wherein dwelleth righteousness. We have seen the *harmony* of creation; all its parts linked together in loving oneness, the animate and inanimate, the intelligent and irrational; no jar, no dissonance in any. Man is the head, the lord, appointed to exercise holy dominion under Jehovah as his Head and Lord. We have seen the *beauty* of creation, with its flowers and dew, its gems and gold, its sunshine and starlight above; its green stretch of hill, plain, forest, below. We have seen it as a world without a sin, or a shadow, or a sigh, or a wrinkle; neither decay nor disease have entered it; there are no tossing sickbeds, no heartbreaking deathbeds, no severing bonds, no bitter farewells, no heaving tombs. It is a world altogether good; a world which angels might visit; over which God might delight, and in which He might dwell with man. We need not say of it, as has been done, 'Fit haunts of gods;' we may at once say, 'Fit dwelling of Jehovah.' A visible dwelling for the invisible God is that which was designed. This has always formed one special part of God's purpose in all its unfoldings.

We have now to learn the story of its change; its change from being the seat of life and righteousness and joy, to becoming the region of death and evil and sorrow; from being the dwelling of God, to becoming the haunt, nay, the regal residence of Satan, and the sphere of peculiar action to his hosts, 'the rulers of the darkness of this world.' From this chapter onwards to the twenty-first of Revelation we have the sad story of its sin. The two first chapters of Scripture tell of its unfallen glory, the two last of its restored perfection; but all between is gloom, a story of ruin and desolation—'written within and without with lamentation, and mourning, and woe.'[1] We have seen a summer's sky overcast in an hour, the heavens putting on sackcloth, and the sun which had

[1] There is a curious old book of the sixteenth century, in quarto, with the following title:—*A Hyve full of Hunnye, contayning the firste booke of Moses called Genesis, turned into English meetre*, by William Hunnis, 1578. From the 'argument' of this work we extract the following verses as a specimen. After describing creation he speaks of man:—

'Who viewing these His gracious gifts,
Should praise His holy name,
And magnify Him day and night,
Entirely for the same.

But man, forgetting quite himself,
And God that rules on high,
Committed sin, displeased God,
And stumbled wittingly.

Who thro' his disobedience
Enthralled himself in woe,
And fell from God, from whom to him
So many gifts did flow.'

risen in calm going down in storm. So was it with our world, as this chapter proceeds to record; once holy, yet only for a day. How sudden and sad the change! Yesterday it was paradise; to-day, the wilderness. Yesterday it neighboured heaven; to-day it is the suburb of hell. Yesterday it was God's footstool; to-day it is Satan's throne. Yesterday it was linked to the sanctuary above by a bond that seemed everlasting; to-day that bond is broken, and it commences a swift descent into the uttermost darkness.

This third chapter records the manner in which this change was effected; the different steps which led to it. And here we have the *true* origin of evil—God's own account of the way in which tares were first sown in the field in which God had sown the finest of the wheat.

The passage takes for granted that there was already *an enemy* in existence. There had been *sin* before, *somewhere*, though *where* is not said. There had been an enemy somewhere; but how he had become so, or where he had hitherto dwelt, or how he had found his way to this world, is not recorded. That he knew about our world, and that he had some connection with it, is evident; though whether as its original possessor, or a stranger coming from far in search of spoil, we cannot discover. All that is implied in the narrative is, that there did exist an enemy,—one who hated God, and who now sought to get vent to that hatred by undoing His handiwork.[1]

[1] 'If creation is the first wonder of time, the second is the origin of that new element which extends through all generations, the en-

This enemy now makes his appearance. He has not been bound; he has not been prohibited entrance: he gets free scope to work. He shall be bound hereafter, when the times of restitution of all things commence, but not yet. He shall not be permitted to enter the 'new earth,' but he is allowed to enter and do his work of evil in the first earth. In order to deceive, and in order to prevent any suspicions arising, or any questions being put as to what he was, or whence he came, or what he sought, he takes the form of one of those animals with which man was surrounded; he selects that which possessed more intelligence than the rest,[1] not only to excite less suspicion, but probably because,

trance of evil into the pure creation, the defilement of that which was formed good, by the first sin. As the history of creation can possess complete truth only where the idea of the Creator and the creature is a true one, so also can the history of the fall only where the idea of good and evil may be discovered, in its true form, where the history proves itself to be true in its idea.'—Hävernick *On the Pentateuch*, p. 100.

[1] 'Quum instrumento opus haberet, delegit ex animalibus quod sibi aptissimum for videbat.'—CALVIN. This expositor, after showing that the serpent was but 'the mouth of the devil,' goes on to consider the question why Moses does not explicitly state Satan's agency in this scene. He gives various reasons for this, such as 'puerilis ecclesiæ ætas,' etc. They do not satisfy. May not the true reason be just the very opposite of these suppositions? May it not be, that from the beginning men so thoroughly understood the thing to be *Satan's* doing, that there was no need for using other language? The personality and agency of Satan were far better understood and realized in early days than in our own. Hence, not only all Jewish, but all heathen traditions, while making mention of the serpent as helping in the origination of sin, introduce also along with him the evil spirit as the great agent. Serpent-worship was universal among the heathen. (See Faber's *Horæ Mosaicæ*, vol. i. p. 71, etc.)

according to the nature of things, he could more easily and more fully take possession of it, and wield it more successfully as the instrument of his deception.

It is, however, only from other parts of Scripture that we directly learn who the real tempter was. It is simply said here,

Ver. I. '*Now* (or *and*) *the serpent was more subtle than any beast of the field which the Lord God had made.*'

This language is too simple to be allegorized or perverted. It obviously refers, in the first place, to the literal serpent.[1] This was the visible instrument through which the enemy spoke and acted. Nor is it a greater difficulty to suppose that Satan spoke to Eve through the wisest of animals, than that God spoke to Balaam through the stupidest, when He opened the ass's mouth to utter His message. The description here given is, as usual, of the matter just as it *appeared*.[2] It was the *serpent* that was seen and heard. It was the *serpent* that acted throughout, so far as Eve or Adam understood at the time. Hence it is the serpent alone that

[1] 'Ille insatiabilis homicida. . . . non ursos, non leones, non fortia terræ animalia delegavit, sed tortuosum et callidum serpentem. . . . serpens non fortior erat sed callidior cunctis animantibus.' —BERNARD, *Serm. de Septem Spiritibus.* As Adam had just been naming the animals according to their natures, Eve would know that the serpent was more subtle or cunning than the rest. (See Lord Barrington's *Dissertation on the Temptation and Fall*, p. 4.)

[2] 'As Satan can change himself into an angel of light, so did he abuse the wisdom of the serpent to deceive man.'—*Bishops' Bible.* The *original nature* of the serpent is evidently referred to as being 'more subtle' than other animals.

is mentioned. Yet that it was Satan assuming the disguise of a serpent, is evident. No mere animal could thus of itself reason of good and evil; could thus plot man's ruin, and show such hatred of God. Besides, the sentence afterwards pronounced on it *implies* this, just as the apostle's statement does[1] (2 Cor. xi. 3. See also Rev. xii. 9–14, xv. 20–22).

Thus we learn, even at the outset, that God is not the author of sin. It is the creature that introduces it. God, no doubt, could have hindered it, but for wise ends He allows it. We know also how sin spreads itself. It is always *active.* It multiplies and propagates itself. Every fallen being becomes a tempter, seeking to ruin others,—to drag them down to the same death into which he has himself been driven.

Nor is it merely the upper orders of being that become

[1] The plague of the fiery serpents seems to point to this, showing us the way of man's ruin by Satan, and the way of restoration by Christ (John iii. 14). We may notice the other allusions to the serpent. 1. Its *bite* (Gen. xlix. 17; Jer. viii. 17; Prov. xxxiii. 32). 2. Its *tongue* (Ps. cxl. 3). 3. Its *voice* (Jer. xlvi. 23). 4. Its *poison* (Ps. lviii. 4). 5. Its *wisdom* (Matt. x. 26). 6. Its *hatefulness* (Matt. xxiii. 33). Such are the Scripture references. They preserve an awful uniformity throughout, presenting to us this one animal as pre-eminent above the rest for its evil qualities, and associating that one creature with Satan himself; with the introduction, propagation, and punishment of sin, giving us in it the emblem of sin's exceeding sinfulness, and of the ruinous results of contact or connection with it. See a very full collection of passages from the Fathers relating to the serpent and his subtlety, in Suicer's *Thesaurus*, vol. ii. pp. 535–537. He thinks that πανοῦργος, not φρόνιμος (as the LXX. render it), is the proper translation, citing in proof the words of the apostle, 'As the serpent deceived Eve by his cunning' (πανουργία), 2 Cor. xi. 3.

snares or tempters. The lower parts of creation can be made instruments of ruin. God cannot tempt, but the creature does, in all its parts. The smallest, commonest thing—a leaf, a tree, an animal—may become Satan's instrument. Whatever can touch or affect any of our desires or feelings, may be made use of by Satan for our injury, just as the serpent was made use of here. How watchful ought we to be in such a world, where so many things minister to the lust of the flesh and the lust of the eye! Flee sin; flee its very shadow; flee its most distant approach under any guise! Say not the temptation is a feeble one. That cannot be. The strength of the temptation lies in *yourself*, far more than in the tempting object. Get as far from sin and as near to God as you can; that is your only security. In God you are safe, but nowhere else. In Him who is God manifest in flesh, you are beyond the reach of danger. No tempter can succeed; no enemy can reach you there.

Ver. I. '*And he said unto the woman, Yea, hath God said, Ye shall not eat of every tree of the garden?*'[1]

The angels fell *untempted*. Man's case was different.

[1] The use of 'God' (Elohim) here and in what follows, instead of the Lord God (Jehovah-Elohim), gives rise to the following striking remark of Hengstenberg:—'The masterstroke of the tempter's policy was then, as it is still now, to change *Jehovah* into *Elohim*, the living, holy God into a *nescio quod numen*. (With what vagueness the term Elohim is used by the serpent, is shown by the expression, Ye shall be as Elohim, ye shall be raised to an unearthly nature and dignity.) Having done this, and not before, he could venture upon deluding

A tempter ensnared him. That tempter took the form of a serpent. Hence he is named so specially, 'that old serpent, which is the devil and Satan' (Rev. xx. 2). He had himself fallen *untempted*, but this did not make him less willing to tempt. He had become the enemy of God, and thus became the enemy of man. A ruined being himself, he sought to ruin others, that so he might have companions in guilt and woe, and thus avenge himself upon God.

From the first clause regarding the serpent's *subtlety*, we are prepared for a well-laid plot, manifesting consummate art and guile.[1] The temptation will be well disguised; the snare will be well laid. The tempter must speak fair, if he hopes to succeed at all. He must veil *himself* as well as his object; for if he be recognised, or if his object be discovered, the victim will elude his grasp.

them with a downright falsehood. Jehovah is not a man that He should lie. The woman should have employed the name of Jehovah as an impenetrable shield to repel the fiery darts of the wicked one. The use of the name *Elohim* (that this was not from ignorance of the name Jehovah, is proved by chap. iv. 1) was the beginning of her fall. First, there was a depression or obscuration of the religious sentiment; then the tree appeared good to eat and pleasant to the eye; God died in the soul, and sin became alive.'—*On the Pentateuch*, vol. i. p. 317.

[1] 'Magis metuendus est cum fallit quam, cum sævit,' says Augustine (on Ps. xl.). This will remind the reader of Rutherford's well-known remark, 'Brother, since we must have a devil to trouble us, I love a *raging* devil best.' Hence the apostle speaks of the 'wiles of the devil;' and hence the serpent seems to have been fixed on by God as the animal of all others fitted to set forth Satan's characteristic,—deadly cunning. The violence of the 'roaring lion' is subordinate to this.

It is the *woman* that he assails, as being 'the weaker vessel,'[1] and therefore more likely to yield, and, in yielding, to draw the man with her. Then, as now (as, for example, in Popery[2]), he avails himself of woman's weakness and woman's influence.

He comes up to Eve, as one may suppose that a stranger might do, seeking information. He feigns to be one who has just heard a rumour that has greatly surprised him,—a rumour which he cannot credit, so insulting does he deem it to God's character, so injurious and unkind to man.[3] It is evident that he had heard God's prohibition. *How*, we know not; but we see here that he has access to learn what is taking place amongst us. He can hear and see the things that we hear and see! He is on the watch to gather them up,—ever listening, ever looking, ever following us, that he may discover alike what we say to God, and what God says to us. At one time he is the beguiling serpent, at another the devouring lion, but always 'walking about,'—'walking to and fro throughout the earth,'—to learn what may serve his purpose of malice towards man and revenge against God (Job i. 7; 2 Cor. xi. 3; 1 Pet. v. 8).

[1] ἀσθενεστέρου σκεῦος,—weaker than the man,—less capable of resistance. 'Imbecilla res est fœmina,' says Quintilian; and Hilary speaks of 'sexus mollioris.'—*Comment. on Matthew.*

[2] For striking illustrations of this, see *The Secret Instructions of the Jesuits*, and Michelet's *Priests, Women, and Families.* Satan, through the priest, does now to the daughters of Eve what, through the serpent, he did to Eve herself.

[3] 'The devil feigneth that he believeth God had wholly forbidden them the use of the fruits of the garden, to make way to talk with the woman, and to induce her to give ear to him.'—DIODATI.

With well-feigned surprise and incredulity he puts the question, 'Yea, hath God said, Ye shall not eat of every tree of the garden?' meaning thereby to insinuate the harshness of the injunction which he pretended hardly to believe.[1] Is it possible that God can have said so? Is it conceivable that He who has just made you, and provided you with such abundance, should grudge you a little fragment of that plenty, and debar you from the garden's choicest fruits; making you lords of creation, yet not allowing you to put forth your lordship; nay, refusing you access to that tree, the fruit of which would enable you rightly to exercise wise dominion?[2] In this his object was to calumniate God; at least, cunningly to suggest an idea which would misrepresent His character to man. He keeps out of sight all that God had done for man, all the proofs of love, so manifold, so vast; he fixes on one thing which *seemed* inconsistent with this; he brings up this before man in the way most likely to awaken evil thoughts of God.[3]

[1] The Jewish rabbis affirm that this is but the conclusion of a long conversation held between the woman and the serpent. Bush remarks, 'The probability is, that this was not the commencement of his discourse, but that something, which the historian does not record, had been previously said.' The words are literally, 'Yea, surely, has God said?' Mercer translates them, 'Itane verum est eum dixisse;' Calvin, 'Etiamne dixit Deus?'

[2] Some have thought that Satan really began with a *lie:* insinuating that God had forbidden them the use of *every* tree of the garden. The woman's answer does seem to confirm this; only it is more likely that Satan took advantage of a *truth*, in order to misconstrue it, than that he framed a *lie*, which could be at once denied and disproved.

[3] 'He begins by calling in question the *truth* of God. Is it true

Not as if *he* wished to say one word against God, nor even as if he needed to say anything; but as if the thing itself were too plain to be mistaken; as if, on the supposition of its being true, it could admit but of one interpretation. He leaves the fact to speak for itself. His object is to isolate the one fact, and so to separate it from all God's acts of love as to make it appear an instance of harsh and unreasonable severity.[1] Man had hitherto known the prohibition; but he had put no such construction on it; he had not imagined it capable of being so interpreted. Now Satan brings it up, and sets it out in an aspect likely to suggest such constructions as these:—'God is not your friend after all; He but pretends to care for you. He is a hard master, interfering with your liberty, not leaving you a free agent, but constraining you, nay, fettering you. He mocks you, making you creation's head, yet setting arbitrary limits to your rule; placing you in a fair garden,

that God has prohibited the use of any tree? For what was it created? Such are the inquiries of wicked men to this day. "For what are the objects of pleasure made," say they, "but to be enjoyed?" We might answer, among other things, "to try them that dwell on the earth"' (FULLER *On Genesis*). Calvin suggests the same idea: 'Mulieri scrupulum injicere voluit ut verbum Dei non esse crederet, cujus non palam extabat plausibilis ratio.' He hints also at another shade of meaning: 'Can your eating or not eating of a tree be of any concern to God? do you think He would take the trouble of forbidding you?'

[1] 'It seems to contain an insinuation that, if man must not eat of *every tree*, he might as well eat of none. Thus discontent overlooks the good, and pores upon the one thing wanting. "All this availeth me nothing, so long as Mordecai is at the gate."'—FULLER *On Genesis*.

yet debarring you from its fruits. He grudges you His gifts, making a show of liberality, while withholding what is really valuable.'

Thus Satan sought to calumniate God, to malign His character, to represent Him as the enemy, not the friend, of man. If he can succeed in this, then man will begin to entertain hard thoughts of God,—then he will become alienated from Him; then he will disobey; and then come the fall, the ruin, the guilt, the doom, the woe! Man is lost! Hell gets another inmate. The devil gets another companion. God's second work is marred, and He Himself is left to grieve over His new-made child torn from His embrace. In this way Satan thrusts in the wedge between man and God,—breaks the link between the creature and the Creator. How simple, yet how successful the process![1] A single question is put. God's character is maligned. The lie is believed. Man suspects God and perishes! Such is the dark process still by which Satan seeks to hinder our return to God. His

[1] 'Fallax diabolus et ad traducendum artifex calidissimus,' says Hilary (on Matt.); and again (on Ps. cxli.), 'Quicquid iniquitatum homines gerunt a diabolo suggeritur.' Thus it is that the Fathers speak of Satan. They always seem to see him and to contend with him hand to hand. He is always personal to them,—their great enemy; no mere figure or personification of the evil principle, but a living agent of perilous power and craft. In their days men calling themselves Christians had not learned to speak of 'extinct Satans.' Chrysologus has a singular passage, setting forth the evil agency of Satan. We can only quote part:—'Diabolus mali auctor, nequitiæ origo, rerum hostis, secundi hominis semper inimicuo; ille laqueos tendit, lapsus parat, foveas fodit, aptat ruinas, stimulat corpora, purgit animas,' etc.—*Serm.* xi., *on Christ's Fasting and Temptation.*

aim is to misrepresent God to man; to prove God to be unkind in what He has prohibited, and a liar in what He has declared. The gospel is the full representation of God's gracious character made known by God Himself that the sinner may be induced to return. Satan perverts it or says it is untrue. Man believes the tempter, stands afar off, and dies!

Vers. 2, 3. '*And the woman said unto the serpent, We may eat* (or *we shall eat*) *of the fruit of the trees of the garden:* 3. *But of the fruit of the tree which is in the midst of the garden, God hath said, Ye shall not eat of it, neither shall ye touch it, lest ye die.*'

Had the woman fully understood the wicked suggestion of the serpent, or had she seen who it was that was speaking to her under the guise of the serpent, she would perhaps have fled at once. But not fully realizing either, and wishing perhaps to vindicate God for imposing, and herself for submitting to, such a restriction, she stood still to reason with the tempter. To a certain extent she was not so inexcusably guilty in this thing as we are in parleying with Satan instead of resisting him at once, and placing God's armour between us and his assaults; still there was enough to leave her without excuse. Even though she might not fathom the malignity of the suggestion, still it touched the question of obedience or disobedience to God, and this she ought at once to have resented and flung off with abhorrence.

Yet she does not yield at once. On the contrary, she defends her position. She makes ready mention of God's kindness and wide liberality, reminding the tempter that there was but one tree forbidden, and that all the rest were free for use.

Still she alters the words of the prohibition, and in this we see her beginning to waver. The change may be a slight one, yet we cannot help thinking that there is a meaning in it. She *adds* to it, for God had not said, 'Neither shall ye touch it;' she *takes from* it, for she greatly softens the threat, making it not 'thou shalt surely die,' but 'lest ye die.'[1] She thus exaggerates the restriction, as if wishing to prove it to be a hardship, and she dilutes the penalty, or at least the awfulness of its certainty, as if trying to persuade herself that it was not quite such a certainty as she had once thought it. Thus does sin work still. It magnifies God's prohibitions into hardships, in order to find an excuse for disobedience, and then it tries to underrate both the certainty and the greatness of the penalty. Simple obedience is what man does not like. Simple acquiescence in God's commands is what he is slow to learn. He altered God's words in order to get an excuse for departing from God, and so he still alters 'the word of the truth of the gospel' for the purpose of excusing himself for not returning at once to God, and taking advantage of the free welcome of His abundant grace.

[1] Calvin does not admit the former alteration to be an indication of apostasy already begun, but contends for the latter being so. He thinks that she was overlooking the penalty, or at least its certain infliction: 'Mortis periculum procul et frigide sentire se demonstrat.' Bernard has brought out the same sense: 'Ista (Eva) sub dubio supponit, ne forte, inquiens, si comederimus moriamur.' And again: 'Deus affirmat, mulier dubitat, Satan negat.'—*Sermones.*

Vers. 4, 5. '*And the serpent said unto the woman, Ye shall not surely die:*[1] 5. *For God doth know, that in the day ye eat thereof, then your eyes shall be opened; and ye shall be as gods* (or *as God*), *knowing good and evil.*'

The tempter immediately catches up the words of the woman, in which she had spoken of death as being the penalty of eating. Professing to act as her friend,[2] he speaks as one attempting to undeceive her as to a mistake under which she was labouring. 'You speak of the tree as dangerous to eat, or even to touch; nay, as involving the penalty of death to the eater. You have been quite deceived in this matter; there is no such deadly penalty; it is a mere threat on the part of God to prevent you eating of a tree which He knows would open your eyes and make you as Himself, knowing good and evil.'[3]

Thus he proceeds with his design of calumniating God, and questioning His veracity as well as His goodness. He goes a step further than in his former suggestion. He openly denies the *certainty* of the threatened penalty;

[1] Coverdale's translation is very expressive: 'Tush, ye shall not die the death.' An old writer notices that the devil says *ye*, not *thou*, having his eye on Adam as well as Eve.

[2] One of the Fathers remarks: 'Diabolus plures decipit blanditiis quam terroribus.'

[3] 'Knowing good and evil.' To know good and evil is sometimes a general expression for knowing *everything*, just as not to know good or evil is the expression for total ignorance,—the ignorance of infancy. (Deut. i. 39.) Or the expression may refer to 'sitting in judgment on good and evil;' as in Eccles. viii. 5, 'A wise man's heart discerneth (knoweth) both time and judgment;' and in 2 Sam. xiv. 17, 'As an angel of God, so is my Lord the king, to discern good and bad;' and 1 Kings iii. 9, Solomon prays for a heart to 'discern between

he questions its reality, and casts suspicion on God's intention in announcing it. Nay, more than this, he goes on to affirm that God knew well that, instead of a curse, there would come a blessing from the tasting of the tree; and that it was because He was jealous of man, and envious of the blessing thus to be reached, that He had shut him out from the tree. Thus he insinuates that God was a being of mere craft and falsehood, bearing no kindly feeling towards man, standing between him and a treasure-house of boundless blessing.

In this answer to the woman he speaks as one conscious that he was *making way.* He sees from *her answer* that he has made an impression by his indirect suggestion; and he now follows it up by something bolder and more direct.[1] 'Ye shall not surely die!' God neither can nor will execute His threat. Do not be alarmed. Do not let a mere fancy hinder you reaching out after such blessings as lie before you. So says Satan to the sinner still. 'There is no hell; the second

good and bad.' The temptation then would be that they should be as God in *judging*, sitting on His judgment-seat. In the world as it stood, they were only to be rulers of what God had pronounced 'good:' they are tempted to seek to be judges of 'evil'—to enter on a new domain both of rule and of judgment. Into this new region they sought to be introduced, not in God's time or way; and hence they found it only a region of shame and darkness. But the time is coming when we shall possess it in a different way, the way of faith and obedience; the obedience of Him who 'grew in wisdom,' waiting God's time for filling Him with knowledge; not like the first Adam, snatching at it impatiently. Then we shall 'judge all things;' we shall 'judge the world;' we shall 'judge angels.'

[1] 'Nemo cum serpente securus ludit, nemo cum diabolo jocatur impune.'—CHRYSOLOGUS, *Serm.* 155.

death is a mere dream; eat, drink, and be merry; sin as you like, and don't fear punishment.' Thus he beguiles the soul, and leads it onward to the second death. Strange that men should believe him; that they should listen to his voice in preference to God's. They *want* to be persuaded, and so they are persuaded; they want to be deceived, and so they are deceived! Yet can all this deception quench the flame of the burning lake, or set aside death, or make the wrath of God less true or terrible? Let him say there are no diseases, no pains, no sicknesses, *now*, would men believe him? No. And will they believe him when he tells them, there is no death *hereafter?*

'Your eyes shall be opened.' They shall be opened by that very act which you so much shrink from. It is God who is keeping them closed. He is drawing a curtain round you, excluding you from visions of brightness on every side. What a prospect spreads round you! A little boldness in disobedience, and all this fair region shall be yours, as it is already mine.

'Ye shall be as God, knowing good and evil.' No lower level than that of God Himself shall you rise to. All His height of honour shall be yours. Nay more, all His *knowledge.* Ye shall know, and judge, and see, even as He knows, judges, and sees. From all this wide circle of knowledge God is shutting you out. He wants the throne wholly to Himself; He cannot bear a rival.

Thus Satan sowed the seeds of mistrust, unbelief, atheism, hatred of God. Thus the 'evil heart of unbelief' was produced, and separation from God was the immediate result. It is thus that he still keeps the sinner at a distance from God, and prevents his 'submitting to the righteousness of God.' He sows and waters the seed of dark distrust in the sinner's soul, by persuading him that God is not sincere either in His wrath or in His grace. He leads the sinner to exalt, nay, to deify himself; to think so highly of himself, that he will not consent to God's terms at all. And hence the first thing that the Spirit does to a man is to *make him stoop*, by convincing him of sin, and bringing him to forget all his ideas of self-deification. Then he is glad of another's righteousness, and takes it eagerly. But till then, he will not take even heaven itself on God's terms. He looks on God as his enemy; or at least as not so entirely his friend that He will at once receive him and bless him as he is. Strange that it should be so now! Whatever our first parents might plead in excuse, we are inexcusable. God's gift of His Son,—the cross, the death, the grave of that Son,—have all unfolded in its fullest breadth the love of God, proving that He is the sinner's true and real friend. Yet who believes this? How few take God's word concerning this, and enter into peace and friendship!

Nay, more than this, Satan tells us that *sin* is a blessing, not a curse; that its consequences are good, not evil; and under this aspect the sinner pursues it. He sees in the command not to sin a restriction of his liberty, and he spurns it! He sees in sin itself the attainment of what is pleasant, and he pursues it. What is sweet in sin is *present*, what is bitter is *future;* so he drinks the cup, and bids the future care for itself. Yet that future involves in it the favour of Jehovah Himself, and the joys of an eternal heaven. Is he prepared to say that that favour is a mere dream, and the loss of it a trifle? Is he prepared to say that there is no heaven as well as no hell,—no joy as well as no sorrow for eternity?

Ver. 6. '*And when* ("when" is not in the Hebrew) *the woman saw that the tree was good for food, and that it was pleasant to the eyes* (Heb. *a desire to the eyes*), *and a tree to be desired to make one wise*[1] (Heb. *to cause to understand*), *she took of the fruit thereof, and did eat; and gave also unto her husband with her, and he did eat.*'

The tempter has now thrown a new and peculiar interest round the tree. He has riveted the woman's eye upon it, and what shall hinder her heart from following her eye? She had stood still to reason with him. This was her first false step. She now stood still to gaze upon the object reasoned about, and to wonder why she should be shut off from it. He had thus succeeded in fixing her eye on the tree; he had succeeded in shaking her belief as to the penalty; and now what remained but that she should wholly yield? Nay, is she not already overcome? The fascination

[1] 'Pleasant to the eyes,'—Vulg. pulchrum oculis. Sept. ἀρεστὸν τοῖς ὀφθαλμοῖς. Coverdale, 'lustye unto the eyes.' The word means delight, or pleasure, and refers here to something that the eye delights in. 'To be desired to make one wise.' This is a still stronger word: 'flagrantius appetendus,' says Robertson. This author derives the word 'to make wise' from one signifying 'to ripen,' implying that the meaning in the present passage is 'to bring to maturity in knowledge.'

becomes stronger and stronger. She lets it carry her unresistingly along. She consults neither her husband nor her God. She hurries into the commission of the sin.[1]

There were three things that wrought upon her.

1. *The tree was good for food.* A strong reason, had she been famishing, but none when surrounded with the plenty of the rich garden. Strange that she should have cared for it on such an account! She is in no need of food, yet it is on this account that she covets it! She is without excuse in her sin. It was the lust of the flesh that was at work (Eph. ii. 3; 1 John ii. 16). She saw in the tree the gratification of that lust, and in God a hinderer of it. Thus she fell.

2. *It was a desire of the eyes.* And had she no other objects of beauty to gaze upon? Yes; thousands. Yet this forbidden one engrossed her, as if it had acquired new beauty by having been prohibited. Or can she not be satisfied with *looking?* Must she *covet?* Must she touch and taste? It is plain that hers was no longer the natural and lawful admiration of a fair object, but an unlawful desire to possess what she admired.[2]

[1] Though it is evident that she consulted not with Adam, yet the words 'with her' would lead us to suppose that he was present, or within sight. Calvin gives reasons against this, but they are very slight. The Jewish writers seem to have believed that he was with her at the time.

[2] Jerome will have it, that we are not even to gaze upon what we may not desire: '*Intueri non debet quod non licet concupisci*' (on Jerem.). This is too much; it is ascetic rigidity, making restrictions where God has made none. *Admiring* and *coveting* are two very different things. When reading such remarks, we cannot help

It was 'the lust of the eye.' Job understood this, and 'made a covenant with his eyes' (xxxi. 1); the Psalmist knew it, and prayed, 'Turn away mine eyes from beholding vanity.'

3. *It was a tree to be desired for imparting wisdom.* This was the crowning allurement. She must have wisdom, and she must have it at all risks, and she must have it without delay. She made haste to be wise. She would not in faith wait for God's time and way of giving wisdom. So strong was the craving for knowledge, and so strangely did the divine prohibition sharpen the appetite for it! She could not but know that nothing would be withheld from her that was really good; that she would get all knowledge in due time, and in God's own way; but her confidence in God had wavered; she could no longer trust Him for this; she was in haste to be wise; and now that all wisdom was within her reach, she can no longer wait. Such was the desire (or lust) of the mind! (Eph. ii. 3.)

These three reasons prevailed. She plucked the fruit, and did eat. Nay, more, she gave also to her husband, who was with her, and he did eat. She was not content to sin alone. Even the dearest on earth must be drawn into the same snare.

believing that we find the prototype of them all in Eve's 'neither shall ye *touch* it.' Jerome, however, adds truly, 'Neque enim Eva lignum vetitum contigisset nisi hoc prius *incaute* respiceret.' And then he remarks, 'Hinc ergo pensandum est quanto debemus moderamine erga illicita visum restringere, nos qui mortaliter vivimus, si et mater viventium per oculos ad mortem venit . . . concupiscendo visibilia, invisibiles virtutes amisit.'

Let us mark here such lessons as the following:—

1. The danger of trifling with objects of temptation. To linger near them; to hesitate about leaving them; to think of them as harmless,—these are the sure forerunners of a fall. Beware of remaining within sight. Get beyond the circle of the spell. 'Flee youthful lusts.' 'Look not on the wine when it is red' (Prov. xxiii. 31). Your only safety is in instant flight. If the tempter can get you to *look*, he has secured his victory.

2. The three sources of temptation: the lust of the flesh, of the eye, of the mind. Strictly speaking, they are not in themselves sinful, but in their excess, or disorderly indulgence. There is no sin in relishing food, nor in looking at a fair object, nor in desiring knowledge; yet through these channels our temptations come. Things lawful in themselves are our most subtle seducers.[1] There is nothing to taint the ear in 'the concord of sweet sounds;' and yet how often does music become our wiliest tempter! There may be nothing to defile the eye in the fairest imitations of nature that art has ever flung upon her canvas; yet has not painting but too frequently ensnared the soul, and drawn it away from the Creator to the creature? What is there in the widest range of science that can be branded as evil? yet do we not see it in the present day supplanting the knowledge of God Himself, and used by Satan as his mightiest instrument for leading men captive at his will? Is not poetry the highest form of word and

[1] 'Fallimur oculis, decipimur auditu, capimur odore, et sapore vitiamur.'—CHRYSOLOGUS, *Serm.* xxvii.

thought? yet man has corrupted it into the utterance of his own wild passions, or the idle breathings of his fond affections. In the scenes of nature there is nought but what is good, and fair, and bright; yet these has man made use of to shut out God, either saying, with the Atheist, 'There is no God in nature;' or maintaining, with the Pantheist, that nature itself is divine.

3. The swift progress of temptation. She listened, looked, took, ate![1] These were the steps. All linked together, and swiftly following each other. The beginning how small and simple; the end how terrible! 'When lust (desire) hath conceived, it bringeth forth sin; and sin, when it is finished, bringeth forth death' (Jas. i. 15). And therefore, adds the apostle, 'Do not ERR,[2] my beloved brethren;' that is, do not turn aside one step out of the right way, as you know not where you may end. You begin with a *look*, you end in apostasy from God. You begin with a touch, you end in woe and shame. You begin with a thought, you end in the second death. Yet of all these steps God protests solemnly that He is not the Author (Jas. i. 13). It is *man* that is his own ensnarer and destroyer. Even Satan cannot succeed unless seconded by man himself.

4. The tendency of sin to propagate itself. No sooner has the tempted one yielded than he seeks to draw others

[1] 'Creditus est serpens, contemptus est Deus; tactum est vetitum, mortuus est homo.'—AUGUSTINE on Ps. lxxiv.

[2] μὴ πλανᾶσθε, 'do not go astray;' do not let temptation allure you one step out of the way. This word is used eight times in the Apocalypse in connection with Satan and his seductions.

into the snare. He must drag down his fellows with him. There seems an awful *vitality* about sin; a fertility in reproduction, nay, a horrid necessity of nature for self-diffusion. It never lies dormant. It never loses its power of propagation. Let it be the smallest conceivable, it possesses the same terrific diffusiveness. Like the invisible seeds that float through our atmosphere, it takes wing the moment it comes into being, flying abroad, and striking root everywhere, and becoming the parent of ten thousand others.

Ver. 7. '*And the eyes of them both were opened, and they knew that they were naked; and they sewed fig-leaves together, and made themselves aprons.*'[1]

Their eyes were opened! They in that moment saw things which they saw not and could not have seen before. They saw into a new region, but that region was a sad and dark one. Their eyes were opened, and they seemed as if suddenly placed before a mirror, for the first object that met their view was,—THEMSELVES.[2] And the first thing that struck and startled them about themselves, was their nakedness! They were naked before, but nakedness had brought with it no sense of shame. But the moment they disobeyed, the conscious-

[1] 'Sewed' is too strong and definite a word; it is simply 'wrought or fastened together.'

[2] We all know something of this 'opening of the eye' immediately on the commission of an act of sin. Up to the moment of the commission we are blind to the sin and its consequences. The moment it is done a strange feeling seizes us, we become aware of the sin, conscience stirs, and we wish the deed undone. In addition to this, however, there might be something in the actual tree affecting the moral nature, and stimulating conscience.

ness of being *unfit to be seen* arose within them. Formerly, all parts of their body were 'comely;' now certain parts became 'uncomely' (1 Cor. xii. 23). Just as certain animals were afterwards set aside as unclean, so were certain parts of man's body, that there might be about man the perpetual token and remembrance of sin. It would seem as if, when Adam ate of the fruit, the grosser passions of his nature were let loose, and rose into mastery. All parts of his nature had hitherto been in equal and harmonious proportions; now the flesh rose up, and sin revealed shame. As, in the case of bodily disease, the general *virus* which may be pervading the whole frame fastens or settles down upon some special part, so was it in the case of the moral poison which now shot through the whole man, in consequence of that fatal act of disobedience.

A sense of shame either in regard to soul or body is not natural. It does not belong to the unfallen. It is the fruit of sin. The sinner's first feeling is, 'I am not fit for God, or man, or angels to look upon.' Hence the essence of confession is, *being ashamed* of ourselves. We are made to feel two things; first, a sense of condemnation; and secondly, a sense of shame; we are unfit to receive God's favour, and unfit to appear in His presence. Hence Job said, 'I am vile;' and hence Ezra said, 'I am ashamed, and blush to lift up my face to Thee, my God' (ix. 6). Hence also Jeremiah describes the stout-hearted Jews, 'They were not at all ashamed, neither could they blush' (vi. 15). Hence Solomon's reference to the 'impudent face' of the strange woman (Prov. vii. 13), and Jeremiah's description of Israel, 'Thou hadst a whore's forehead, thou refusedst to be ashamed' (iii. 3). It was the *shame* of our sin that Christ bore upon the cross; and therefore it is said of Him that He 'despised the shame.' It was laid upon Him, and He shrank not from it. He felt it, yet He hid not His face from it. He was the well-beloved of the Father, yet He hung upon the tree as one unfit for God to look upon; fit only to be cast out from His presence. He took our place of shame that we might be permitted to take His place of honour. In giving credit to God's record concerning Him we are identified with Him as our representative; our shame passes over to Him, and His glory becomes ours for ever.

It was this sense of shame that led Adam and Eve to have recourse to fig-leaves for a covering. Suddenly possessed with the awful thought that they were unfit to be seen, even by each other, they eagerly betook themselves to the first thing that lay within their reach, glad to get hold of anything which would hide them from each other's eyes, or prevent that strange feeling of shame which had thus arisen.

It is to the *eye* that the sense of shame appeals, and it is only in the *light* that its appeal can be made good. To prevent this appeal the sinner seeks the *darkness*, and hence it is that deeds of shame and deeds of darkness are the same in import. Hence it is also that our Lord speaks of men hating the light and loving the darkness because their deeds are evil. But whether it is to fig-leaves or to darkness that the sinner betakes himself, the feeling that leads to the act is the same. His object is to get where no eye can see him. He forgets the eye above, that can look through every human covering; and hence, as Adam tried his fig-leaves, so he tries his good deeds, his prayers, and his repentance; forgetful that the eye of flame (Rev. ii. 18) can look through them. The covering he needs is one which will hide his shame from the eye that is *divine.* He learns this when the Holy Spirit begins His work of conviction in him. For then it is as if God's eye of awful holiness were piercing through his coverings and flashing through the darkness in which he had wrapt himself. Then he learns that the covering he needs must be *divine.* It must be as divine as that eye which is looking into him from above. It must be something which will hide his shame even from the eye of God; something that will do for him not merely in the darkness or the twilight, but under the brilliance of a cloudless noon.

What is it but this same consciousness of shame that leads man to resort to *ornaments?* These are intended by them to compensate for the shame or the deformity under which men are lying. They feel that shame belongs to them; nay, confusion of face. They feel that they are not now 'perfect in beauty,' as once they were. Hence they resort to ornament in order to make up for this. They deck themselves with jewels that their deformity may be turned into beauty. But there is danger here;—danger against which the apostle warns us, specially the female sex (1 Pet. iii. 3, 4). There is nothing indeed innately sinful in the gold, or the silver, or the gems which have been wrought by the skill of men into such forms of brightness. But in our present state they do not *suit* us. They are unmeet for sinners. They speak of pride, and they also minister to pride. They are for the kingdom, not for the desert. They are for the city of the glorified, not for the tent of the stranger. They will come in due time, and they will be brilliant enough to compensate for the shame of earth. But we cannot be trusted with them now.[1]

[1] We add the following extract from a work already quoted, which helps to illustrate the whole passage over which we have gone :—

'Those who are so averse to admit the figurative language of Scripture, are puzzled extremely to account for the vehicle of Satan's first temptation—*a serpent.* Let such writers and readers as feel so disposed, amuse themselves with answering the cavils of critics and the sneers of fools on this subject; it shall be our province to attempt a plain and scriptural investigation of it. We have already stated that it appears the situation of Adam in paradise corresponds with our situation now; he lived by a commandment, as we do; for "this is His commandment, that we should believe on the name of the only-begotten Son of God," who is the true *tree of life.* In like manner we observe, that there is nothing uncommon, nothing contrary to what is daily experienced, in the first temptation; otherwise Paul was wrong to say, "But I fear, lest by any means, as the serpent beguiled Eve through his subtilty, so your minds should be corrupted from the simplicity that is in Christ" (2 Cor. xi. 3). As the serpent is characteristic of guile, subtilty, and deceit, so his form was assumed by Satan, as his character daily is by the tempter, corrupting the truth of the gospel. God had placed our first parents in paradise, setting before them life from the tree of life, and death from the tree of knowledge. There are no proofs mentioned as adduced, simply the *Divine Word,* as to these trees. Satan, by the serpent, reasoned their minds out of the belief of the simple truth God had set before them. And he gradually persuaded them, not only that they should *not* die from eating the tree of knowledge, but that the brightest happiness and most perfect

Ver. 8. '*And they heard the voice of the Lord God* (*Jehovah-Elohim*) *walking* (or *who was walking*) *in the garden in the cool* (Heb. *the wind*) *of the day: and Adam* (Heb. *the man*) *and his wife hid themselves from the presence* (Heb. *the face*) *of the Lord God amongst* (Heb. *in the midst*) *the trees of the garden.*'

Scarce had the transgressors twisted their girdles, and thus completed the hasty covering which was to hide their shame from each other's eyes, when they heard the voice of the Lord God, and trembled as they were thus reminded that there was another eye to hide from. It was not, indeed, a long-known, but still it was a well-known voice. They had heard it before, and they recognised it at once. 'It is the voice of Jehovah! He is coming,—whither shall we flee?' It was no mere sound; no casual blast or rush of the meeting streams; it was a living voice,—the voice of a being as true and personal as themselves. To them God was a real being,—a person; and His voice a real voice.[1]

attainments would infallibly ensue. So is it at this hour; the gospel sets the tree of life before us, as connected with present and future bliss; the tempter sets this world, and assures us that everything gratifying to man is to be found in it, while certain death is by no means the penalty. In every age and nation, Satan's temptation has had the same object—we had almost said, the same language. Believing this father of liars, as we are all most prone to do,—persuading herself that every gratification would follow,—Eve ate and gave her husband, who partook in her transgression, and became subject to the same penalty. Their conduct under the impressions of guilt was the same as in all future ages: their eyes were opened; they found themselves naked and exposed to shame and everlasting disgrace; they therefore betook themselves to the only frail covering they could devise—fig-leaves.'—MORRISON'S *Key to the Pentateuch.*

[1] 'We conclude that the *Logos* did not only appear in a visible

Whether any *form* were seen we know not. There might be; for God did always, in after ages, as to Abraham, reveal Himself in a form. But this matters not. A distinct and intelligible voice addressed them; and they recognised it as the voice of Jehovah-Elohim,—'the Lord God.' They 'heard' it, and they knew it. They had 'heard' it before, and they are now to hear it again, though in circumstances far different.

When the Lord God thus uttered His voice, He was 'walking in the garden,' for it seems not to be the *voice* that was moving or walking (as some think), but Jehovah Himself. Elsewhere He is spoken of in the same way. When speaking to Israel of Canaan, as their promised dwelling, He not only says, 'I will set my tabernacle

manner, but conversed also with Adam and Eve, audibly and by an articulate voice.'—FLEMING'S *Christology*, vol. ii. p. 249. The word 'voice' is used in several senses in Scripture. Sometimes it denotes a distinct articulate sound (Deut. iv. 12, 36, v. 22; Ezek. i. 24, 25, 28, x. 5); sometimes a commandment (the thing proclaimed by the voice) (Ps. xcv. 7); sometimes thunder (the sound accompanying the voice) (Ex. ix. 23, 28, 29; Job xxxvii. 5). It was this voice that spoke to Cain (Gen. iv. 9), to Noah (Gen. vi. 13), to Abraham (Gen. xv. 1). It is said (Ex. xix. 19) that 'Moses spake, and the Lord answered him by a *voice*.' It was God's voice that shook Sinai and its wilderness; that shook the posts of the temple (Isa. vi. 4). It is by this voice that 'the Assyrian is to be beaten down' (Isa. xxx. 31). It was this voice that Isaiah heard (vi. 4), and Ezekiel (i. 24, x. 5, 9), and Daniel (x. 6). It was this same voice that was heard at the baptism of Christ (Matt. iii. 17), at His transfiguration (Matt. xvii. 5). It is interesting to trace this 'voice' throughout Scripture, so generally in connection with the 'cloud,' or 'glory' (2 Pet. i. 17). It is sometimes terrific as the thunder; sometimes a 'still small voice;' sometimes as the noise of a 'multitude;' sometimes like many waters, — by all these figures setting forth 'the majestic, melodious, mighty voice of God.'

among you,' but 'I will *walk* among you' (Lev. xxvi. 12). Or, when referring to their desert-sojourn, He gives, as a motive to entire purity in their habits, 'The Lord thy God *walketh* in the midst of thy camp, therefore shall thy camp be holy' (Deut. xxiii. 14). As the reference here is obviously to God's presence, as manifested in the Shekinah, or visible glory, so it might have been in Eden by some such visible form that the Lord revealed Himself and 'walked' in paradise.

It was 'in the wind of the day' that Jehovah was heard. Meaning thereby, either at the time that the breeze was blowing, or *in* the breeze; or, more probably, *both*. It is generally in connection with the wind, or whirlwind, that Jehovah is said to appear (Ezek. i. 4). In 2 Sam. xxii. 11, we read, 'He was seen upon the wings of the *wind*;' in Ps. xviii. 10 we read, 'He did fly upon the wings of the *wind*;' in Ps. civ. 3 we read, 'Who walketh upon the wings of the *wind*.' In these passages we note the difference of expression, yet the identity of the general idea,—He was *seen* upon the wind; He did *fly* upon the wind; He did *walk* upon the wind; which last is the very expression in the passage before us.[1]

As soon as Jehovah appeared and His voice was heard,

[1] Yet, as in our passage it is ל and in others על, and as the former is the usual expression for *at*, or *at the time of*, we must take 'at the breeze of the day' as the primary sense. (See Gen. xlix. 27; Josh. x. 27, etc.) The Vulgate gives it, 'ad auram post meridiem;' the Sept. τὸ δειλινόν, *i.e.* the evening. Symmachus renders it, διὰ πνεύματος ἡμέρας; Theodotion, ἐν τῷ πνεύματι πρὸς καταψύξιν τῆς ἡμέρας. Jerome paraphrases it 'declinante sole.' (*Works*, vol. v. p. 269.) Calvin thinks that, after their sin, they slept all night, and that it was in the *morning* that the voice awoke them. So also Diodati. (See Morrison's

the transgressors fled. Terror took hold of them, and shame covered them.[1] Fig-leaves might hide them from each other's eyes, but when God comes nigh they must try something more effectual. They *flee.* That is their first effort. Their object is to get as far from Him as possible. But they need something else. They flee to the thickets, that there the gloom may render them invisible.

It was from the 'presence,' or 'face,' of God that they fled. It is evident that something was seen by them,

Introductory Key to the Scriptures on this passage.) The following passage from a writer formerly quoted may interest the reader:—

'It is evident from Scripture that Jehovah the Son, the only visible God, appeared to Adam so soon as he was created, and on many after occasions. Adam heard His voice, and held familiar conversation with Him, as a man does with his friend. Then and ever afterwards, in all the ages previous to His incarnation, Jehovah seems to have made the sound or rushing of wind the visible symbol of His appearance. Thus He announced His approach to Job (xxxviii. 1). So He appeared to Ezekiel (i. 4). This also was the sign by which David knew that Jehovah was gone out before him to smite the host of the Philistines (1 Chron. xiv. 15). And, as this had always been the sign of the divine approach, the coming of the Holy Ghost upon the apostles was announced in the sound of a rushing mighty wind (Acts ii. 2). Hence God is said to walk on the "wings of the wind." Now, as this was the usual token whereby Adam knew the approach of his Maker, so soon as he heard the sound of wind issuing from a cloud, walking among the trees of Eden, he was apprized of the approach of the offended Jehovah; and, alarmed by his fears, he ran to hide himself from the divine presence among the thickets of the garden.'—*Pirie's Works*, vol. iii. p. 68.

[1] Our readers will perhaps remember Spenser's line—

'All wrongs have mends, but no amends of *shame*.'
—(*Faerie Queene*, book ii. cant. 1)

Most true! No 'amends of shame,' but through Him who took our shame upon Himself.

here and elsewhere called by this name. It was from this 'face' of God that they turned away, just as the wicked are said hereafter to be 'punished with everlasting destruction *from the presence* of the Lord.'[1] This name seems to be given because the manifestation (whatever it might be) was that which, in God, corresponded to the face of man,—the part which reveals most of the man himself. It was a visible glory indicative of a personal presence,—the presence of the second Person of the Godhead, who, from eternity, was the brightness of Jehovah's

[1] *ἀπὸ προσώπου τοῦ κυρίου*. This, of course, refers to the presence of Christ. But it was to this 'presence' that all former 'presences' pointed. All these were but prefigurations of His glory,—the bright raiment which was to invest the person of the God-man in the fulness of time. It is to this 'presence,' or 'glory,' or 'Shekinah,' that reference is made in such passages as the following :—Gen. iv. 14, 16, xviii. 22, xix. 13; Ex. xxvii. 21, xxviii. 12, 30; Lev. i. 3, 5, 11. It is to the second Person of the Godhead that 'presence,' or 'face,' refers. He is essentially and eternally the 'off-shining,' or radiance, of Jehovah's glory (*ἀπαύγασμα τῆς δόξης*), and the express image of His person (*χαρακτὴρ τῆς ὑποστάσεως αὐτοῦ*, the impression or stamp of His person). He is also the 'Word,' as being the utterance or expression of the mind of Godhead,—the communication between the invisible and the visible. Thus Owen calls Him 'the essential image of the Father,' and says, 'were He not the *essential image* of the Father in His own divine Person, He could not be the *representative image* of God to us, as He is incarnate' (on the Person of Christ). Thus the voice that spoke in Eden was the voice of the WORD; and the presence that was seen was the presence of Him who is the radiance of Jehovah's glory. 'The Logos,' says Fleming, 'according to the agreement of the sacred Trinity, was He that acted even to created intelligent beings as their immediate Head, in the name of God, essentially considered. The Logos, being infinite in regard of essence, could never be seen or known, even by the most glorious created spirits, had He not condescended to assume some created form,—such as that which the Jews called the Shekinah, or

glory and the express image of His person. This visible glory (like the Shekinah in the wilderness pursuing the rebels) seems to have advanced towards them; and as *it* advanced *they* retreated,—the voice and the glory from which the voice issued combining to terrify them, for they were the voice and the glory of that God whom they had disobeyed. Their own refuge is the trees of the garden; yet what shelter could they be from a glory so bright, or from a voice which makes the mountains to shake? (Ps. xxix.)

That voice! It pierces the sinner's ear in a moment. It forces its way into the conscience. Nothing can withstand it. It is specially to the *conscience* that it speaks, alarming, convincing, overpowering. When it speaks in the *law*, then the commandment comes (Rom. vii. 9); the sinner is smitten, he flees before it or falls under it. It

the glory of God; and it seems plain to me, that the Logos appeared thus in heaven to the angels. And I look upon it to be more than probable, that this assumed image was not barely light, or something like a luminous cloud, but was something likewise of a determined shape, appearing as an animated being. And I believe, from what I can judge by laying things together, that it was the exact representation of a man clothed with a most glorious garment of wonderful light. And I make no question but this ancient image was the very same with that wherein Christ appears now in glory, excepting that He has now a real animated body of human flesh, whereas before He had an ethereal one only, or one of some such sort of composition. But, excepting this, I make no question but that the features and lineaments of the one body and the other were as exactly, and more exactly, the same, than ever any picture was like an original. And when Christ was transfigured, I believe He appeared the very same to Moses that He appeared to be to him formerly, when he and the elders of Israel, as well as the angels then present, saw Him upon Mount Sinai (Ex. xxiv. 1, etc.).'—*Christology*, vol. ii. p. 255.

sweeps through him and lays him in the dust. His mouth is stopped; he is compelled to plead guilty. 'By the law is the knowledge of sin.'

And then, that glory! It terrifies the transgressor. He cannot bear it, even afar off. Its approach overwhelms him. Even the saints have trembled at it,—Job (xlii. 5), Isaiah (vi. 5), and Daniel (x. 7, 8),—how much more the sinner! The 'presence' of Jehovah is *light*, and that he cannot bear, for he loves the darkness. Israel got a glimpse of it on Sinai, and trembled; the ungodly shall see it in the day of wrath, and flee to the rocks for shelter.

And then the insufficiency of human coverings. Till God came nigh, the fig-leaves seemed safe enough; but He shows Himself, and then the covering is found 'narrower than a man can wrap himself in it' (Isa. xxviii. 20). He flees, and tries another covering (for *leaves* will not do; he must have the whole *trees*), still 'making lies his refuge, and under falsehood hiding himself' (Isa. xxviii. 15). For whither can he flee from God's 'presence'? (Ps. cxxxix. 7.) Neither fig-leaves nor thickets will do. It is God that is the sinner's terror; and the nearer that He comes the greater is that terror.[1] No human coverings can avail. Darkness will not do. Distance will not do. The wrappings of man's merits will

[1] Jerome, in commenting on the first verse of the 82d Psalm,—'God standeth,' or, as he has it, 'Deus stetit,'—has a curious passage, in which he attempts to show the difference of the expressions, 'God stands,' 'God walks,' 'God sits;' referring the first to His posture in reference to man innocent; the second to God's posture in reference to man guilty, as if He were moved out of His place to come to him; and the third in reference to God's posture to men before the judgment-seat.

not do. To be *naked* before God is what he shrinks from; and none of these can hide his nakedness. That which alone can remove his terror and his shame is a shelter that is divine,—a covering that is infinite,—the righteousness of the Son of God.

In the day of wrath this scene of Eden will be repeated, —man fleeing from the presence of God. In the absence of thickets he will betake himself to the rocks and hills (Hos. x. 8; Rev. vi. 15, 16). But what will these do? Can His eye not pierce these? Can His hand not pluck them thence? For thus the Lord has spoken, 'Though they dig into hell, thence shall mine hand take them; though they climb up to heaven, thence will I bring them down; and though they hide themselves in the top of Carmel, I will search and take them out thence' (Amos ix. 2, 3).

Ver. 9. '*And the Lord God* (Heb. *Jehovah-Elohim*) *called unto Adam* (Heb. *the man*), *and said unto him, Where art thou?*'

The voice which had been heard was no inarticulate noise such as tempest or thunder. It spoke explicitly and articulately. It addressed itself to Adam,—to 'the man.' The words are not 'He *said* to,' but 'He *called* to,' Adam. And there could be no mistake as to who was meant. He proceeds by making inquiry after him, that, step by step, He may make sin unveil itself, and draw confession from the sinner. He does not at once lay hold of the offender and extort a confession by terror. Neither does He proceed upon His omniscience and say, 'Thou art the man.' His object is so to speak to the conscience that the man may confess, and be led without compulsion to survey his own devious steps. 'Where art thou?' was the question. Simple, yet, like the Lord's words to the woman of Sychar (John iv.), effectual for bringing all to light. As if He would say, 'I expected to find thee at the appointed meeting-place, but I find thee not. How is it so? What has led thee away? Where art thou?' Thus He goes in quest of the sinner.[1]

Ver. 10. '*And he said, I heard Thy voice in the garden, and I was afraid, because I was naked; and I hid myself.*'

The man replies immediately. God has met him face to face, and he cannot evade Him or decline an answer. He had heard the voice. He had known it at once. It was 'in the garden' that he heard it, and terror took hold of him. He admits that he had fled from God, and that he was not where he ought to have been found. He excuses himself for fleeing because, being naked, he was afraid of the majesty of God; and feeling that he was unfit to stand before Him, he had hid himself.[2] In so speak-

[1] 'Graciously calling him to return, who would otherwise have eternally fled from God.'—*J. Wesley's Sermons*, vol. ii. p. 25.

[2] Fleming supposes that man, before he sinned, had a sort of 'luminous vestment,' which disappeared the moment he sinned (*Christology*, book iii. chap. 3); and adds, 'Adam turning apostate, was no way fit that he should wear the livery of the Shekinah any longer, and therefore the luminous garment with which he and Eve were clothed is taken away, and they are left naked.' Mede has a somewhat similar idea, when he speaks of their 'nakedness' as being an 'obscuration of that glorious and celestial beauty which he had before his sin; the difference whereof was so great, that he could not endure afterwards to behold himself any more, but sought for a covering, even to hide himself from himself.'—*Works* (folio), p. 233.

ing, he seems to take credit to himself for having fled, and rather suggests that the blame lay with God, who had made him naked. In this there is no confession of sin; there is fear and shame; but that is all. Instead of 'declaring his transgression,' he first attempts to hide it by hiding himself; and when that is vain, he shifts the blame from himself to God. It seems to be to this that Job refers, when he says, 'If I covered my transgression as Adam, by hiding mine iniquity in my bosom' (Job xxxi. 33). Covering sin in any such way avails not. There is but one covering which is effectual,—the covering of the *blood*. It is by blood alone that sin can be 'covered.' Man, however, knew not this. He thought he could cover it himself. He had yet to learn that the only thing that can *cover* sin is that which can *absorb* it and make it to be as though it had never been. God had yet to unfold His own method, and to teach man the efficacy of the blood as a covering; so that when he came to understand this he would feel that, in order to cover sin, it is not necessary to flee from God or to resort to thickets, but that, receiving God's testimony to the covering efficacy of the blood, he may meet God face to face without shame or fear, reversing the words of his first father, and saying, 'I heard Thy voice, and was not afraid, for I had found a covering; and, instead of hiding myself, I returned to Thee.'

Ver. 11. '*And He said, Who told thee* (or *declared to thee*) *that thou wast* (or *art*) *naked? Hast thou eaten of the tree, whereof I commanded thee that thou shouldest not eat?*'

God pursues the inquiry. His object is to make man

convict himself. He has touched the conscience already, and He now sends the arrow deeper. Thou speakest of being 'naked.' How is this? Thou didst not feel thus at first. Hitherto thy nakedness has been no barrier between thee and me. Who, or what, has suggested the thought that it is so? Who, or what, has made thee afraid or ashamed to come? Whence hast thou got this knowledge, by means of which thou excusest thyself from drawing near to me, and palliatest thy guilt in fleeing from me? Man is silent. He answers not a word. No one has told him. The thought has started up from within. A strange but irresistible feeling has taken possession of him,—'I am naked; I cannot look upon God; God cannot look upon me.' Without noticing man's silence, God proceeds with His inquiry. 'Hast thou eaten of the tree which I prohibited?' This is the only thing that could have done it. Is it possible that thou hast already transgressed? Thus, by question after question, he leads man to the acknowledgment of his sin, making him feel that his sin is already known, that the true cause of his fear is no secret, and 'that all things are naked and open unto the eyes of Him with whom he has to do.'

Ver. 12. '*And the man said, The woman whom thou gavest to be with me, she gave me of the tree, and I did eat.*'

He feels that God has had His eye upon him, and that what He says is true. It is the tree that has given him this knowledge of 'evil.' Had he waited God's time, the eating of it would have given him the knowledge of only good; but he has refused to wait; he has disobeyed God; he has made haste to be wise; and it has opened his eyes only to the *evil.* Still, however, he will take no blame to himself for doing what he has done. He makes no direct and honest answer to God, in freely confessing that he had eaten; yet he cannot deny the deed, and therefore, in the very act of admitting (not confessing), he casts the blame upon the woman,—nay, upon God, for giving him such a tempter.[1] Here let us mark such truths as these.

1. The difference between *admitting* sin and *confessing* it. Adam admits it,—slowly and sullenly,—but he does not confess it. He is confronted with a Being in whose presence it would be vain to deny what he had done; but he will go no further than he can help. He will tacitly concede when concession is extorted from him, but he will make no frank acknowledgment. It is so with the sinner still. He does precisely what Adam did; no more, till the Holy Spirit lays His hand upon his conscience and touches all the springs of his being. Up till that time he may utter extorted and reluctant *concessions*, but he will not *confess* sin. He will not deal frankly with God. He is sullen, and admits that he is a sinner because others do it,—because it would be

[1] Jerome has an ingenious comment on Lam. iii. 65. 'Give them sorrow of heart' is our translation, the margin giving 'obstinacy;' and Jerome translating it 'scutum cordis,' as the text had given ὑπερασπισμόν. He represents Adam as holding up this shield when God came nigh, flinging back the blame not only upon the woman, but upon God: 'Ut quasi reatum suum oblique in auctorem redideret.' Eve also holds up the shield: 'Hoc scutum etiam requisita mulier tenuit. . . . ut ipsa quoque reatum suum oblique in creatorem duceret.'—*Works*, vol. iv. p. 323.

thought pride in him not to do it,—because he cannot help it,—because he is conscious there is something wrong; but still there is no open-hearted confession. If there is not actually the 'keeping silence' (Ps. xxxii. 3), or the 'covering of sin' (Prov. xxviii. 13), there is nothing of the ready spirit: 'I acknowledged my sin unto Thee, and mine iniquity have I not hid. I said, I will confess my transgressions to the Lord; and Thou forgavest the iniquity of my sin' (Ps. xxxii. 5; Prov. xxviii. 13; Luke xv. 18–21; 1 John i. 9).

2. The artfulness of an unhumbled sinner. Even while admitting sin, he shakes himself free from blame; nay, he thrusts forward the name of another, even before the admission comes forth, as if to neutralize it before it is made. How artful! yet how common still! Men do not only give a mere reluctant admission,—they do not merely in so doing try to shift the blame from themselves, but they attempt, by introducing the name of another, *before the admission is made*, to give the impression most cunningly that this other is the really guilty person. Thus, by mentioning another first, they hope to draw away all the attention from themselves to him, so that, before their own guilt has been conceded, attention has been directed to him as the guilty one; and thus not only is there a bare admission of guilt instead of an honest confession, but there is a most cunning endeavour to undo that very admission by the peculiar way in which it is made. It is difficult to say whether such a method be more cunning or cowardly. It is certainly the procedure of a man who is, on the one

hand, afraid to confess; and, on the other hand, afraid not to confess, and who compromises these two opposite fears by a most artful declaration, which shows how sorely he shrinks from the consequences of his own poor admission. Ah! where do we find honest, unreserved acknowledgment of sin? Nowhere, save in connection with pardon. Up till the moment that we learn the 'forgiveness that there is with God,' there will always be reserve,—a cowardly reluctance to confess, an unmanly shifting of the guilt from off ourselves, a desire to palliate our sins, or lessen their number. There will always be 'guile,' for there will always be a motive to hide our sins; but when the free pardon comes, it takes away all reserve, it renders us 'guileless.' We confess freely, for the reasons for restraint are done away. And in coming to receive the pardon we put forward the name of our Surety first, before even mentioning our sins, that, like Adam, though not with his guile, we may call attention to Him on whom we cast our guilt: 'For THY NAME'S SAKE, O Lord, pardon mine iniquity, for it is great' (Ps. xxv. 11).

3. The self-justifying pride of the sinner.[1] He admits as much of his guilt as cannot be denied, and then takes credit to himself for what he has done. He is resolved to take no more blame than he can help. Even in the blame that he takes, he finds not only an extenua-

[1] The contrast between this and David's feeling in Ps. li. 4 is very striking. Adam's object was to justify *himself;* David's was to justify *God* 'That THOU mightest be justified when Thou speakest, and be clear when Thou judgest.'

tion, but a virtue, a merit; for he fled, because it was not seemly for him to stand before God naked! Nay, even in so much of the blame as he takes, he must divide it with another, thus leaving on himself but little guilt and some considerable degree of merit. Had it not been for another, he would not have had to admit even the small measure of blame that he does! There is pride here, but no godly sorrow; nothing of the 'broken spirit;' nay, not even *despair*. His self-righteousness elates him, buoys him up, and makes him think his case not so bad as to be hopeless. Till the sinner sees the cross it will be always so. Law will not humble him. The voice of God will not humble, though it may alarm him. He must see the utter condemnation of himself in the cross, and at the same time God's provision for meeting his case and removing the condemnation, ere he will throw away his confidences. It is only the knowledge of the Divine righteousness that can remove either his pride or his shame, just as it is only the knowledge of the 'perfect love' that can cast out fear.

4. The hardened selfishness of the sinner. He accuses others to screen himself. He does not hesitate to inculpate the dearest; he spares not the wife of his bosom. Rather than bear the blame, he will fling it anywhere, whoever may suffer. And all this in a moment! How instantaneous are the results of sin! Already it has rooted out affection, and broken the nearest tie, and made man a being of dark selfishness. He has ceased to 'love his neighbour as himself.' SELF

has now risen uppermost within him. He is steeled against his dearest of kin. He does not hesitate to expose them to the wrath of God; he cares not what their doom may be, provided *he* escape! 'Hateful, and hating one another,' is the inscription on the forehead of our fallen race. It is this that we here read upon the brow of Adam.

5. The sinner's blasphemy and ingratitude to God. 'The woman whom Thou gavest me,' said Adam. God's love in giving him a help meet is overlooked, and the gift itself is mocked at. God's earnest pains in providing for him a companion so suitable are forgotten, nay, turned into an occasion for casting the blame of his fall upon Him. Had it not been for *Thee*, I should not have sinned;—she whom Thou gavest me has become my seducer. *Thou* didst it, in giving me such a companion. Thus it is that Israel taunted God with being the author of their sins and woes (Ezek. xxxiii. 10): 'If our transgressions be upon us, and we pine away in them, how should we then live?' That is, 'If we die, we must just die; we cannot help it; and God is only mocking us with broken promises, speaking to us of life, yet sending only death.' And in reference to this it was that God cleared Himself upon oath, refusing to lie under the imputation, or to take the blame of man's death: 'As I live, saith the Lord God, I have no pleasure in the death of the wicked.' Thus it is that scoffers in these last days pervert the gifts of God into an excuse for sinning, or into reasons for believing that there is no such thing as sin at all. When we speak of their sin

in following their lusts, they ask, 'What sin can there be in the indulgence of those desires that God has given? or if there be sin in these things, who is to blame but He who gave them?'

6. The sinner's attempt to smooth over his deed. 'The woman gave me the fruit, and I ate of it; that was all. Giving, receiving, and eating a little fruit; that was all! What more simple, natural, innocent? How could I do otherwise?' Thus he glosses over the sin. He speaks smooth things to himself regarding it, and would fain make God think as little of it as he does himself. And so men still trifle with sin. What harm is there in it? What harm is there in the song, the dance, the laugh, the gaiety, the glitter? Are not these amusements *harmless?* Ah! it was thus that the first sinner tried to reason with his God. But did he succeed? Did God accept his plea of harmlessness? Did He turn away His wrath, or dilute the curse, or justify the transgressor? So long as man persists in smoothing down his sin, and trying to make God think as lightly of it as he does himself, he must fail in finding favour. It is not till he acquiesces in God's verdict, and, accepting condemnation as his due, takes the sinner's place before God, that he can hope at all. For all hope to a sinner begins in the acknowledgment of his hopelessness, and in consenting to take his hope, not from the idea that wrath is not his due, but from the knowledge of that wondrous grace that has stretched its blessed circle far beyond the uttermost limits of human sin.

Ver. 13. '*And the Lord God said unto the woman, What is this that thou hast done? And the woman said, The serpent beguiled*[1] *me, and I did eat.*'

The trial proceeds, and the investigation is carried on with all judicial calmness. Adam's sullen answer awakes no wrath, and calls forth no remark. The Lord God now passes on to the woman. She had been accused by the man, and He turns to her to see how the man's accusation stands. He takes him at his word, and proceeds with the inquiry: 'What is this that thou hast done?' Is it really true that thou hast done this thing with which thy husband charges thee?

In Eve we mark the same self-justifying spirit. She does not, indeed, retaliate upon the man, and say, 'How am I to blame for *his* sin, seeing he need not have eaten unless he had pleased?' She admits that she had done the deed, though, like her husband, she does so most sullenly, and not by a direct or frank confession. She does not deny the deed, but she will not take the blame.

[1] It is the same word as is used in Ps. lv. 15: 'Let death seize upon them;' literally, 'Let death beguile them;' that is, stealthily and craftily lay hold of them, as did he who has the power of death, of our first parents. Robertson (*Clavis*, p. 44) refers also to Ps. lxxxix. 23, 'The enemy shall not seduce him,' as he did Eve. In 2 Cor. xi. 3 we read, 'As the serpent beguiled Eve through his subtilty,' ἐξηπάτησεν ἐν τῇ πανουργίᾳ; and in 1 Tim. ii. 14, 'Adam was not deceived (ἠπατήθη); but the woman, being deceived (ἀπατηθεῖσα), was in the transgression.' In Eph. vi. 11, the apostle speaks of 'the wiles (τὰς μεθοδείας) of the devil.' Of the Lord Jesus (the woman's seed, and therefore the opposite of the serpent's seed) it is said, 'Neither was guile (δόλος) found in His mouth' (1 Pet. ii. 22); and of His seed it is written that they were like Him: 'In their mouth was found no guile' (δόλος) (Rev. xiv. 5).

It was the Serpent that beguiled her! How could she help it? As if she would thus indirectly cast back the blame on God. 'It was Thine own creature, the Serpent; he is the real cause; blame *him*, not *me;* why was he allowed to beguile me?'

Thus it is that the sinner refuses to accept the *guilt*, even when he admits the *deed*. He dares not say, I did not do the deed; but he does not hesitate to affirm, 'I was not to blame in doing it.'[1] He affirms, either 'the sin was not a very great one,' or, 'there were many excuses for me;' and the greatest of all is this, that 'it was a creature of God's own making that seduced me.' See how fatally sin works. It makes him a liar,—a liar to his own conscience, to his fellows, to his God. It makes him a coward. It makes him an accuser of others. It makes him a blasphemer of God Himself. To own himself totally a sinner,—made so, not by God, nor by any fellow-creature, nor by education, nor by circumstances, but solely by himself,—is what he will not stoop to. Yet on any other terms God cannot deal with him. As a confessed sinner, he may at any moment go to God, assured of finding favour and pardon; but on any other footing, approach to God must be wholly in vain.

[1] In all this process of inquiry there is no *grace* manifested. And hence the sinner flies from God, unrepenting and unconfessing. Nor will terror ever do aught but drive a man from God. No amount of it will ever draw him nigh, or unlock his breast, or soften him into repentance. Nothing but *grace* can do this. Besides, terror only appeals to the *coarser* feelings of our nature; grace touches the finer chords. Terror contracts the spirit, grace enlarges it. Terror drives man into the thicket, only grace can draw him out.

Half-confessions will not do; concealments will not do; extenuations will not do; there must be the full acknowledgment of entire guilt, otherwise God can have no dealings with him at all.

And here again, let us mark the forbearance of our God. Even before grace is directly announced to man, we can observe the dawnings of it in the way in which God approaches man, and in the difference between His dealings with man and His dealings with the serpent. How slow to anger! How loth to find the woman guilty! How anxious to hear all that she has to say for herself before pronouncing sentence! How condescending, too, in all this; for He comes Himself in person to make the inquiry, not trusting it to another; and comes most graciously to seek after man, when man was fleeing from Him; not hastily putting a harsh construction upon his flight, but waiting to hear his excuse and defence; not threatening nor upbraiding, but, in the words of calm and friendly inquiry, asking, 'What is this that thou hast done?'

Such is the God with whom we have to do,—'the God of all grace;' not hating, but loving; not cursing, but blessing; not hasty, but slow to anger; not upbraiding, but dealing tenderly; not condemning, but pardoning. How manifestly is this the same God who so loved the world as to give His only-begotten Son! How perfect the harmony of character in this God, from these first words, spoken to fallen man, to the last which His book contains! How blessed to learn that this God, who sought out Adam when he fled from Him, is seeking the sinner still, unprovoked by his wanderings and resistances and self-excuses; waiting, with undiminished patience and forbearing love, to receive, and to love, and to bless!

Vers. 14, 15. '*And the Lord God* (Heb. *Jehovah-Elohim*) *said unto the serpent, Because thou hast done this, thou art cursed above all cattle, and above every beast of the field: upon thy belly shalt thou go, and dust shalt thou eat all the days of thy life.* 15.' *And I will put enmity between thee and the woman, and between thy seed and her seed: it shall bruise thy head, and thou shalt bruise his heel.*'

Though both of these two verses refer, in a measure, to Satan himself, yet they do embrace separate subjects; the former pointing more especially to the curse upon the literal serpent, the latter predicting the curse upon the great Tempter.[1] They seem but one prophecy, and yet they take in two objects, the near and the distant, the literal and the figurative. Commencing, like all double prophecies, with the near and the literal, they end in the distant and the figurative. As in the 72d Psalm, the singer begins with the actual Solomon and ends with the greater Solomon; and as in several burdens the prophet Isaiah begins with the Babylon then in being upon the plain of Shinar, and ends with Babylon the great, upon the seven hills; so is it here. He begins with the serpent, He ends with Satan. The figure used is taken from

[1] See Usher's *Body of Divinity*, chap. ix., where, after giving an exposition similar to the above, he says, 'If God did punish a poor worm, which had no reason nor will to choose or refuse sin, how much less will He spare us, which have both!' 'As an argument of the detestableness of the sin, and a constant memorial of it, the abused beast is cursed. Compare Ex. xxi. 28, xxxii. 20; Lev. xx. 15; Gen. ix. 5.'—Bishop KIDDER *On the Pent.* vol. i. p. 15.

the serpent; but the prophetic picture thus given concerns a far greater personage. For it is evident that one main object gained by employing such a figure in such a way as is done here, is to bring before us the *personality* of that being who is here introduced to us. The words, no doubt, are *figures*, but they are figures of what is *literal*, —precise and personal. They are not figures of abstractions or principles or truths, but of a *person*. They do not set forth God's condemnation of error or of evil, but His judgment upon a *person*. They do not denote the mere conflict between evil and good, with the triumph of the latter after a brief depression, but they foretell the battle between two *persons*. The nature of the combat is not declared, but the personality and literality of the combatants is vividly, and beyond mistake, set forth.[1]

This much is plain. Let us now look at the words themselves.

God had, in His dealing with our first parents, proceeded in the way of judicial inquiry, step by step. He had taken nothing for granted, but had calmly questioned them, allowing them full opportunity of defending themselves; loth to condemn, nay, giving out His accusations

[1] German rationalists, denying the personality of Satan, make this a conflict between the good and evil principles in man! See Dr. S. F. N. Morus' *Comment. Exeg. Hist.* vol. i. pp. 417-419. The literary scoffers of the age, who set aside the truths of Scripture as overdated and obsolete,—unsuited to an era of intellectual progress, —mock at the personality of the Evil One, talk of 'extinct Satans,' and treat the ancient belief in the devil's true being as an old fable. If the Bible testimony to a God and a Christ be plain, equally plain is that testimony to the being and personality of Satan. 'No God' and 'no devil' generally go together.

simply as questions, no more.[1] But when He comes to deal with the serpent and with Satan, we find nothing of this. They were dealt with as already condemned, and only waiting their sentence. Such is His grace to man, and such the intimation of His purpose to deal with him in grace, not in judgment. Wondrous contrast between the two races of creatures and His purposes concerning them! With the one all is grace, with the other all is righteousness and wrath! Even in the lower creation this difference is shown. That animal that had sided with Satan, and become his instrument in ruining man, is cursed with Satan's curse, and for *Satan's sin;* while the other animals are cursed with a less heavy and less abiding curse, and that for *man's sin.*[2] As if God would thus from the beginning proclaim the pre-eminent guilt

[1] 'Serpens vero jam non requiritur, quia nec ejus pœnitentia quærebatur.'—JEROME. 'As for the Serpent, He vouchsafes not to ask him one question, nor to expect what he should say for himself; but presently, without examination, proceeds to judgment against him.' —MEDE, *Works*, p. 221.

[2] Satan's connection with the serpent is a subject of great difficulty. The serpent's punishment was on account of Satan's sin, not man's sin. Hence the heavier curse,—a curse not only heavier in itself, but longer in duration, not removed even in millennial days, when blessing returns to the rest of creation (Isa. lxv. 25). Dust shall *still* be the serpent's meat. 'Dum plenam naturæ integræ ac bene constitutæ instaurationem promittit sub Christi regno inter alia commemorat, pulverem serpenti pro pane futurum esse.'—CALVIN. We think it may be made a question whether the animal creation at large were cursed for *man's sin* or for *Satan's sin.* No doubt they were involved in the former, but still was it not for their participation in the latter, through their representative the serpent, the wisest of them all, that they have fallen under the curse? Is not this implied in the words, 'Thou art cursed *above all cattle*'? etc. The ground is said to be

of every ally of the Evil One; and the swift doom of all that, in the day of doom, shall be found upon his side. The serpent was but the involuntary agent, yet he was cursed; how much more they who have 'yielded their members instruments of unrighteousness unto sin' (Rom. vi. 13),[1] nay, 'run greedily' in the way of the Evil One!

Though the serpent was but the instrument, yet he is cursed.[2] And the words, 'above all cattle,' imply that the rest of the animal creation were made to share the curse which had come down upon it as Satan's special agent in the plot against man. And why this universal curse?

1. *To show the spreading and contaminating nature of sin.*—One sin is enough to spread over a world. There is something in the very nature of sin that infects and defiles. It is not like a stone dropped in a wilderness,

cursed for man's sake, as it was by eating its fruit that he fell; but the animals seem cursed on Satan's account, as they were connected with his temptation. Yet in the end they are separated from him and his doom, and made to share the grace in store for man, their head and king.

[1] The word 'yield' poorly expresses the Greek παρίστημι, which forcibly implies the willing, nay eager, *presentation* of our members to be the instruments of sin.

[2] 'Shrunk from its erect and probably lofty stature; deprived of its limbs; reduced to grovel on the earth and seek its food in the dust; mute henceforth, and abject; the baneful serpent sunk beneath this awful curse, and glided away to hide itself out of sight; and from that day the miserable reptile has ever slunk from the eye of man.'—HEAD'S *World and its Creator*, p. 124. In these figures of the *humiliation* of the serpent, we read the *utter humiliation* of the tempter himself. The *posture* and the *food* of the serpent most aptly set forth the present degradation of the Evil One, just as the remaining words denote his final ruin.

upon the sand, there to lie motionless and powerless. It is like that same stone cast into a vast waveless lake, which raises ripple upon ripple, and sends its disturbing influence abroad, in circle after circle, for miles on every side, till the whole lake is in motion. We do not understand the activities and energies of sin. We are slow to credit them. Still less do we understand or believe the strange connection between one sinning creature and another; so that it seems unrighteous to us that one should involve another in evil. Yet it is evident that there is such a thing as a union, not only of nature, but of *responsibility*. I do not profess to explain this. But God proceeds upon it as *a law of being*. The passage before us takes it for granted; nay, the whole Bible assumes it. It is not some casual or some arbitrary proceeding. It is the law, the righteous law of creaturehood, which unfolding itself first in the curse, has consummated its development in the blessing, when 'He was made sin for us, who knew no sin, that we might be made the righteousness of God in Him.'[1]

[1] We cannot in this place discuss the doctrine of the imputation of sin or righteousness. This much we may say, that not only does the Bible assume them, but they are evidently wrapt up in the history of man. Why is disease transmitted? Why does woman suffer in child-birth? Why do infants die? Because sin has been imputed. There has been previous guilt somewhere. Many admit the transmission of evil, but deny the transference of guilt. Now we may ask, could there be the transmission of evil, if there were not a transmission of guilt? Would the one be a righteous thing without the other? However difficult it may be to demonstrate the justice of making guilt transmissible, yet it is much more difficult to prove the justice of transmitting suffering, if the transmission of guilt be un-

2. *To show how all the manifold parts of creation hang together and depend upon each other.*—One being displaced, all are ruined. There is a unity in creation which we have not yet learned to understand,—a unity of the closest kind, yet quite compatible with individual responsibility and separate action. The arch is not more dependent on the keystone than are the different parts of creaturehood dependent on each other for stability and perfection. It is as if the unity of the Godhead had its counterpart in the unity of creation. And, strange to say, it is the fall that has so fully discovered this oneness, and made us acquainted with its manifold relations.

3. *To be a monument of the evil of sin.*[1] Sin needs something visible, something palpable, to make known

righteous. That law of being which transmits suffering or death can only be just upon the supposition of a previous law of being, transmitting guilt. Hence it is not the compensation afforded us in Christ's righteousness that makes the imputation of Adam's sin an equitable thing. But it is the great original law of creaturehood, as to the transmission of moral and legal liabilities, that makes both of these strictly and truly righteous.

[1] 'Because the excellency and sagacity of the serpent had been the occasion of man's confusion, by being made the lying counterfeit of the devil's excellency and wisdom, and the mask whereby he so covered his vileness that the woman took him not to be as he was indeed; therefore God in His wisdom thought good to change the copy, and henceforth to blur and deface that unhappy physiognomical letter, and, by abasing the serpent for the time to come, to make him an everlasting emblem and monument wherein man might hieroglyphically read the malice, vileness, and execrable baseness of that wicked spirit that had beguiled him; to hate him (as now we do the serpent) with mortal hatred, and by his unlucky fortune to expect the devil's deadly destiny. In a word, that which was once used for a mask to cover the devil's knavery, should for the future be a glass wherein to behold his villany.'—*Mede*, p. 229.

both its existence and its 'exceeding sinfulness.' It must exhibit itself to our senses. It must stand forth to view, branded with the stroke of God's judgment, as the abominable thing which He hates. Thus He has strewn the memorials of sin all over the earth. He has affixed them to things animate and inanimate, that we may see and hear and feel the vileness and the bitterness of the accursed thing. Before God can proceed to unfold His purpose of pardon, He must rear upon the soil of earth an enduring monument of sin, that thereafter there may be no mistake on the part of man; that it may never be supposed that in being gracious to the sinner He was trifling with the sin.

While the serpent is thus cursed above all the rest of creation, he is made to understand the reason why he is so dealt with. 'Because thou hast done this.' God takes care that there shall be no mistake. The curse is no accidental and no arbitrary evil; it is traceable to one distinct cause. The serpent has beguiled man, and therefore judgment lights upon it. 'The curse causeless shall not come.' 'Because thou hast done this,' is God's preface to His sentence on the serpent. It is His preface to the judgment pronounced upon the sinner. 'Because thou hast done this,' are the awful words with which he will be sent into the everlasting fire.

Such is the *visible* curse on the serpent. Let us now mark (ver. 15) the *invisible* curse on Satan. There was to be, from that moment, war between Satan and the woman, enmity between his seed and her seed. Nay, there was to be warfare,—open warfare. This warfare would consist of two great parts, or stages. In the first, the woman's seed would be wounded; in the second, the serpent would be destroyed. The length of his warfare is not stated, or how near its two great parts might be to each other. They might be near, or they might be far off, we are not told, for it was not needful that we should learn this at first. Simply the two things are presented to us, but the question of time is kept out of view, that, from the very first, there might be not merely a looking for the arrival of the woman's seed, but also a *watching* for Him. We get here but the far-off glimpse of a great mountain-range. Its lofty peaks seem all clustered together, as if there were not a step between: yet, when we reach them, as now in their last days we have done, we find them separated from each other by valleys, and plains, and precipices of vast extent and height. We could not gather from the brief words of this verse whether the battle was to be the conflict of a day or of ten thousand years. After ages were to unroll the detail; to reveal to us the suffering and the triumph, the shame and the glory. So closely are the first and second comings of the Lord here brought together, that we should have supposed that there was no interval between them.

But though the times and seasons were not given, and therefore much was hidden from man, yet enough was told to let him know that God had taken his part against his enemy; that Divine love had interposed and pledged itself to the final discomfiture of Satan, and the final blessedness of the victim which he had counted on as his own. Here sounds the first note of gladness in the ear of man. It sounds in many respects indistinctly and inarticulately; but in this respect, at least, is it most distinct and articulate, that it announces the free love of God, and that free love not simply as displayed in the sending of a deliverer; but as making for itself a righteous approach to man through the sufferings of that deliverer Himself. *Now* the great thought of God's heart, the idea of *grace*, began to be unfolded, not only to man, but to the universe. But oh! what a mighty apparatus requires to be constructed ere that one idea can be made plain, and man trusted with it! What an apparatus must be raised (and that gradually, age after age) for carrying out as well as for exhibiting the whole adjustment of righteousness and grace, holiness and grace, wrath and grace, punishment and grace, ere the sinner can be made to comprehend the new, the strange idea, or to distinguish it from mere indifference to sin, or be trusted with the application of it to himself! This was the first step to the unfolding of 'the mystery which was hid in God, who created all things by Jesus Christ; that now unto the principalities and powers in heavenly places might be known by the Church the manifold wisdom of God, according to the eternal purpose which He purposed in Christ Jesus our Lord' (Eph. iii. 9–11). And it is in reference to this that the epistle thus concludes: 'Unto Him be glory IN THE CHURCH, throughout all ages, world without end. Amen' (Eph. iii. 21). And at the consummation of the glorious mystery shall this song be sung: 'Oh the depth of the riches both of the wisdom and knowledge of God!' (Rom. xi. 33.)

Having briefly sketched the meaning of these two verses, let us now look at them more in detail. They are too important to be slightly passed over. They contain the root of all redemption-truth.

1. *Let us mark how God proceeds in His inquiries after sin.*—He first traces it out step by step, tracks it in all its windings, ere He utters one word of judgment. His dealings hitherto had been with Adam, as the head of creation. Therefore He speaks first to him. Then from Adam sin is traced to the woman, then from the woman to the serpent. By this process, it was brought solemnly before the conscience of the transgressors, that they might *see* what they had done. In this process God takes no advantage of the sinner. He does not make use of His omniscience or omnipotence to convict or overawe the sinner, or to extort confession from him. He proves all by the sinner's own admission, that his mouth may be stopped, and that the Judge may be acknowledged as righteous in all He does; that He may not only be the just God, but that He may be *seen* to be so by His creatures (see Job xxxiv. 23; Ps. li. 4; Rom. iii. 4). And as is the process of inquiry, so is the judgment. The sentence is judicially announced, not in anger, but in righteousness. Having traced the sin to its source, God begins with the serpent, the source of the evil, or rather with Satan and the serpent jointly, as the twofold source. He began with the transgressor in His inquiry, He begins with the tempter in His judgment; for the

first word of condemnation must be directed against the originator of sin, the first stroke of wrath must fall on the prime mover of the deed. Thus, even in the minutest things, showing His truth and justice! Even in the *order* of judgment, how careful to mark His sense of the different kinds of criminality! Such is a specimen of the way in which He will judge the world in righteousness!

2. *Let us mark the circumstances in which the sentence was given.*—It was given in the hearing of our parents. It was not specially directed to them. They were but *hearers.* Yet the scene was designed for them. This curse on the serpent was spoken in their ears, because it contained in it God's purpose of grace towards them. God's design was, that they should learn His gracious intentions without delay, and thus their fears be quieted and their confidence in God restored, but still that they should learn them in a way which should completely humble them, and make them feel that the grace did not arise from anything in themselves. They learn this grace of God in a sort of side way, as if God turned away His face when making it known. They get it in the form of a curse against the serpent for the evil done by him, thereby learning that the evil done must all be undone before man can be blest! This awful curse against the being that had ruined them intimated such things as these: (1.) That God meant to save them, and not to give them up to the snares of their enemy; (2.) That they could only be saved by their enemy being destroyed; (3.) That this destruction would be attended

with toil, and conflict, and wounds; (4.) That it was easy to ruin a world, but hard to save and restore. How affecting the thought, that God could not preach the gospel directly to Adam, but that he must be left to gather it from the curse against the Evil One,—as if he could not be trusted with the full glad tidings of grace till he had learned the exceeding sinfulness of sin! How different now with us! God preaches that gospel directly to the sinner in all its largeness; saying to each of us, There is grace enough for thee, come thou and be reconciled, come thou and be saved!

3. *Let us mark how God hated that which Satan had done.*—'Because thou hast done this,' are the words of awful preface to the sentence. God had no pleasure in the snare or the ruin it had wrought. He had no satisfaction in the marring of His handiwork, no pleasure in the death of the sinner, no joy in the desolation of His world. His words are the expression of deep displeasure against him who had done the horrid deed, and at the deed which had been done. And let us not forget how much of that which Satan has since then been doomed to suffer, as well as of that which he shall hereafter suffer, has its origin here. 'Because thou hast done this!' No doubt he was ruined and doomed before, for his own transgression; but now he is to be sunk to a lower level of condemnation, and loaded with a weightier curse, for being the tempter of man, the destroyer of a world. This is the brand upon his burning forehead; this is the millstone round his neck. God will have him understand how He abhorred that which he had done. And when here-

after he is seized, and bound, and shut up by the strong angel in the abyss, shall not these words ring in his ears as he is thrust down into his dwelling of darkness, 'Because thou hast done this'? His sin, by means of which he succeeded in casting man out of Eden, shall be the sin by which he himself shall be cast wholly out of earth, to deceive the nations no more.

4. *In undoing the evil God begins at its source.*—The drying up of the stream will not do; the source must be reached. If man is to be saved at all, it must be by the removal of sin; and if sin is to be removed, God must begin at the very root. There must be a complete undoing of the evil,—an undoing which shall not only sweep off the actual sin, with its sad results, but which shall strike at the very nature of sin itself. Thus God's hatred of sin is the foundation of the sinner's deliverance; and no deliverance can be sure or permanent, if not founded upon this. God's purpose of grace does not treat sin as a light thing, but as an infinite evil, which must be met at its first uprising; nay, which can only be rightly met when met there. Grace cannot come forth to the sinner, save in connection with the utter condemnation of the sin. There can be no true love to the sinner, which does not extirpate and utterly make away with the sin. Sin was the real enemy, and love to the sinner must proceed at once against this enemy, not resting till it is utterly destroyed.

5. *God shows that Satan shall not be allowed to triumph.*—He has gained a mighty advantage, but his victory is only temporary and partial. God is seen

interposing and setting His face against the adversary. God is taking the sinner's side; and this is the assurance that Satan's victory shall be reversed! His doom is sealed. Degradation, shame, ruin, are his portion. What might have been his doom hitherto on account of his former sin we know not; but here we learn the superadded penalty which he was henceforth to bear. Man hears the condemnation of his enemy, and knows that this defeat is his deliverance. And of this he is to have a *visible pledge* in the serpent's form and habits. This very curse upon the serpent is the declaration to man of his own deliverance from the curse, for it is God's declaration of displeasure against the enemy that had seduced him. Thus Satan's ruin and the sinner's deliverance are bound up together. It was to 'destroy the works of the devil' that the Son of God was to come; nay, it was 'to destroy him that had the power of death, even the devil.' And we now, in these days, know that He has come. He has done His mighty work. He has led captivity captive.

6. *God Himself undertakes man's cause.*—'I will put enmity between thee and the woman, and between thy seed and her seed.' It is not, 'there shall be enmity;' but 'I will put it.' God Himself will now proceed to work for man. The serpent's malice and success have but drawn forth the deeper love and more direct interposition in man's behalf.

7. *God promises a seed to the woman.*[1]—All that this

[1] How *literally* was this fulfilled in the Son of Mary! He was the seed of the *woman*, not of the man.

implied she could not know at the time. But it is evidently declared, that she was not to die immediately. The sentence, 'In the day thou eatest thou shalt die,' was to be suspended in so far as death temporal was concerned. She was to have a seed, and that said, Thou art not to die immediately.[1] This suspension was, of itself, an intimation of grace. The seed of the woman might be supposed to be three. First, there is the whole race of man. Secondly, there is the Church. Thirdly, there is the Messiah. To this last, more especially, does the promise point. On Him, as the woman's seed, He sought to fix man's eye from the beginning. Through Him deliverance was to come. For whatever might be the mystery hanging over this, still it was indicated that it was in this way, and through this seed, that sin was to be undone. The woman's seed was to be God's instrument in destroying Satan, and avenging the wrong he had done to man. Here let us mark, (1.) The honour put upon the woman, even though she was first in transgression.[2] This is grace indeed,—grace in its largeness. And thus, while the woman is taught not to be overmuch cast down, the man is hindered from triumphing over her. (2.) The confounding of Satan. It is the seed of his victim that is to be his destroyer. It is thus that he is put to shame, and the

[1] Hence to Messiah Himself the promise was, 'He shall see His *seed,* He shall prolong His days,' Isa. liii. 10.

[2] May we not say, that thus the man was *reproved* for casting blame upon the woman? He was prevented from boasting. If the woman had the dishonour of being the chief transgressor, she had the honour of being the instrument of deliverance.

success of his wiles made the means of his own ruin. His triumph is his destruction. (3.) The directing of the Church's eye to a *person* as the instrument of blessing; nay, to a *man*, — very flesh and blood. The salvation was to come *from* God, and yet it was to come *through man*.

8. *God is to put enmity between the serpent and the woman, and between the serpent's seed and the woman's seed.*—The woman and the serpent had joined together in rebellion; and so long as this friendship lasted, there could be no hope for her or for the race. But God steps in to break this bond. This 'covenant with death shall be disannulled, and this agreement with hell shall not stand.' The woman and the serpent had been fellow-accomplices; but henceforth this league was to be broken. As if God had said to the tempter, 'Thou hast beguiled her to be an accomplice with thee against me, and thou thinkest to get her seed to join thee; but it shall not be so. I will break the alliance. I will not only separate between thee and her, but I will raise up deadly hatred.' Let us notice here such things as these: (1.) The enmity between Satan and the Church. There can be no friendship with him, and no sympathy with his works. Thus the distinction between the Church and the world is as old as Eden; and it is not merely distinction, it is hostility. (2.) The enmity between Christ and Satan; between Him who is the representative of heaven and him who is the representative of hell; between Him who is the friend and him who is the enemy of man. (3.) The name given to the ungodly,—

'the seed of the serpent.' And it was this expression that Christ took up when He spoke of the 'generation of vipers,' and said to the unbelieving Jews, 'Ye are of your father the devil.' By birth we are the serpent's brood, till grace transforms us, and we become the woman's seed; then our friendship with the accursed race is for ever broken. (4.) The name of the Church, —'the seed of the woman.' Yes, the seed of her who sinned, who 'was in the transgression,'—offspring of Eve, —of her who was first in apostasy. What tender favour is thus shown to her! (5.) The name of Christ. The same as the Church's, the 'seed of the woman.' Yes, He was indeed 'born of a woman,'—the Son of Mary, —the Son of Eve,—the Son of her that had transgressed. We sometimes wonder that Jesus should have allowed such names as Tamar, and Rahab, and Bathsheba to be in the roll of His ancestors; but is not all this implied in His being called at the outset the seed of the woman? What grace is there in His taking to Himself such a name! What oneness with us does such a name imply; oneness with *all* the redeemed! Ah, surely He is not ashamed to call us brethren! Truly the Son of man did come to seek and to save that which was lost.

9. *There is not only to be enmity, but conflict.*—That these two parties should keep aloof from each other was not enough. There must be more than this. There must be alienation and hatred; nay, there must be warfare, and that of the most desperate kind. Satan and the Church must ever be at open warfare. The world and the Church must ever be foes to each other. It

cannot be otherwise. No concession, no compromise, can ever make it otherwise, or alter the declared purpose of Jehovah. Neither Satan nor the world can change. They may hide their vileness, they may mask their hatefulness, and seek to win us with flattery, or beguile us with lies; but they change not. They are still 'from beneath,' not 'from above;' and woe be to us, if by silence, or unfaithfulness, or compliance, we dishonour our Lord before them, and act unworthy of our calling, and name, and hope!

The beginning of this warfare we see in Cain and Abel. Its progress we find in the history of succeeding ages. In Christ Himself we see that warfare at its height. Since then it has still proceeded, and perhaps more than before, in the open field. Babylon was Satan's citadel at first, round which his armies were gathered, and from which, as from a centre, he assailed the Church in her citadel, which, in former days, was exclusively Jerusalem. In each of the seats of the four successive monarchies Satan found a citadel. These were his four great encampments, from which he launched his squadrons against the army of the living God. Especially in the last of these empires has he found at once a city and a fortress, from which he assails the hated followers of the Lamb, and 'wears out the saints of the Most High;' shedding their blood like water, and scattering their bones upon the earth. In a threefold form does this great anti-Christian armament take the field,—as Paganism, as Popery, as Infidelity,—the last the most terrible of all, as the product and combination of the others,—

the concentration and embodiment of all the various forms of evil from the beginning. In its ranks will be found 'the seed of the serpent' in fullest development,—the truest offspring of the Evil One to which earth has given birth. This conflict is made up of two great parts,—two events, each of which is the crisis of a long series preceding, and the commencement of another series arising out of it. They are widely different in their nature, though forming part of one great development. They are thus referred to by our Lord, 'Ought not Christ to have suffered these things, and to enter into His glory?' (Luke xxiv. 26); and by the Apostle Peter, when he speaks of 'the sufferings of Christ, and the glory that should follow' (1 Pet. i. 11); and again, when he speaks of himself as a 'witness of the sufferings of Christ, and also a partaker of the glory that shall be revealed' (1 Pet. v. 1). They form the two mighty events, known to us as the first and second comings of the Lord,—the first coming embracing that part of the conflict which consists in His 'suffering,' the second coming embracing that which is consummated in His 'glory.' Let us notice the two divisions.

1. *The bruising of the heel of the woman's seed.*[1]—It is not the *woman's* heel that is to be bruised, but the heel of *her seed;* neither is it the *woman* that is to bruise the

[1] The serpent, as it were, cunningly steals behind and seizes the *heel.* (See Gen. xlix. 17.) 'The serpent,' says Turrettine, 'can only lay hold on and bite the heel, that is, the humanity and flesh of Christ, by which He trod the earth ; and by means of temptations, persecutions, and death, afflict Him,' etc. 'Thus it is also,' he adds, 'with believers. The old serpent bites their heels.'—(Vol. ii. p. 242.)

serpent's head, but *her seed;*—'it shall bruise thy head, and thou shalt bruise his heel.'[1] It was an inferior part that was to be wounded, not a vital one. Yet still there was to be a wound. The serpent's seed was to have a temporary triumph, and this was fulfilled when Jesus hung on the cross. Then the heel was bruised. Then Satan seemed to conquer. That was the hour and power of darkness. Then 'He was wounded for our transgressions, He was bruised for our iniquities.' Then that wound was given which defeated him who gave it, and began our victory. Thus it was that the Church was taught to look forward to the 'bruised heel,' and out of that symbol to gather the great truth which alone can heal the conscience, that God had provided a *substitute*, by the shedding of whose blood there was to be deliverance. It was not salvation by mere love that was taught; it was not salvation by mere incarnation; it was salvation by *sacrificial substitute*, salvation by *vicarious bloodshedding*, salvation by a surety's endurance and exhaustion of the penalty which was our due. In no other way could love find its way to us, and in no other could our consciences have been pacified. The 'bruised heel' was not the mere display of love; it was *the judicial removal of the righteous barrier*, which would otherwise have for ever hindered that love from reaching the sinner. In the man with the 'bruised heel' we see the sinner's substitute, and, at the same time, the sinner's pattern,—

[1] It is not, '*she* shall bruise thy head,' but 'it' or 'he,' הוּא. It was not to be Eve herself, or any daughter of Eve. And this was perfectly understood all along from the beginning.

his 'leader and commander.' We are followers of the Man with the bruised heel! Let us not be ashamed of Him or of His cross! Let us not expect for ourselves anything better than He had to pass through. Tribulation was His entrance into the kingdom. It must also be ours. The servant is not greater than his Lord.

2. *The bruising of the serpent's head.*[1]—It was his most vital as well as his most honourable part that was to be bruised. An intimation this of utter defeat and ruin. He has received many a stroke. His deadly wound was given upon the cross, in that very stroke by which he bruised the heel of the woman's seed. So that from that moment our victory was secure. But the final blow is reserved for the Lord's second coming. Then it is that the great dragon, that old serpent, is to be bound in chains, and shut up in the abyss. And it is to that day of triumph that the apostle's words specially refer, 'The God of peace shall bruise Satan under your feet shortly.'

Such was the curse upon the tempter; such the glad tidings to man which it contained; such the grace it

[1] There is evident reference to this not only in Rom. xvi. 20, but in the promise to Messiah (Ps. xci. 13), 'Thou shalt tread upon the *adder* . . . the *dragon* shalt Thou trample under feet;' and in the promises to the apostles, 'They shall take up *serpents*,' etc. (Mark xvi. 18); and especially in Luke x. 18, 19, where, after saying, 'I beheld Satan as lightning fall from heaven,' our Lord adds, 'Behold, I give you power to tread on SERPENTS AND SCORPIONS, AND OVER ALL THE POWER OF THE ENEMY;' as if He would say, 'I, the seed of the woman, the bruiser of the serpent's head, delegate this power of mine to you; I, who am specially appointed to carry on the enmity between the two seeds, *I* give you power over *the enemy*.'

manifested; such the victory which it pledged; and such the process through which that triumph was to be reached. It was this display of an infinite but most unexpected grace that made Adam throw aside his fig-leaves, leave his thicket, and draw nigh to God. He could have expected only avenging wrath; he meets with pardoning love; love that would not rest till it had undone all the evil that had been brought into the world by man's sin; that would spare no cost, not even the blood of the Only-begotten of the Father, in accomplishing this end; and would press forward through every enemy and every barrier, till it had taken the spoil from the mighty, and delivered the lawful captive; till it had overthrown the adversary in righteous battle; till it had won back man and man's forfeited inheritance; till it had compensated for all the dishonours done to God by Satan's victory; nay, till it had secured glory to God in the highest, peace on earth, and good-will to man.[1]

Ver. 16. '*Unto the woman He said, I will greatly multiply thy sorrow and thy conception: in sorrow thou shalt bring forth children; and thy desire shall be to thy husband, and he shall rule over thee.*'

In the sentence on the woman there are no words of preface, serving as a link to connect the special sin with the special penalty. In the case of the serpent, the preface was, 'because thou hast done this.' In the case

[1] In this first promise, which so fully contains the gospel, not one word is said of anything being done by *man*, He is set aside, and God does everything for him. 'Salvation is of the Lord.' Man stands still and beholds it. The gospel is no command enjoining us to do anything; it is God's declaration that He has done all for us.

of Adam, it was, 'because thou hast hearkened to the voice of thy wife;' but in the case of the woman, it is not, as might have been expected, 'because thou hast hearkened to the serpent;' but, without any such introduction, the sentence goes forth at once, 'I will greatly multiply thy sorrow.' The want of this introduction, taken in connection with the peculiar sentence, seems to show that the woman's punishment was something special, superadded to her share in the punishment of the race, because of her leading her husband into the transgression. As one with the man, she was to partake of his sentence; but, as having misled the man, she was to have a penalty that would always remind her of this. Adam, as the representative of the race, is made to bear the *general* penalty; and in this the woman, as one of the race, has her part. But, apart from this, as the beguiler of her husband, when given him as his help-meet, she is to have her sorrows multiplied.[1] Yet though her sentence implies this, God, in His tender love to her, does not actually

[1] May there not be in the words, 'I will greatly multiply,' a reference to the well-known physical law, that adverse circumstances, such as hardship or feebleness in the human race, or a poor soil in the case of plants, tend to increase the propagative power, and multiply, instead of diminishing, the numbers produced; as if nature, inwardly conscious of more precarious life, and anticipating a speedier end, were putting forth every effort to prevent the cutting off of the peculiar race or kind, by hastening the process of propagation, and multiplying the numbers produced? In that case, it would be as if God, when inflicting the sentence which gave weakness and hardship to woman as her lot, threw around her, as an amelioration and compensation, the protection of a new law—the law which was to regulate her fruitfulness, not by the extent of her healthfulness, and ease, and comfort, but by the amount of her feebleness, and hardship, and oppression; a law

announce this with a 'because,' lest the man should think that God was confirming his accusation against her (ver. 12), and thereby lessening his guilt. Thus she gets something which the man does not, because she was first in transgression, and because she was both the deceived and the deceiver. 'Adam,' says the apostle (1 Tim. ii. 14), 'was not deceived (by the serpent); but the woman, being deceived, was in the transgression. Notwithstanding, she (even she!) shall be saved (no less than Adam) through her child-bearing (by means of that very child-bearing which contained her sentence and her sorrow), if she continue in faith, and love, and holiness, with sobriety;' for without holiness no man shall see the Lord.

Thus it was made manifest, (1.) That God looked upon the serpent as the great origin of the sin and the evil in both woman and man. (2.) That God treated *Adam* as the representative of the race, through whom sin entered, and passed over to posterity, so that it was not Eve's sin that effected *our* ruin (though it brought woe upon herself), but that (if we can suppose the case), had Eve sinned alone, no evil would have followed to mankind (Rom. v. 12, 14; 1 Cor. xv. 22). (3.) That the very penalty inflicted was connected with *grace;*[1] the child-bearing in sorrow, which was the penalty, being the channel through which

which, while it multiplied her grief, multiplied her joys also, giving her ten children, though in sorrow, for one without it, and compressing within the brief period of shortened life on earth the whole strange story of a woman's heart, and a mother's tears.

[1] 'A promise of mercy, and forgiveness of sin, and great afflictions, or rebukes for the same, may and shall attend the same soul; "I

the seed was to come by whom deliverance was to be wrought. (4.) That God wished it to be known that this sentence of evil, as well as the previous sentence of blessing, came directly *from Himself*. He is the Almighty, the Sovereign *doer* as well as *purposer* of all. 'I will greatly multiply.'

This sentence takes for granted the previous promise of 'the seed.' As if God were saying to the woman, 'Yes, thou shalt have a seed, and from it deliverance shall come, and come through *thee*, the introducer of the evil; but the bringing forth of that seed shall be a perpetual memorial of thy sin, so that thou shalt be continually humbled, and solemnized, and saddened, by the very thing which seemed fitted only to lift thee up, and make thee rejoice; with thy joy shall grief be mingled, so that thou shalt not be allowed to forget thy sin, but be perpetually reminded of it; and if at any time thou shouldst exult unduly, and say, "I am the deliverer," thou shalt hear a voice saying in thine ears, "But thou wast the transgressor."' Thus the memorial of the deliverance and of the sin is *one*. The two things are kept before our eyes by the same token; and we are taught that,

will greatly multiply thy sorrow" comes after the promise of grace.' —BUNYAN'S *Exposition of the first ten chapters of Genesis*.

'God does not cast Eve off, or curse her as He had done the serpent. All this was fatherly chastisement, rather than a satisfactory punishment. God might have inflicted the mulct of sudden death upon her, which she had merited; He might have taken away the blessing of fruitfulness before promised, but He only mingleth it with dolours.'—CHRISTOPHER NESS, *History and Mystery of the Old and New Testament*, vol. i. p. 52.

whilst there is a redemption and a Redeemer, it was an awful sin that needed such a redemption and such a Redeemer. On each portion and fragment of this ruined world has God written the evil of sin.[1]

His sentence on the woman is, in part, a reversal of the first blessing: 'Multiply, and replenish the earth.' God's blessing alone went out at first with the command to multiply; but now some drops of the curse are to be infused into it, in remembrance of sin. The race was still to go on increasing; but henceforth it was to be in sorrow. The very perpetuation of the species was to be accompanied with marks of the displeasure of God. The dark cloud of sorrow was to take up its station above each man as he came into the world. There was henceforth to be pain and danger, fear and trembling, the shrinking of woman's feeble nature from the greatness of the conflict which lay before her, ere the desire of her eyes was attained; and that which was meant to have been an unmingled joy, became the sorest trial of humanity; one of Nature's sharpest struggles; one of the bitterest ills that flesh is heir to. And, kindred to these pangs of her corporeal frame, are the other varied sorrows which overshadow her lot—the weakness, the dependence, the fear, the rising and sinking of heart, the bitterness of disap-

[1] Bernard, in alluding to this passage, notices, on the one hand, the pains of child-bearing, and on the other, the disgrace that was attached to barrenness, as if woman were now placed in a strait betwixt the two. After speaking of the 'hard necessity and heavy yoke laid on the daughters of Eve,' he adds, 'Et si pariunt cruciantur; et si non pariunt maledicuntur. Et dolor prohibet parere, et non parere, maledictio.'—*Homil. III. de Adventu.*

pointed hope, the wounds of unrequited affection;—all these, as drops of the sad cup now put into her hands, woman has, from the beginning, been made to taste.

The sentence falls on her specially as *woman*, not as one with the man, and part of the human race, but as woman. The things which mark her out as woman are the things which the sentence selects. It is as the *mother* and as the *wife* that she is to feel the weight of the sentence now pronounced. A mother's pangs (which otherwise would have been unknown); a wife's dependence (which, in all save Christian countries, is utter degradation); sorrow, not joy, in that appointed process through which the promised seed is to be born into the world;[1] inferiority, instead of equality, in that relationship in reference to which it had been said by her husband, 'Bone of my bone, and flesh of my flesh;' not henceforth the husband 'cleaving to the wife,' as at the first (ii. 24), but the wife cleaving to the husband, and the husband ruling over the wife. Such are the sad results of sin![2]

[1] An old commentator gives four reasons for the sorrow, among which are not only the prospect of the temporal ills of her offspring, but the foreboding of the eternal ruin of so many of those whom she brings forth: 'eorum qui generantur, pauci sunt electi et prædestinati, plerique propter eorum flagitia æternis suppliciis destinati.'—Vol. i. p. 678 of a *Commentary on Genesis*, in four quarto volumes, by Benedictus Pererius Valentinus, A.D. 1599. This may be somewhat strained; yet it is a solemn thought for either man or woman.

[2] 'She must pay the penalty of her sin before she can rejoice in her child,' says Chrysologus; and then adds, 'What must be the end of that of which the beginning is penal? Shall joy be the life-portion of the man who begins that life in sorrow?'—*Sermones in Ps.* i.

In the helplessness of clinging dependence, as well as in the fondness of blind attachment; in the consciousness of needing an arm to lean upon, as well as in the irrepressible overflow of passionate and unreasoning love, 'thy desire shall be to thy husband.' Nay, more, 'he shall rule over thee.' His the lordship, thine the submission; his the rule, thine the obedience. Such, henceforth, is to be thy condition; such the principle on which the domestic constitution is to be reared.[1] So God has ordained it; not only as the penalty of woman's sin, but as that which best suits a fallen world, and which best carries out His design in regard to the families and kingdoms of the children of men. And what can that family expect where this divine ordinance is overlooked, nay, perhaps reversed? Hence the apostle utters the command so strongly, 'Wives, be in subjection to your own husbands' (1 Pet. iii. 1); 'Submit yourselves unto your own husbands in everything. Let the wife see that she reverence her husband' (Eph. v. 22, 24, 33).[2]

[1] The 'natural subordination in innocency,' as Fuller calls it in his *Exposition of Genesis*, was to be greatly increased, so as to become afterwards a *yoke*. It is not merely that she who had thus 'gone' beyond her bounds' should be 'forced back into her own proper rank' (in ordinem suum cogitur), as Calvin remarks, but she was henceforth to occupy a still lower place than before; not necessarily 'bondage,' as he says, but still such a position as would eventually lead to bondage, unless counteracted by higher principles. Yet it is to be noticed (says Trapp), that though the apostle bids wives submit themselves to their husbands, he does not say, Husbands, rule over your wives.—TRAPP *On Genesis*, A.D. 1650.

[2] 'A just law unto her, who, having given way to her own inordinate phantasie and appetite, had undone both herself and husband. And yet a rule given her for her own good and safety, who, having by

Yet, as if to comfort her spirit under this heavy prospect; as if to elevate woman's lowly lot, and to sanctify a mother's pangs, God has taken this very fact concerning her as the groundwork of figures wherein He sets forth the world's coming deliverance and the Church's promised glory. To this He refers when He speaks of creation's groans and travail-pains (Rom. viii. 22); and of His people's joy when the day of present sorrow shall have passed away (John xvi. 21, 22). Again, as if to dignify woman's humbling dependence on another, the figure of the wife is made use of in illustrating the relationship between Christ and His redeemed (Eph. v. 23–32). He, the lover; she, the loved one; he, gazing on her beauty (Song vi. 4, vii. 1–6); she, leaning on his strength

experience found how ill she was able to moderate her own desires, must needs be the more secured, by having a moderator set over her.' —WHITE *On the first three chapters of Genesis*, 1656. A tolerably thick folio, containing abundance of practical instruction deduced from these chapters. Poole thus paraphrases the words: 'Seeing, for want of thy husband's rule and conduct, thou wast seduced by the serpent, and didst abuse that power I gave thee, together with thy husband, to draw him into sin, thou shalt now be brought down to a lower degree; for he shall rule thee, not with that sweet and gentle hand which he formerly used, as a guide and counsellor only, but by a higher and harder hand, as a lord and governor, to whom I have now given a greater power and authority over thee than he had before.' Jackson remarks: 'That is, thy desire shall be subject to thy husband. Upon his will and pleasure all thy desire must depend. For in this sense the same phrase is used (Gen. iv. 7) concerning Abel's subjection to Cain as the first-born. It is true, by the law of creation, the woman should have lived in subordination under her husband, and should have been governed by him; but being here denounced as a chastisement for sinne, it implieth a further degree of subjection than that which should have been by the law of nature and creation.'—JACKSON *On the Pentateuch*, A.D. 1646.

(Song ii. 6, viii. 5); he, decking her with jewels, as the partner of his throne and heart; she, 'sick with love,' yet reverently looking up to and rejoicing in the strength and honour of her husband-king; he, putting on his royal state and raiment of glory, to win her eye yet more; she, though conscious of the infinite inequality, not saying, as human love in such circumstances is represented as doing:

> 'It were all one
> That I should love a bright particular star,
> And think to wed it; he is so above me,
> In his bright radiance and collateral light
> Must I be comforted, not in his sphere;'

but saying, in the conscious security of well-proved affection, 'My beloved is mine, and I am his.'

Under the figure of woman's birth-pangs, the whole creation is described as travailing and groaning, pressing forwards with eager longings to the glorious birth which lies before it, in the day of the 'regeneration.' Israel, too, is spoken of under the same figure, as anticipating a wondrous birth in the same day of 'restitution' (Isa. lxvi. 7, 8); and the Church also is represented as, with like pangs and groanings, longing for her expected hour of blessing (Rev. xii. 2).[1]

[1] Now be it observed, there is not in nature such an image as woman's travail for expressing that event which, looking to the substance of it, is the bringing again of the Son out of the womb of the invisible into the visible world, for ever to abide therein; which, looking to the circumstances of it, is, with long-deferred hope, growing towards the consummation into longing desire, and accomplished with rending pangs, yet issuing in joy, transport of joy, that the Man-child

And as this sentence on woman as a *mother* is thus made use of to set forth the process of bitter grief and anguish through which the coming glory is to be reached, so the sentence on her as the *wife* is referred to in connection with the Church's relationship to Christ; for though she is spoken of as the Bride, the Lamb's wife, spouse of the second Adam, yet to her it is said, as if to keep her in mind of her subject condition, 'He is thy Lord, worship thou Him' (Ps. xlv. 11); so that, though in one sense she seems raised to an equality with Him, and placed upon His throne, yet she is ever to keep in mind her inferiority to Him who is 'God over all.'

Church of God! Bride of the Lamb! keep in remembrance thy heavenly calling, thy relationship to the Son

is born into the world; which, again, for the time of it, is fixed and definite, but as it approaches, all uncertain to the very hour, inducing continual preparation and readiness, yea, and longing, until the fierce trial be overpast, and the joy be come. By this most expressive similitude, dignifying and sanctifying that sorest trial of humanity, having expressed the condition of the parturient Church, and the weakness to which at length she is brought, and her own lamentation over her own unprofitableness in the earth,—'We have, as it were, brought forth wind; we have not wrought any deliverance in the earth;' the Holy Spirit comforteth the Church with these words, spoken in the person of the Christ: 'Thy dead shall live; my dead body shall they arise;' which words, without any gloss whatever of an interpreter, convey their own meaning to be, that the deliverance which the Church lamented she had not wrought upon the earth, should be wrought by the rising of her dead men, who are promised this, among other things, that they should rule the nations with a rod of iron, and break them in pieces like a potter's vessel. These dead men of the Church He honours by the name of His dead body, according to the universal symbol of the Apostle Paul, which representeth the Church as the body of Christ, the fulness of Him that filleth all in all.

of God, that thou mayest be cheered, and gladdened, and quickened; yet keep in mind thy lowly origin, thy unworthiness of character, thy unlikeness to the Holy One who has bethrothed thee to Himself, that thou mayest be humbled and abased. He is thy Lord, worship thou Him; forget not the adoration that is due to Him for His high majesty and condescending love. He is thy Lord, let thy desire be to Him. Love Him as He hath loved thee, and let His name be written on thy heart. He is thy Lord, let Him rule over thee! Serve Him as He hath served thee, when for thee He took on Him the form of a servant. Rejoice in being reigned over by one whose sceptre is love. He is thy Lord, look for His appearing, for He comes to complete the espousals. Long for that marriage-day; the day of nearness, and union, and vision, when the bridal-blessing, the bridal-glory, the bridal-crown, shall all be thine. In spite of the 'much tribulation' that lies before thee, be of good cheer, for thus He Himself has spoken: 'A woman when she is in travail hath sorrow, because her hour is come; but as soon as she is delivered of the child, she remembereth no more the anguish, for joy that a man is born into the world. And ye now therefore have sorrow; but I will see you again, and your heart shall rejoice, and your joy no man taketh from you' (John xvi. 21, 22).

Vers. 17-19. '*And unto Adam He said, Because thou hast hearkened unto the voice of thy wife, and hast eaten of the tree, of which I commanded thee, saying, Thou shalt not eat of it: cursed is the ground for thy sake* (or *on thy account*); *in sorrow* (or *with pain*) *shalt thou eat of it all the days of thy life:* 18. *Thorns also and thistles shall it bring forth to thee* (Heb. *and thorns and thistles shall it cause to bud to thee*); *and thou shalt eat the herb of the field.* 19. *In the sweat of thy face shalt thou eat bread, till thou return unto the ground; for out of it wast thou taken: for dust thou art, and unto dust shalt thou return.*'

God now turns to Adam, to pronounce sentence upon him. In his case, as in that of the serpent, He begins with 'because,' making him feel the special point on which his punishment is made to turn. Adam had cast the blame of his sin on the woman, as if to palliate his own guilt, or at least to divide it with another. God begins at that very point, and takes up the excuse thus made as the very aggravation of the sin. Had the case been that of the woman hearkening to the man, there would have been some excuse for her, for she was under him; but it was Adam, *the head*, hearkening to the voice of her whom he ought to have led, instead of suffering himself to be led by her. God had made him the head of the woman as well as the head of creation, and therefore his sin was aggravated, not extenuated, by its being done at the woman's suggestion. For thus Adam left his place of rule; he forgot his headship, he overlooked his responsibility both to his wife and to his posterity; he set his wife's voice above the voice of God. Thus he made haste to sin; and, as he aggravated the sin by doing it at the suggestion of her whom he ought to have restrained, and guided, and watched over, so he aggravated it still more by trying to make that a palliation which was an increase of heinousness.

The sentence then follows: 'Cursed is the ground for thy sake.' It is not a direct one, as in the case of the serpent and of the woman, but a sentence in the form of a curse upon the earth. The king is punished by a curse upon his kingdom, in addition to the personal woe falling on himself, just as Pharaoh was cursed in the plagues inflicted on his people.

The ground, out of which he was taken, is cursed on his account, as if all pertaining to him had become evil. It is not he that suffers on account of his connection with the soil, but it is the soil that suffers on account of its connection with him, affording proof that it is not from matter that evil flows into spirit, but that it is from spirit that evil flows into matter. That soil from which he had sprung, that soil which God had just been strewing with verdure and flowers, that soil whose fruitfulness had produced the tree whose beauty and desirableness had been the woman's beguilement and his own ruin, that soil must now be scourged and sterilized on his account; as if God had thus addressed him: 'I can no longer trust thee with a fruitful soil, nor allow the blessing with which I have blessed the earth to abide upon it; *thou* art to remain here for a season, but it shall not be the same earth; in mercy I will still leave it such an earth as thou canst inherit, not a wilderness nor a chaos as at first, but still with enough of gloom, and desolation, and barrenness, as to remind thee of thy sin, to say to thee continually, O man, thou hast ruined the earth over which I had set thee as king.' God's blessing on the soil at first proclaimed the commencement of an age of holiness on earth; His curse proclaimed the entrance of sin; and, in the latter day, His blessing shall again descend, restoring it to former excellence and beauty. It was for man's sake that it was made a blessed earth at first; it was for man's sake that it was transformed into a cursed one; and for man's sake it shall be restored to a blessed world again. The first Adam's connection with it (being made of dust) drew on it all evil when he fell; but the second Adam's connection with it—for He also has a body formed out of it—shall undo the evil, cancel the curse, and perfect it again.[1]

Let us mark the details of the curse.

1. The earth is to bring forth the thorn and the thistle. Whether these existed before, we do not undertake to say, nor whether they are given here merely as the representatives of all noxious plants or weeds, nor whether the object of the curse, in so far as they were concerned, was to turn them into abortions, which they really are. Taking the words as they lie before us, we find that the essence of the curse was the multiplication of these prickly abortions, till they should become noxious to man, and beast, and herb of the field; mere nuisances on the face of the ground. Elsewhere in Scripture they are referred to as calamities. As the effects of judgments, Job refers to them, xxxi. 40, and Jeremiah, xii. 13. As the

[1] See Ps. xcvi. 11–13, xcviii. 7–9; Isa. xi. 6–9, xxix. 17, xxxii. 15, xxxv. 1, lxv. 17, lxvi. 22; Ezek. xlvii. 8–12. It is to this period that our Lord refers when He speaks of 'the regeneration' (Matt. xix. 28), and Peter when he speaks of 'the restitution of all things' (Acts iii. 21), and Paul when he refers to the deliverance of the 'reluctant' (οὐχ ἑκοῦσα) creation (Rom. viii. 19-23), and Peter when he speaks of the new heavens and earth (2 Pet. iii. 13), and John when he describes the same (Rev. xx. 1).

true offspring of a barren soil, the apostle speaks of them, Heb. vi. 8. As injurious to all around, our Lord Himself alludes to them, Matt. xiii. 7–22. And it is evident that all these passages connect themselves with the original curse, and are to be interpreted by a reference to it.[1] They are tokens of God's original displeasure against man's sin, so that the sight of them should recall us to this awful scene in Eden, and make us feel how truly God hates sin, and how impossible it is for Him to change in His hatred of it. These tokens of His anger have not been rooted up, neither have they withered away. They have survived the changes of six thousand years. They are God's monuments of sin, and must stand till He who erected them shall take them down, and that come to pass which is written, 'Instead of the thorn shall come up the fir-tree, and instead of the briar shall come up the myrtle-tree: and it shall be to the Lord for a name, for an everlasting sign that shall not be cut off' (Isa. lv. 13).

Christ, in bearing our sins, was 'made a curse for us'

[1] Thorns are always spoken of in connection with evil. The word occurs twelve times in the Old Testament. We have such an expression as 'thorns of the wilderness,' as if the two things were congenial. We have the coming up of the 'thorn and brier,' which is spoken of in connection with the desolation of Judea (Isa. xxxii. 13); and the 'grieving thorn' is used as the figure for Israel's enemies (Ezek. xxviii. 24), as Paul speaks of the 'thorn in the flesh.' The anti-Christian confederacy is to be 'as thorns thrust away' (2 Sam. xxiii. 6). And as Jeremiah had said, 'Sow not among thorns' (iv. 7), so our Lord had spoken of the good seed being choked by thorns. The word 'thistle' only occurs once elsewhere (Hos. x. 8), and Gesenius makes it to mean some 'luxuriantly growing but useless plant.' If thorns be really, as is said, abortive branches, the curse of barrenness appears in them more remarkably.

(Gal. iii. 13). He took our curse upon Him in all its parts. He was treated as the accursed One. In token of this He sorrowed, and was crucified, and died, and went down into the grave. It was our curse that wrought all these evils for the sinless One. And it was in token that He was truly the *curse-bearer* that He allowed Himself to be crowned with thorns. In wearing a 'crown,' He was saying, 'I am a King—earth's King, as the first Adam was;' and His enemies, in crowning Him, were unconsciously owning His royalty and dominion; in wearing a crown of *thorns*, He was announcing Himself as the willing sufferer of the sentence which attached not only to Adam, but to His inheritance, the earth; He was saying, 'Lo, I have come to stand in the first Adam's place, to bear the first Adam's penalty, to endure the first Adam's curse, to redeem the first Adam's forfeited kingdom, and in token thereof I accept this crown of thorns.'

2. Man is to eat the herb of the field. Originally, the fruit of the various trees was to have been man's food; the 'herb' was for the lower creation, if not exclusively, at least chiefly.[1] But now he is degraded. He is still, of course, to eat fruit, but in this he is to be restricted.

[1] 'When the curse, the heavy curse, passed upon him, he had to betake himself to the herb, which heretofore was the property of the lower creatures for browsing on, to which they were created prone, and bowed down. Now, he is truly of the earth earthy, his origin dust, his food gathered from the dust, his eye cast upon the dust, and his bed at length made in the lap of dust; his life a circle from dust to dust, a series of sensations, of animal impulses, of animal gratifications, of animal actions, until, like the animals, he yield up the animal life which, with sore toil and labour, he hath been endeavouring to maintain.'—IRVING *On the Curse as to Bodily Labour.*

Whether it were that, the earth being less productive in fruit, he must betake himself to inferior sustenance; or whether it might also be from a change in bodily constitution, requiring something else than fruit, we cannot say. The sentence is, 'Thou shalt eat the herb of the field, not the pleasant fruits of paradise.' In the ages to come, when the better paradise arrives, every vestige of this is swept away, and we 'eat of the tree of life which is in the midst of the paradise of God' (Rev. ii. 7).

3. He is to eat in sorrow. There was to be no glad feasting, but a bitter eating, or, if there might be feasting, it should be like Israel's, 'with bitter herbs,'—the sweet and the bitter mingling. A cloud of sorrow was to hang not only over his dwelling, but especially over his table; and perhaps to this we may trace the divinely instituted practice of *fasting*, as if not only man's eating was to be in sorrow, but as if at certain times he was specially to connect his common food with the remembrance of sin, and to put it away from him altogether, as if not worthy to be sustained by God at all.

Does not man mock all this by his feastings, making them to be special seasons of merriment and pleasure, and forgetting that God had thrown over them a dark shadow, as the memorial of sin! Yet the time is coming when joy shall take the place of sorrow. The great festival is at hand; the feast of fat things for Israel (Isa. xxv. 6), the marriage-supper for the Church (Rev. xix. 9), and the great feast of tabernacles at Jerusalem for the nations of the earth (Zech. xiv. 16). Of this day of happy festival—this time of the removal of the curse—we have an earnest in the supper of the Lord, when we show His death till He come; nay, more, we may be said to have an earnest of it each time that, like the early believers, we eat our bread with gladness and singleness of heart (Acts ii. 46), as men who by faith have already tasted their deliverance from the curse.

4. He is to eat it with toil. He is to wring a stinted subsistence out of the reluctant earth with sore labour and weariness; and the 'sweat of his face' is to attest the hardness of the conflict.[1] The earth will not yield even the herb of the field without heavy toil, toil in every department of the preparation of his food—tilling, sowing, reaping, grinding. He cannot live but in a way which reminds him of his primal sin. Each day he hears the

[1] Is not the following a true picture of man's toil?—'If you are up by times, you will hear, in the grey of the morning, the footsteps of the labourer beneath your casement pacing heavily on to the scene of his daily labour. As the dawn makes progress upon the rear of night, the din slowly increases, and ascends until the first watch of the day. One constant volume of sound inspheres the city like the noise of the neighbouring ocean, through which the rattling sound of chariot-wheels, and the rolling din of heavy vans, and the shrill discord of oaths and angry men, break incessantly like waves which dash upon the shore. It ceaseth not the livelong day. It ascendeth into your ears, a ceaseless tide of sound, in which no instant of silence is to be discovered. A voice of men and cattle, and of the instruments of their toils, which are all day long employed in bearing burdens from place to place, and in returning to bear more, until the shades of evening come to loose them from their harness, and allow them to rest their weary limbs. And these burdens which they bear are not the enjoyments of men, but the subject-matter of their toil, as you will discover if you follow them to their landing-places.'—IRVING *On the Curse as to Bodily Labour.* The whole book of Ecclesiastes is an illustration of this part of the curse.

original sentence ringing in his ears. And yet all this hard toil serves barely to sustain a 'dying life;' and even that only for a little, until he return to the dust. This is the end of his earthly toil!

5. He is to die. Grace does not remit the whole penalty. It leaves a fragment behind it, in pain, weakness, sickness, death, though at the same time it extracts blessing out of all these relics of the curse. Besides, in thus leaving men subject to death, it leaves open the door by which the great Deliverer was to go in and rob the spoiler of his prey. By death is death to be destroyed. Man must die! He came from the dust, and he must return to it.[1] The grave must be his portion. Yet, like everything else in the great purpose of grace, this is but the occasion for bringing in larger blessing—that is, resurrection, and all that resurrection comprises. Far beyond our original possessions, are those which flow to us through this channel. Resurrection-life and resurrection-glory are things higher far than that which Adam knew ere he fell.

Thus has sin degraded man; bringing him down to a lower level; introducing toil, and sweat, and weariness;

[1] Had we room, we might find an interesting subject in the various connections in which the word 'dust' occurs. Abraham speaks of himself as dust and ashes (Gen. xviii. 27). It was 'dust' that was to be mingled with the water in the trial of jealousy (Num. v. 17). It was 'dust' that was sprinkled upon the head in the time of sorrow (Job ii. 12). It is in the 'dust' that we are said to 'rest' (Job xvii. 16), to 'lie down' (xxi. 26), and it is out of the dust that we are to awake and arise when He who is our Life appears (Isa. xxvi. 19; Dan. xii. 2).

infusing sorrow into every part of our lot; nay, making us to be 'born to trouble as the sparks fly upward' (Job v. 7, xiv. 1); making our very food to be the memorial of the curse, and existence only to be maintained by a daily warfare with it; bringing in death, preparing the grave, tearing asunder soul and body; ruining this globe itself, and making its very soil the abode of evil.

Where the actual seat of the curse lies we cannot say. Whether it is in the ground itself, from which noxious influences ascend; or whether it is from the air, in consequence of its being the abode of 'the prince of the power of the air,' so that the soil is impregnated with evil by these ever-descending influences, we cannot say. The subtle processes of atmospheric action are only half discovered, and even science itself is not prepared to say what is the cause of earth's strange fruitfulness in evil and barrenness in good. But the disease is there, though man may not detect the seat. God's purpose subjected the creation to 'vanity.' We know this. We know also that it is subjected 'in hope' (Rom. viii. 20), and that that hope will ere long become a reality.

What efforts man makes to shake off the curse, both from himself and creation!—by means of science healing his own body, alleviating his sufferings, lessening his toil, and fertilizing the earth. To a large extent has he succeeded.[1] Marvellous discoveries have been made, by

[1] One cannot fail to notice that the various discoveries of the present day all tend in these directions. Chloroform in one direction, agricultural chemistry in another, and Liebig's investigations on the subject of diet in another. Compare the words of the curse, and mark the resemblance.

means of which, for a season, the body may be made insensible to suffering, so that the severest operations may be performed—nay, even woman's travail passed through, without the consciousness of a pang. Marvellous progress has been made in tillage, so that with less toil the soil is made more fruitful; in producing the various articles needed for subsistence or clothing, mechanical power has been brought in, to lighten or supersede the toil of man. In many such ways has man succeeded in lightening the curse. Nor in any of these efforts is there sin. It is not sinful to endeavour to heal disease, or alleviate pain, or ease labour, or wipe the sweat from the brow. No. Man is to use all those facilities and advantages which God has given, and to be thankful that any part of the burden can be thus relieved.

If man, indeed, were in these endeavours defying God, and proclaiming his purpose of effacing what God has written so legibly upon creation, then it would be *sin;* it would be rebellion. But it is evident that God has allowed man to seek alleviations of the curse; He has allowed him to seek to prolong life by medicine; and, in doing so, He has told him that there is no sin in these endeavours, so long as God is recognised. When Paul said to Timothy, 'Drink no longer water, but use a little wine for thy stomach's sake and thine often infirmities,' he was seeking to lighten the curse. And so, when we take measures either for healing disease or relieving pain, we are only acting in the spirit of that grace which has been dealing with our world since sin intruded, and showing us that God has not wholly given it over to the evil one; nay, we are acting in the spirit of Him who came not to destroy men's lives, but to save; who was anointed by the Holy Spirit for the very purpose of healing diseases, as well as of preaching the gospel to the poor.

But what then becomes of the curse? Is it to be disregarded wholly? Alas! after man has done his utmost, how very little of it has he removed! How much remains behind! And if those who sometimes are startled at the progress which man is making in soothing pain and healing disease, and who are at times afraid to make use of his remedies, would but consider how very little is, after all, effected; how in most cases it is a mere transient suspension of pain, a mere shifting of the burden from one shoulder to another, a mere relief such as that which rest gives to the body when it is weary; they would not be under any serious apprehension of man's interfering with the curse. That curse is too sore and deep for any to remove save He who laid it on. He will, in His own way and time, remove creation's curse, and stay its groans; He will bring to an end man's toil and woman's travail; He will swallow up death in victory. For that glorious day of hope let us wait in faith, knowing that not till then will the 'regeneration' come; not till then will all things be restored. Man may wipe off the tear, but he cannot dry up its source. He may hide himself from the billow and the blast, but he cannot say to either, 'Peace, be still.'

Ver. 20. '*And Adam* (Heb. *the man*) *called his wife's name Eve* (Heb. *Chavah*) ; *because she was the mother of all living.*'[1]

The sentence has now been pronounced, the criminals have heard it and have left the place of judgment, each, doubtless, occupied with his own thoughts and pursuing his own way. Satan goes out from the presence of the Lord to begin his 'going to and fro in the earth' (Job i. 7), to lay his snares, to prepare his wiles, to forge his fiery darts with double malignity, because he has been foiled in his purpose utterly to ruin the race. The woman retires to brood over coming grief, yet to mingle happier thoughts with her darker musings in the anticipation of the promised offspring which was to be the issue of her pain and travail. The man departs to look round upon a blighted paradise and a ruined earth, to brood over the days and nights of toil that awaited him, till this brief day here be done; yet to cheer himself with the thought that there was love even now for him, and the undoing of the evil in the end.

What space may have intervened between the announcement of the sentence and the scene in this 20th

[1] Was this her first name? or was she called *Ishi* before, and now, like Abraham, had her name altered to express her new circumstances as mother not of the dead, as she might have been, but of the living? The Septuagint translate the Hebrew name and call her Ζωή. Perhaps it would have been as well had we done the same; for surely to an English reader the meaning of the passage would have been better expressed thus, 'And the man called his wife's name *Life*, because she was the mother of all *living*.' There seems no reason for De Sola's change of tense here, into 'now the man had called;' nay, it appears from the way in which the statement is introduced, that he had *not* called her so before.

verse, we know not. We may suppose it to have taken place when Adam and his wife retired from the present vision of Jehovah. They talked or silently mused together over what had just befallen them,—over the evil and the good, the falling and the rising, the condemnation and the pardon, the curse and the blessing, the past, the present, the future of their life. Then the man, as if catching up the notes of grace which were just dying away amid the trees of the garden, adds his Amen, and embodies them in the name of her who was now doubly knit to him, doubly one with himself.

The fact that it was not God but Adam that gave the name to the woman, teaches us much. Why did not God give Eve her name, as He had done to Adam? God did not allow Adam to name himself, even in his innocence; yet now in his fall He permits him to name the woman, nay, sanctions his so doing. This was for such reasons as the following:—(1.) To show His grace. What grace, what tender love is displayed in allowing man to give a name to his wife,—and such a name,—Eve,—LIFE! (2.) To show that Adam was not to be deprived of his headship. He was still to be 'head of the woman,' even in his fall, and as such he names her. (3.) To show, that though Adam had so cruelly flung blame upon her before God, yet no estrangement had followed. She was still bone of his bone. They had been companions in guilt, they were to be companions in sorrow, and they were fellow-heirs of the hope just held out to them. Thus they were reunited in new bonds of mingled sadness and joy. (4.) To show the direction in which Adam's thoughts were running, that from this manifestation of the current of his thoughts we might learn how the promise had taken hold of him. This verse gives us unequivocal insight into the state of Adam's feelings. It exhibits him to us as one who understood, believed, prized, rested on the divine promise which he had just heard. He stands before us as a believing man; and we might say of him, 'By faith Adam called his wife's name Eve.' It is the voice of a believing man that speaks. One cannot mistake either the word or tone. Unbelief could not have spoken thus; none but a believer could have thought on such a name; a name that takes all its significancy from the promise,—*Life*, or the Living One,—doomed, and yet living; nay, dead by law, yet living; mother of the living; mother of a spared race; mother of one who is the Prince of life, 'the resurrection and the life;' mother of a family of men, alive from the dead! He takes the promise, he ponders it, he receives it as a faithful saying and worthy of all acceptation; and, on thus receiving it, he gives vent to his feeling, and utterance to his faith, in this expressive name. What can this verse be but the solemn utterance of Adam's faith in the divine promise? Surely this is one of the most simple and child-like, yet one of the most expressive ways of proclaiming his faith; and as Abraham expressed his faith by calling his son *Isaac*, 'the child of gladness,' so did Adam by naming his wife *Eve*, 'the mother of the living.' He looks at her and says, 'I see in thee the divine promise all realized,—life, not death, coming from thee; God carrying out His purpose of grace in thy seed, though afar off; I see in thee the pledge and embodiment of divine forgiveness and love, and I proclaim my faith in all this before God and before posterity, by naming thee *Eve*.'[1] This name is not the mere burst of feeling or a vague expression of acquiescence or wonder; it is the explicit confession of his faith. It is as a believing man that he speaks; a man strong in faith, and wishing to hand down to posterity a declaration of his confidence in the promise of a gracious God.

How simple is his faith! He has just been listening to the voice of God announcing grace, and life through grace; and forthwith he believes. He cavils not, questions not. A dark cloud had come between him and God; but now that cloud has passed, and the true light is shining again. He has just for a moment tasted the bitter cup of separation from his God (and who can tell the agony of that interval?), and straightway he is brought back to his father's love and bosom. The child has but wandered a few steps from the parental door, when it is snatched up by the fond mother's arm and replaced beneath the happy roof, never more to stray. The sheep has but gone a little way from the fold, enough to let it feel the bleakness and famine of the desert, when it is seized by the shepherd's strong hand and carried back in joy.

How immediately and how simply he believes! 'Faith comes by hearing;' he heard and believed, taking God at His word, and giving Him credit for speaking nothing but the truth, though no sign was given. God had spoken;

[1] 'He manifests his faith in the promise of the Messiah by whom he was delivered from death, and in whom he and his posterity should live for ever.'—WHITE *On Genesis*.

who was he, that he should doubt or hesitate, or reckon it presumption to return to God at once? He has spoken but *dimly*, no doubt; it is a very brief word of promise; yet he sees in these few words the free love of a forgiving God, and that is enough. He tastes that the Lord is gracious; and how sweet must that cup of grace have been to the parched lips of Adam! God has spoken *once;* but that once suffices, for He with whom he has to do is the God that cannot lie. We, with a thousand promises and assurances of love, doubt and tremble; Adam, with but one word, unratified by sign or token, believes.

If any one might have needed a sign, it was Adam. If any one might have said, 'I am too great a sinner, I dare not at once believe,' it was Adam. For his was deep guilt indeed: he had ruined a world; he had let in the flood of evil upon the earth; he had banished God from it; he had helped God's enemy to triumph; he had known what holiness was, and therefore knew what sin was. If any might have shrunk from trusting at once, it was Adam. Yet he believed, and it was counted unto him for righteousness. Nay, he not only believed, but he 'confessed with his mouth;' he testified his faith; he proclaimed his sure hope of everlasting life.

Go, sinner, and do likewise! Go, and like a child receive the simple word of God, speaking to you in love. Go and take forgiveness at His hands, and sonship, and the kingdom, and the glory. Do not, in the pride and presumption of your heart, speak of your unfitness and unworthiness, as if you would fain be fitter or worthier of the favour of Jehovah. Go, and as you are by birth a child of Adam, rebelling and departing from God, become by the second birth a child of Adam returning and reconciled. Take God's promise of life,—life through the living one,—the seed of the woman; take it and be saved, take it and be blest; and when thou hast thus received God's record, confess with thy mouth, as thy first father did. Make it manifest thou art a *believing* man; not a doubting, distrusting, wavering man, but a *believing* man.

Ver. 21. '*Unto Adam also* (Heb. *and unto Adam*), *and to his wife, did the Lord God make coats of skins,*[1] *and clothed them.*'

Adam's faith, so far as it went, was true and firm, but it was dim. The extent of his own wants he knew not. The kind of remedy which his case required he understood not. The way in which the promised deliverance was to come he could not foresee. All that as yet he knew was, that God had revealed Himself as gracious, and had pledged His love; therefore he could trust Him entirely, not merely for showing favour to the sinner, but for providing a way in which grace and righteousness might be reconciled.

Adam, however, having now made solemn confession of his faith, God proceeds to take another step by which some further insight into the process of deliverance was to be given. Adam had believed at once, without sign or

[1] כתנות עור, coats of skin. Tunicas pelliceas, Vulg.; *Χιτῶνας δερματίνους*, Sept. The word denotes properly, under-garments, fitting closely to the body. Thus there are three points of contrast: (1) skin contrasted with fig-leaves; (2) close-fitting garments with the loose fig-leaves; (3) the self-made fig-leaf clothing with the God-made skin-clothing.

pledge exhibited, and God honours his faith by a further revelation of His purpose, making him to know that 'blessed is he that hath not seen, and yet hath believed;' that 'to him that hath shall be given;' that 'if any man is willing to do the will of God, he shall know of the doctrine.'

In Adam's first estate no shame was felt, but as soon as he sinned shame covered his face. He showed this by his fleeing to the thickets, and he showed it by the fig-leaves with which he covered himself. God now deals with him as one *ashamed*, and who has just cause of shame. He takes for granted that Adam's shame and sense of sin were right things, and He proceeds to deepen them, to make him *feel* his sin more bitterly, to unfold the evil of sin, to spread out before him the infinite wants which sin had occasioned, to make him understand how largely as well as how entirely he must be indebted to God, and to teach him how great that redemption must be, and that Redeemer who was to accomplish his deliverance.

He begins by taking off their fig-leaves—for, doubtless, this act was *His*—and then giving them coats made by His own hand, coats of *skin* for their covering.[1] In so

[1] The utter blindness of most of the Fathers to the real meaning of this, is one of the many proofs that might be given that they neither prized nor knew the truth of salvation by another's righteousness, and life by the death of a substitute. Some of them affirm that the garments were made of 'skins of trees;' others, such as Origen, that it is Adam's *body* that is meant, as having become fleshly by his sin. This absurdity Epiphanius refutes in a letter, which Jerome has translated, and left among his own works, calling it *frivolam expositionem*

doing was He not saying, 'Look at your sin; it is far deeper and darker than you reckon, so deep and dark that no fig-leaves can cover it or hide your shame; there must be something else even for your bodies than coverings derived from the trees of the garden; something which I only can provide and put on; not the growth of the fields like these fig-leaves, but obtained by the *death* of the being from which it is taken; something which costs *life*, which points to blood and death; something which will continually remind you that a sinner's covering must be a thing planned by God, provided by God, made by God, put on by God, yet a thing of *earth*, not of *heaven*, a thing not outwardly comely or bright, yet *costly*, so costly that even God can obtain it only by taking that which is more precious than gold or gems, the life of the creature which He has made'?[1]

Thus was man taught that one great point in his coming deliverance would be the covering. He needed to be covered, else he could not look up to God, nor could God look upon him; nay, he could not look upon himself

(JEROME'S *Works*, vol. i. p. 210). Theodoret and Athanasius come nearer the truth, maintaining the garments to be really from slain animals, and to be intended to point out to man his sin and its penalty, death. But the idea of sacrifice does not seem to have occurred to them; σύμβολον ὄντας, τῆς διὰ τὴν ἁμαρτίαν νεκρώσεως αὐτῷ προσγένομενης. ATHAN. *On the Cross and Passion. Works*, vol. i. p. 1012.

[1] Man was not left to provide this clothing, for the right to use animals for such a purpose could come only from God, and because 'God would teach man that it belongeth only to God to cover sin with the clothing of the Redeemer's righteousness.'—DIODATI. Some suggest that Adam was thus to be humbled and made to feel how low he had fallen when the beasts of the field must furnish him with clothing.—FAGIUS.

without shame. One awful feeling of the sinner is, that he is naked before God, and this feeling is met by the clothing provided by God. But as this feeling of shame is the result of sin and a consciousness of guilt, the covering must be one which will assure him of forgiveness; for if the covering does not of itself proclaim pardon, it will not remove the sense of shame. It did this even in symbol when Adam was clothed with the skins; it does so more truly when we see in it the righteousness of Him who was delivered for our offences, and raised again for our justification.[1] Man's raiment will do nothing; his goodness, his repentance, his prayers, his feelings, these cannot cover sin, nor hide shame, nor purge the conscience; it must be through death that all this is to be done.

God Himself must do it all. He selects the victim, He slays it, He makes the clothing, He puts it on.[2] From first to last, salvation is of Jehovah! It is salvation by death, by sacrifice, by the substitution of life for life. Nor could Adam fail to trace here a connection between the slaying of the animal from whose skin the garment was made, and the bruising of the heel of the woman's seed.

[1] Athanasius, referring to Christ being stripped of His garments, remarks strikingly, 'It became Him when leading man into paradise to put off the garments which Adam received when he was cast out' (*Works*, vol. i. p. 1012), as if Christ thus took more completely our shame as well as our sin upon Him.

[2] At this time, no doubt, sacrifice was instituted, and the coats were the skins of the slain victims. Adam would at once connect these things together, the woman's seed, the bruised heel, the sacrifice, the clothing; and how much of Christ would he learn from this! That sacrifice should originate with *man*, or be a device of his for appeasing

That slain Lamb and that bruised heel were in some mysterious way linked together. Time would evolve the connection; meanwhile, the man ponders it in his heart as he looks upon his clothing and remembers whence it was obtained.

Vers. 22, 23. '*And the Lord God said, Behold, the man has become as one of us, to know good and evil: and now, lest he put forth his hand, and take also of the tree of life* (Heb. *the life*), *and eat, and live for ever:* 23. *Therefore* (Heb. *and*) *the Lord God sent him forth from the garden of Eden, to till the ground from whence he was taken.*'

Adam has now been clothed with the God-provided raiment; not raiment such as he would have devised or felt himself at liberty to propose,—raiment which reminded him of his sin, yet exhibited the way of forgiveness and life through the death of a substitute. He stands before God as an accepted man, covered with a garment which removes his sense of shame, and enables him to look up to God without blushing or wishing to be hidden from His face; teaching us that God's *first* dealings with the sinner are always about the matter of *acceptance*, and that this therefore ought to be our first point in dealing with God.

But the question of acceptance being settled, that of

God, is incredible. How could man suppose that God would be pleased with the slaughter of one of His own creatures, or what connection could man discover between the death of one of these and pardon? Besides, what right had man to take away life? Could he have dared to do so without a command from God? Those who speak of there being a rooted idea in the minds of all men as to the connection between the suffering or death of a creature and the appeasing of God's wrath, have yet to tell us how and when and where such an idea came into their mind.

discipline begins. On this Adam is now to enter. He had much to unlearn as well as much to learn. He had to be taught that, though forgiven, he stood now on a different footing from that on which he stood when a holy being, and that therefore a new line of treatment must be adopted. He might suppose that, being restored to favour, he would be reinstated in his former privileges, remain in Eden, and have access to the tree of life just as before. This, however, cannot be. He is not to be at once placed upon his former footing; he is not to go on eating the tree of life, thus prolonging his days and enjoying an immortality on earth. He has sinned the very sin against which God had warned him; he has gotten 'forbidden knowledge by forbidden means,' and thus far he has gained his end; he has become as God, by eating of the tree of knowledge. God has forgiven him freely and without reserve, yet between his past and his future condition a great gulf must be fixed. He is indeed to 'live for ever,' but not the same kind of life, nor in the same way, as heretofore. The immortality for which he is now destined is to be obtained, not by eating of the tree of life, but through *death*. It is to be reached only by resurrection. Such was God's purpose respecting him and his posterity. It was to a more glorious immortality than that which he had lost that he was now to be led, but its entrance was the grave! Meanwhile he must leave paradise and be shut out from the tree of life.

God's lesson now to Adam was, that he must still return to dust. This part of the doom was to remain, not so much as a remnant of the original sentence, as a chastisement, a needed piece of discipline, and as the necessary passage to the new immortality that lay beyond. Had God allowed Adam to have access to the tree of life, it would have just been saying to him, Thou shalt not return to dust; eat of the tree of life and preserve your immortality here, such as it is on this now blighted earth. To prevent him from entertaining any thought of this kind, and to fix his eye on resurrection, he was sent forth from *paradise* to till the ground from which he was taken, that is, *Eden*.[1] He was to be cast out of the *inner* circle which had been his home, and whose special fertility would have made his toil in keeping it a source of pleasure; but he was still allowed to remain within the *outer* and less fruitful circle, there to remain a toiling man all the days of his life.

Such seems to be the true meaning of the above passage. There is no ground for believing it to be spoken as an interrogation, far less in irony. What more unlike God, than thus to be mocking His creatures at the very moment that He is bending over them in such deep true love? Is this like Him that 'upbraideth not'? Is it like Him who was 'grieved at His heart' because of man's iniquity? It is only once or twice that Scripture speaks ironically, and it is to the daringly ungodly, as to the priests of Baal. But does irony befit a scene like this? Standing on the wreck of a newly-made, newly-ruined world, having just proclaimed to man His grace, and pointed him to the coming Redeemer, is it possible that He can utter irony, and wound without a cause His weeping

[1] Formerly he had but to 'keep and dress,' now he is to 'till;' formerly it was paradise, now it is the outer region.

children? Besides, what follows is so solemnly expressed ('lest he put forth his hand, and eat, and live for ever'), even in its very abruptness so like the solemn oath of God against Israel's entrance on the land ('lest they should enter into my rest'), that we cannot admit of irony in the case at all. There is so much of deep love on the one hand, and of stern judgment on the other, that the introduction of irony here would be quite out of place. Nor will there appear any necessity for such a supposition, if our previous exposition of the tree of life be remembered.

Ver. 24. '*So* (Heb. *and*) *He drove out the man:*[1] *and He placed at the east of the garden of Eden cherubims*[2] *and a flaming sword which turned every way, to keep the way to the tree of life.*'

Man, however reluctant, must leave paradise. Neither God's purpose, nor His honour, can allow him to remain.

[1] גָּרַשׁ. It is the same word as is used for 'driving out' the nations of Canaan, Ex. xxxiv. 11; for 'divorcing' a wife, Lev. xxi. 7; for 'casting out' the bondwoman, Gen. xxi. 10; for the 'thrusting out' of Israel from Egypt, Ex. xii. 39. The Sept. give ἐξέβαλε; the Vulgate, *ejecit;* Tremellius, *expulit;* Orton paraphrases it, 'He drove out the man by violence.' The Jews say that God led Adam gently by the hand till he came to the entrance, and then, as he hung back, He thrust him out by force. 'The double expression of the driving of man out of paradise seems to imply, that God would have special notice taken of that judgment of His upon him.'—WHITE.

[2] The Sept. render the passage, 'He cast out Adam and made him to dwell in front of paradise, and stationed the cherubim,' etc. They must have had another reading before them. But the word 'He placed,' in our translation, does not bring out the full sense. It is literally, 'He made the cherubim to dwell at the east,' etc. It is the same word as in Josh. xviii. 1, 'He *set up* the tabernacle;' Ex. xxv. 8,

Whether ejected by force we cannot say, but his unwillingness to quit seems implied.

His expulsion is not to be viewed, as is generally done, as mere ejection from a happy dwelling, his own special home, as if this were his punishment. No, it is banishment from God and from His presence, that is the true idea which the passage presents to us.[1] Paradise was not so much Adam's home as Jehovah's dwelling. It corresponded to the holy of holies; it was the chamber of the presence of the great King. And Adam's being cast out of this, corresponded to Israel's being kept outside the holiest, and not allowed to enter into the immediate presence of God, where He dwelt between the cherubim.[2] Though Adam's banishment was in some

'that I may *dwell* among them;' Ps. lxxxv. 9, 'that glory may *dwell* in our land;' Ex. xxiv. 16, 'the glory of the Lord *abode*,'—expressions which call to mind similar ones in the New Testament: 'the Word was made flesh, and *dwelt* among us,' 'that Christ may *dwell* in your hearts by faith,' etc. Faber remarks: 'The force of the original Hebrew is, that God placed these cherubim in a tabernacle.'—*Horæ Mosaicæ*, vol. ii. p. 34.

[1] Hence Cain, using the same word, says, 'Thou hast driven me out' (Gen. iv. 14); and Jonah says, 'I am cast out of Thy sight' (ii. 4), both of them referring to being *banished* from the presence of Jehovah.

[2] This 'dwelling between,' or 'sitting upon' the cherubim, refers evidently to the service rendered by the cherubim. Sometimes they are Jehovah's chariot, 1 Chron. xxviii. 18; Ps. xviii. 10; see also Ezek. i. 15–21; sometimes they are His throne, 1 Sam. iv. 4; Isa. xxxvii. 16; in this connection they are referred to in Ezekiel, and in Rev. iv. 5, where the living creatures seem to form the throne. Their presence in paradise is the intimation that it was considered more in the aspect of Jehovah's temple than of Adam's home. The word cherub or cherubim occurs ninety-one times in the Old Testament, and seems to be derived from a word signifying to engrave, so

measure of the nature of a *punishment*, yet its chief object was to announce that truth which it took ages to unfold, that there was a hindrance to man's drawing near to God, that 'the way into the holiest of all was not yet made manifest.'

Man is banished from paradise, yet he is left within sight of it; he is allowed to remain in Eden.[1] He is not driven into some desert, as if there were nothing for him but wrath. There is favour for him in spite of his sin; and the expulsion does not cancel the pardon he has received, or intimate that God has begun to frown. It merely showed that before the full *consequences* of that favour could reach man, time must elapse, and barriers be thrown down. It is not the 'outer darkness,' neither is it the full sunshine, into which he is brought. It is the twilight that surrounds him; and that twilight assures him of the coming noon.

He is left to linger at the gate, or wander round the sacred fences of that forbidden ground. For paradise is not swept off nor swallowed up.[2] It is left as God's temple, now shut up and empty, but still within sight of

that it would thus mean the 'sculptures' or symbols. We need not enter into the fancies either of the Rabbis or of the Fathers on this point.

[1] Adam was formed in *Eden*, outside of paradise, and then taken into paradise, which was the dwelling of God, where God 'walked,' and where the 'voice' was heard. Now, after his sin, he is cast out of the temple and replaced in Eden.

[2] White takes up the point of God's leaving paradise, as a monument both of God's judgment and mercy, and shows how thereby He 'justified Himself, and convinced men of their unworthy carriage towards Him.'—*On the first three chapters of Genesis.*

man. Probably it shared the common blight of creation; though, like primeval man, it took long to wither; till, having waxed old and being ready to vanish away, the deluge came and swept it from the earth.[1] It remained as a specimen of God's original handiwork, reminding man of the glory which he had lost. It stood as a monument of what sin had done in blighting God's perfect creation, and turning man into an exile. It showed how God estimates the material creation, and that *matter* is not the defiling and hateful thing which some conceive it to be. It proclaimed that God had not wholly left the earth, and that in His own set time He would return to it; nay, that *man*, though for a season dethroned and banished, should yet repossess earth as king and lord. Thus God, in preserving paradise for a season, with man a wanderer outside its gates, announced these truths to the ages to come,—truths which were afterwards embodied in types and promises, and unfolded at length to us by His holy prophets. For the prophecies of after ages are but the translation into *words* of the *facts* which these primeval scenes presented to the eye.

Within the sacred enclosure, towards its eastern extremity, God placed, or made to dwell, 'the cherubim.'[2]

[1] Speaking of the cherubim and paradise, Faber says: 'As no hint is given that the paradisaical cherubim were ever withdrawn before the flood, and as the same reason which first caused them to be stationed before the garden still subsisted until the very time of the deluge, we have ample ground for concluding that their manifestation was not temporary, but permanent.'—*Horæ Mosaicæ*, vol. ii. p. 35.

[2] Some have suggested that the rendering might be, 'So He drave out the man; and he inhabited or dwelt between the cherubim, at the

Of this word no explanation is here given; but from the way in which it is introduced, and from the article 'the' prefixed, we conclude that it was quite familiar to Moses, and that the children of Israel would at once understand it as denoting the same thing which they were commanded to place in the holy of holies. No Israelite would understand it of certain living beings moving to and fro, but of a symbolic figure or statue, such as that in their own tabernacle. Just as 'the cherubim' were afterwards set in 'the holiest,' and for the same symbolical ends, so were they placed in paradise. There is nothing more to lead us to suppose that they were living beings (such as angels) in their former abode in the garden, than in their latter in the wilderness. In both they were *symbols.*[1]

Of what, then, were they the symbols? There is no proof of their being representatives of angels, still less of

east of the garden of Eden, the fire unfolding itself to preserve inviolate the way of the tree of life;' or, as Mr. Morison (*Key to the Scriptures*) interprets it, 'to point out the way to Jesus Christ, the true tree of life.' This would bring the scene to a still nearer resemblance of that within the tabernacle; for thus, 'He who was worshipped, dwelling between the cherubim in the temple and tabernacle, was worshipped also at the east of Eden, between the cherubim also, and that accompanied by the visible emblem, the Shekinah or flame of fire.'—MORISON'S *Key*, p. 15.

[1] After showing that the *form* of the cherubim must have been well known to Israel, inasmuch as no special directions are given to Moses or to Bezaleel as to their construction, and after expressing his judgment that they were not withdrawn till the deluge, Mr. Faber adds: 'We can scarcely avoid concluding, when we reflect upon the close analogical resemblance in every particular, that they bore the very same relation to the stated worship of patriarchism as the cherubim of the Levitical tabernacle did to the stated worship of the law.'—*Horæ Mosaicæ*, vol. ii. p. 36.

the Trinity, as some have thought; there are no passages connecting the cherubim with either of these. They are always introduced in connection with man, and man's redemption.[1] They are referred to about a hundred times in the Old Testament, but only in the above connection. In Ezekiel (i. 5, 8, 10) it is said they 'had the likeness of a man,' and the 'hands of a man,' and the 'face of a man.' In Isaiah, also (vi. 2, 6), they have face, and feet, and hands,—being evidently the same as in Ezekiel, though called seraphim. Then, further, we find them connected with the lower orders of creation, with the *lion*, and the *ox*, and the *eagle*,—the representatives of the different orders of animals (Ezek. i. 10). Then we find them associated with the vegetable creation,—the 'palm-tree' (Ezek. xli. 18, 20, 25), the representative of that order of creation, and the well-known symbol of triumph and joy, not only in the case of Israel (Jer. xxiii. 40), but of the redeemed multitude (Rev. vii. 9). Then we observe them in connection with Christ Himself (Ex. xxv. 19, xxxvii. 8), being 'made out of the mercy-seat;' or, as the apostle expounds it, 'He that sanctifieth, and they that are sanctified, are all of one,' literally, 'out of one, made or taken out of one being or one piece;' and in Ezekiel's description (i. 26, 27) we discover 'a man,' evidently the incarnate Son Himself, upon the throne that

[1] See, in reference to the whole subject of the cherubim, Mr. Smith's admirable work, *The Doctrine of the Cherubim* (Longman, 1850); also, though with less satisfaction, such works as the following:—Faber's *Horæ Mosaicæ*, and *Origin of Pagan Idolatry;* Dr. Sharp's *Discourses* in answer to Hutchison, where the etymology of the name cherub is well investigated, pp. 397-407.

was over the cherubim. Further, we find them in closest relationship to the symbols of redemption (Ex. xxxvii. 1, 9). They were part of the mercy-seat; they stood upon the mercy-seat, their feet were upon the blood with which it was sprinkled (Lev. xvi. 14), and, of course, they themselves would share the sprinkling; their abode was a chamber, every part of which was sprinkled with blood; they were enveloped in the incense which went up from the high priest's censer on the day of atonement (Lev. xvi. 12, 13); their eyes, bending downwards, were ever fixed upon the blood of the mercy-seat. And then, in Revelation, where these same symbols reappear, only as in Isaiah and Ezekiel, instinct with life, there can be no mistake as to the beings represented, for they sing the song of redemption (Rev. v. 9), 'Thou hast redeemed us to God by Thy blood.' The whole scene carries us back to the Old Testament emblems as given by Moses, by Isaiah, and by Ezekiel. These are the wings, the mystic faces, the incense, the blood, the throne, and, last of all, the glorious triumph of which the palm-trees were the symbol, 'We shall reign on the earth' (v. 10).

That the cherubim were the symbols of a coming redemption, and foreshadowed re-entrance into that very presence of Jehovah from which man had just been cast out, seems evident.[1] But the peculiar forms and various

[1] Athanasius, though not interpreting the cherubim as we have done, yet notices rather strikingly the Lord's promise to the thief, 'To-day shalt thou be with me in paradise,' as showing that Christ has reopened its gates, so that Adam, in the person of the thief, enters his lost habitation. See his *Exposition of the Faith.* It is as if now the

appendages belonging to them intimate that more than man are concerned in this restitution. The figures of the lion, and the eagle, and the palm-tree indicate that the whole creation is to share in the blessing. The symbol is not merely one of redeemed man, but of a redeemed creation, from man, the head, down to the lowest forms of being. All that God created 'good' is thus symbolized as awaiting deliverance in the day of the manifestation of the sons of God; and thus the three concluding psalms, so minute in their details of praise, so prophetic of the glory of creation in all its parts, and so often sung before that God who 'inhabited the cherubim,' with their commencing and closing hallelujahs, shall be found most wondrously to harmonize with that burst of universal praise from 'every creature in heaven, and on the earth, and under the earth, and in the sea' (Rev. v. 13),—to 'Him that sitteth upon the throne, and unto the Lamb for ever and ever.'

But while the symbols of redemption are thus set up in paradise, they are not to be too nearly approached.[1] In front of them there is placed 'a flaming sword which turned every way;' or, more exactly, 'the flame of the

gates of paradise were thrown open, and the second Adam enters with the chief of sinners at His side, leading the way. Who is there on this sinful earth that may not follow?

[1] Lactantius, in his book on the *Origin of Error*, alluding to man's expulsion, says: 'Paradise itself He surrounded with fire (*igne circumvallavit*), that man might not approach till the time when He shall set judgment on the earth, and recall the righteous who serve Him to that same spot (paradise), when death has been taken away.'—Book ii. sec. 12.

sword which turned itself.' This self-revolving flame was the symbol of Him who is 'a consuming *fire;*' of Him who appeared as 'devouring *fire*' on Sinai (Ex. xxiv. 17); of Him who sent forth to Israel His '*fiery* law' (Deut. xxxiii. 2); of Him whose throne is like the *fiery flame*, and His wheels like *burning fire* (Dan. vii. 9); of Him who is to be 'revealed from heaven in *flaming fire*' (2 Thess. i. 8). That this fiery sword was part of, or at least connected with, the Shekinah, is evident from the first chapter of Ezekiel, which is a description of the Shekinah.[1]

This fiery sword took up its position at the gate of paradise, to bar all entrance to man. It not only, like the veil in the tabernacle, hindered his entrance, but threatened him with death should he attempt it. It was God's awful prohibition of man's entrance into the presence of God until the hindrances which existed should be taken out of the way. Till the woman's seed should arise, and by the blood of His 'bruised heel' remove that flaming barrier, man must remain outside.[2] From that flame came the fire which consumed the sacrifice on the altar, which was doubtless erected in front of paradise, teaching man that it was through the altar, and the sacrifice, and the blood, that the way was at length to

[1] Ezekiel's expression (chap. i. 2), 'a fire unfolding itself,' bears manifest reference to this expression in Genesis. The self-linking flames of Ezekiel and the self-whirling fire of Moses are strikingly similar.

[2] Jerome speaks about Christ removing 'that flaming wheel and fiery sword, which were at the gates of paradise,' and entering in with the thief.—*Works*, vol. v. p. 10.

be opened up, and paradise repossessed in greater blessedness and glory than before. But not till the true altar had been reared, and the true sacrifice slain, and the true blood shed, could there be boldness to enter into the holiest. Not till then would it be said, 'Let us draw near with a true heart, in the full assurance of faith' (Heb. x. 19–22).

The 'tree of life' was not at once uprooted. It remained where it had first been planted. But man was not to touch it yet. He might see it afar off, with the fiery sword between, but access is prohibited. Its fruit is no longer to be tasted. He is to *live*, not to die; he is to be made heir of a more glorious life than he had possessed before, but not by means of that tree of life. His new life is to come in another way, and through another channel, of which that tree was but the symbol; through Him who is the resurrection and the life. So that it was as if that now prohibited tree were pointing his eye to something beyond and above itself, saying, Look not at me, but at Him of whom I am but the shadow.

Man is now to worship outside of paradise. The favour of God is freely given; but intercourse, though not denied, is restricted. Man must now worship in the outer court. The hope of re-admission is vouchsafed, but the time is indefinitely deferred. The tree of life is to be again thrown open to him in far more blessed circumstances (Rev. ii. 7, xxii. 2), but no intimation is made of what lies between.

Man's altar is reared before the gate of paradise, in

front of the flaming sword; and there he lays his sacrifice, at once pleading for re-admission, and preparing the way for it. The cherubim are at the eastern extremity; the tree of life in 'the midst;' the flame at the gate; outside, the altar! Such was God's first outline of a temple; an outline which, though often altered in the course of ages, still preserved its main features throughout.[1] From that day to this we have been worshippers outside paradise. Faith takes us into the holiest of all: and in that sense we have been already re-admitted, for the veil has been rent, and the fiery sword withdrawn, or rather *quenched*—quenched in the blood of the sacrifice. But still we have not yet been actually admitted. We still wait the re-appearance of the woman's seed, and then shall not only our first father Adam, but all the saved seed, a mighty multitude, in one glorious band, re-enter with songs and everlasting joy upon their heads, with no dread before of a second ejection and a second exile.

Then we shall have unhindered access into a better paradise than the first, and be privileged to eat of the tree of life, which is in the midst of it. Then shall the re-deemed from among men, the true cherubim, of which all

[1] One of these changes we may notice, though not able to account for it. Paradise lay at the eastern extremity of Eden, and the cherubim at the eastern extremity of paradise (though some think that the words 'at the east' ought to be rendered 'before,' or 'in front of'—FABER). In the tabernacle this was altered, as it was placed east and west, with its gate to the east, and the holy of holies to the west. On the other hand, the temple was placed on the east side of Jerusalem, as paradise lay east of Eden. Ezekiel's temple is represented as situated on the south side of the mountain (xl. 2), though its position is the same as the tabernacle, the main gate being towards the east.

that have been seen hitherto have been but the shadows, take up their residence in the true tabernacle which the Lord hath pitched for them, where they shall abide in nearest communion, seeing face to face, and knowing even as they are known.

CHAPTER IV.

Ver. 1. '*And Adam knew Eve his wife;*[1] *and she conceived, and bare Cain, and said, I have gotten a man from the Lord.*'

IT is no longer paradise that stands before us. We leave it and its fair scenes behind us, not to see them again till the visions of Patmos bring them before us in more than primal glory. The guarded gate, the sword of fire, the cherubim, the tree of life,—all these are to be lost sight of for a season, and our eye to be directed to the wondrous process by which the lost heritage is to be redeemed, and man put in possession of a home fairer than that which he had lost, yet bearing still the unforgotten name, the paradise of God. It is as if a cloud or veil were flung over Eden, that all concerning it might henceforth be

[1] In maintaining that this was after they had quitted paradise (and not before, as some Jewish and even Christian writers supposed), Augustine reasons, that the temptation and fall occurred *immediately after* the creation of woman, which seems likely. Jerome reasons, in his own ascetic way, that paradise was 'non nuptiis sed virginitati destinatum.' Musculus infers that it *must* have been so, as the fruit of the conception was Cain, showing that he had been shapen in iniquity and conceived in sin. This first clause is to show us, that though Adam had been formed from the ground, and Eve from Adam's side, yet now there was the commencement of God's system for the propagation of the race, in virtue of which each one was to be connected with Adam. 'Memorat neque ex terra neque quovis alio modo hominem nasci sed ex conjunctione maris et fœminæ, quâ per unum hominem peccatum in omnem posteritatem transfunditur.'—RUNGIUS, p. 220.

things of faith to man. That cloud still wraps it; but the fulness of time shall come; the cloud shall part asunder, and, rising upwards, disclose to view not merely paradise regained, but something more excellent and divine,—'the inheritance which is incorruptible, undefiled, and that fadeth not away.' The last glimpse we had of paradise was when the first Adam, with his sorrow-stricken partner, left its gates, which closed behind them; the next is, when the second Adam and His triumphant Bride are entering its unfolded gates, with songs and everlasting joy upon their heads.

We quit paradise, then, and follow Adam to his new home outside its gate, yet not far off from its still visible glory. We have seen him as the first husband: we now see him as the first father. We get a glimpse, too, of Eve, the wife and mother, now first experiencing the bitterness of the curse that sin has drawn down on her. We learn also the first result of the command, 'Be fruitful and multiply;' and we see that, thus far at least, the curse has been repealed or suspended, for the original blessing, 'Be fruitful,' is still in force. Sin has not prevailed to cancel the blessing, though it has embittered and saddened it.

Months, of course, have passed on ere she brings forth Cain; and during these she would be led to meditate much upon the promise. Though she has never yet looked upon the face of infancy, and has only seen the connection between mother and offspring in the animal creation around her, bringing forth their young after their kind; yet she could not but have some idea of what was about to take place, and could not but be anticipating, not only the threatened pangs, but the gladness that follows, making her forget all these in the joy that a man is born into the world.

In the expected fruit of her womb, what could she see but the promised seed? Unless the contrary had been revealed to her, it seems impossible that she could have counted on anything else, if she believed the promise; and, no doubt, with anxious longings did she look forward to the day when the child of promise should be born. What months of solemn thought, and self-humiliation, and earnest hope, and mingled grief and joy, must these have been! The day came at last, and in the hour that she became a mother, her faith, resting on the promise, yet but dimly seeing how it was to be fulfilled, broke forth in the exulting cry, 'I have gotten a man from the Lord,' calling his name *Cain*, which signifies a possession;[1] as if she said, 'Jehovah has fulfilled His promise; I have gotten the deliverer: I will call him the gotten one,—the possession.'

Thus did her faith and hope declare themselves. She recognises Jehovah in this. It is He who has given her joy in the midst of grief; so that, though burdened with the awful consciousness of having ruined a world, she now rejoices in the thought of giving birth to the world's deliverer. She sees how Jehovah has remembered His

[1] The often suggested translation, 'I have gotten a man, even Jehovah,' is not an unlikely one. JEHOVAH was in reality *Messiah's* original name; 'He was to be' the 'coming one.' Enoch knew that name as Messiah's: 'Behold, the Lord cometh' (Jude 14).

promise, and she rejoices, as if now the effects of her sin were to be at once effaced. Her light must, indeed, have been dim. She had little to rest upon; just one brief promise. Yet faith, when simple, makes much of little things; and so did Eve's. The promise had been like a seed sown in the earth. She had been watching its up-springing; and now, when the first traces of it appear, she gives utterance to her joy. She views it, too, as favour shown to herself. Not foreseeing the sword that was to pierce through her own heart, she rejoices that God has thus visited her in her low estate, and manifested His love. She had felt His frown when He proclaimed to her the sorrows awaiting her as a mother; and now she tastes His smile, and receives from His gracious hand the gift of fatherly love;—love that had freely forgiven her, and was now pouring down on her the blessings of its free bountifulness.

We saw Adam's faith showing itself in the naming of his wife; we now see Eve's in the naming of her son. In calling his wife Eve, Adam spake as a believing man; and in naming her first-born Cain, Eve speaks as a believing woman; as one who knows Jehovah, knows Him as her God, and finds in His grace and faithfulness her rest and joy; as one who has understood the promise, and sets her seal to the sure word of the great Promiser. No doubt she spoke in much ignorance; but still it was *faith* speaking; and though, in after years, when she found her sad mistake, she might mourn over disappointed hopes, yet, looking back on the day when she remembered her grief no more for joy that a man was born, she could still say, 'I believed, therefore I spake.' She had been watching the first springing of the seed, and, to her unpractised eye, it seemed now to have sprung up. In its first upbursting, she could not discern the difference between the seed of the woman and the seed of the serpent. She deemed it the former; but it proved the latter. Still her faith was called out; she believed and spake; and though soon undeceived, yet not the less was it faith in her, though it failed to discern the difference at first between that which was from beneath and that which was from above.

Thus simple ought our faith to be,—looking straight to God, and resting on His promises. It will make many mistakes and meet with many disappointments, yet in the end it will not lose its reward; for He on whom it rests shall come at length, though He seem to tarry long. It is not a faith free from mistakes that God expects of us, but a faith which, in spite of mistakes and delays, rests on Himself and His sure word, knowing that all He has spoken will sooner or later come most surely to pass.

Ver. 2. '*And she again bare his brother Abel. And Abel was a keeper of sheep, but Cain was a tiller of the ground.*'

There is no proof that the brothers were twins, though some have thought so. The narrative seems to warrant the common idea, that there was an interval; how long, we know not. It was long enough to let Eve feel what a world of vanity and sorrow she dwelt in; to show that she was a stranger on the earth; and, accordingly, she gave vent to the sorrowful feelings of her heart (as did afterwards the mother of Jabez, 1 Chron. iv. 4) in calling him Abel, that is, vanity. In the name of her first-born, we see her up-springing joy of heart, as if now the wrong she had wrought were to be repaired; in the name of her second-born, we trace the utterance of hope deferred, making the heart sick, yet raising it upwards to something above the vanities of this vain earth. It was the second time that a mother's pangs had been upon her, and in passing through them she is made to feel that this is not her rest.

The boys grew up, and Cain followed the calling of his father Adam, feeling, doubtless, the weight of the curse in the toil and sweat which the tilling of the ground cost him.[1] So that *he* especially ought to have known the evil of sin, seeing that he was made, more than his brother, to endure the curse. That he did not, only shows how desperately he had hardened his heart against the dealings of God, and refused the teachings by which the Holy Spirit sought to convince him of sin. How much might a man's earthly lot teach him, if he would but listen to God's voice in it! But he will not, and so his conscience becomes seared by that very discipline

[1] 'By this, it seems that Cain was the man in favour, even him that should by his father's intentions have been heir. He was nurtured up in his father's employment, but Abel was set in the lower rank.'—JOHN BUNYAN, *Exposition of the first two chapters of Genesis.* An old Latin commentator thinks that Abel chose the shepherd's life as the most remote from sin, and turned from agriculture because the ground was cursed: whereas Cain took to the latter, as not heeding the curse.

which was meant to make it tender. Abel was a keeper of sheep; finding in this occupation something more congenial to his spirit. He had thus a less rugged and toilsome life, as well as one which left him more of leisure and of solitude, in which he might often anticipate the feelings and song of David, 'The Lord is my shepherd.' And if Cain's employment ever reminded him of the curse, and spoke to him of sin, Abel's showed him the Lamb of God, by whom the curse was to be borne, and brought continually into view the 'no condemnation' in which he had learnt to rejoice.

Vers. 3, 4. '*And in process of time* (Heb. *at the division of days*) *it came to pass, that Cain brought of the fruit of the ground an offering unto the Lord.* 4. *And Abel, he also brought of the firstlings of his flock, and of the fat thereof.*'

Each brought his offering to Jehovah; and this was done at what is called 'the division of days,' very probably the Sabbath. The act mentioned here is evidently not *one*, but a series of acts, as if it had been said, 'they were in the habit of bringing.'[1] Here let us mark such things as the following:—

1. Both worship professedly the same Jehovah. They acknowledge Him as Jehovah, their God.

2. Both worship Him at the same place. In all likelihood they worshipped at the gate of paradise, and brought their offerings to the altar at which their father worshipped. They frequent the same temple (if we may say so), and bow at the same altar.

[1] We find Musculus noticing this, 'Non semel tantum sed aliquoties.' —*Explanatio in Genesim*, p. 116.

3. Both come at the same appointed times and seasons. They observe all these outward parts of worship alike.

4. Both bring an offering in their hands, thereby acknowledging the allegiance which was due to Jehovah.

Thus far they are alike. But here the likeness ends, and the difference begins. How great is that difference! In man's eye, the likeness is great, and the difference small; in God's eye, it is the opposite.

1. Abel comes as a sinner, having no claim upon God, and feeling that it is only as a sinner that God can deal with him. Cain approaches as a creature only; not owning sin, though willing to acknowledge the obligations of creaturehood.

2. Abel comes acknowledging *death* to be his due; for he brings a lamb, and slays it before the Lord, as a substitute for himself. Cain recognises no sentence of death; he brings only his fruits, as if his grapes or his figs were all that he deemed God entitled to. His offering might cost him more toil than his brother's, but it spoke not of death. It was meant to repudiate the ideas of sin and death, and salvation by a substitute.[1]

3. Abel comes with the blood in his hand, feeling that he dared not appear before God without it; that it would not be safe for him to venture nigh, nor honourable for God to receive him otherwise. Nothing but the blood

[1] See Smith's *Script. Test. to Messiah*, and Magee *On the Atonement*. Abel brought 'a more excellent sacrifice than Cain' (Heb. xi. 4), πλείονα θυσίαν—which the Vulgate curiously renders 'plurimam hostiam.' It seems to mean, not merely a more excellent sacrifice, but a fuller one; something that had in it much more of a sacrifice than Cain's.

upon his conscience can give him confidence before God. Cain brings no blood,—doubtless scorning his brother's religion as 'the religion of the shambles;' a religion which increased instead of removing creation's pangs.

4. Abel comes resting on the promise,—the promise which revealed and pledged the rich grace of God. Cain comes as one that needs no promise and no grace. His is what men call 'the religion of nature;' and in that religion there is no room, no need for these.

In Cain's worship we see the germ of *man's* religion; a religion which has taken a thousand various and subtle forms; a religion which, in these last days, is assuming yet more varied and subtle forms. In whatever form we find it, we see at least two things invariably absent,—the recognition of the mere grace of God, and of the blood of the substitute as bringing that grace nigh. These are the two elements which Cain's religion sets aside; and these are still the two elements which man's religion abhors.

God's religion turns on these two things; and these have ever been the joy and confidence of those who, like Abel, have learned to worship Him who is a Spirit in spirit and in truth.

Vers. 4, 5. '*And the Lord had respect unto Abel, and to his offering:*[1] 5. *But unto Cain, and to his offering, He had not respect.*'

Jehovah accepts the one brother and rejects the other.

[1] 'Herein are the true footsteps of grace discovered, viz. the *person* must be *first* in favour with God; the person first, the performance afterwards.'—BUNYAN.

He intimated in some explicit way,—such as, perhaps, the coming down of fire from the Shekinah that rested between the cherubim, or the flaming sword that waved at the gate of paradise,—His well-pleasedness with Abel. Of Cain He took no notice, marking most visibly His thoughts regarding the brothers. This *well-pleasedness* and *displeasedness* were, of course, *marked* things—things which Abel knew and which Cain knew, and which their parents knew. Abel *knew* that he was accepted; Cain *knew* that he was rejected;—God, from the beginning, thus showing us that He means us to know even here when we are accepted, and when we are not accepted. There was no uncertainty about either the one or the other. 'By faith, Abel offered to God a more excellent sacrifice than Cain;' and God left him in no doubt as to the acceptance of that offering. He obtained witness that he was justified (Heb. xi. 4), 'God testifying of his gifts'—that is, giving some open testimony respecting their acceptableness, by means of which all men knew that the favour of Jehovah was resting on him. He came to the altar each day, with the blood in his hand, as a believing man, and he was accepted. God made no secret of His love to him; he left him in no doubt as to his acceptance.

Ver. 5. '*And Cain was very wroth, and his countenance fell.*'

Anger took possession of his bosom, and rested there (Eccles. vii. 9). He was 'very wroth:' this was the first effect. Then his 'countenance fell.' It was not the sudden flash of anger that lighted it up, but the gloom of sullen, silent, deep-seated malignity that overshadowed it. Its lines bent downwards; he went hanging his head; he will not look upward to heaven, for God has thwarted him; he will not look around upon his brother, for he hates him, as one who has supplanted him in the favour of God.[1] He broods over his fancied wrong and insult, meditating revenge, not merely against Abel, but against God. He is not led to repentance, or heart-searching as to the reason of God's making such a difference. He is too proud to admit the thought that the fault can be with himself. He cannot bear the thought that God should prefer another, and that one his own brother. Instead of saying, Well, I am glad that Abel is to be blest if I am not, he quenches all natural affection, and scowls upon him in bitter wrath. Nor can he endure to think that another should be preferred on such grounds,—the difference between the fruits of the field and the firstlings of the flock! Had the preference turned upon any other point, it would not have seemed so irritating; had it been because Cain was immoral and Abel moral, it would not have been felt as so insulting; but that it should turn upon the difference between a cluster of grapes and a lamb of the flock, this was intolerable. Such are still the feelings of Cain's successors, the men of this world. They are angry at others being

[1] Yet why be so angry, if he did not care for God's favour? It seems as if no being, however evil, can erase from his mind the idea of God's favour being desirable. Hence the first exhibition of envy and malice was not on account of man's friendship or woman's love, but for the favour of God.

accepted; envious of the peace of believing men; unable to bear the idea of assurance of pardon; enraged at God for bestowing favour on a friend, or neighbour, or brother. O heart of man! what art thou? the seat of every evil passion, the fountain of enmity both against man and God.

Ver. 6. '*And the Lord said unto Cain, Why art thou wroth? and why is thy countenance fallen? If thou doest well, shalt thou not be accepted?*[1] *and if thou doest not well, sin lieth*[2] *at the door.*[3] *And unto thee shall be his desire, and thou shalt rule over him.*'

Jehovah now speaks to Cain.[4] He had given visible indications of the non-acceptance of Cain's fruit-offering; and this had been followed by anger and sullen defiance

[1] The word means lifting up, exaltation, forgiveness, acceptance.

[2] The word signifies either sin or sin-offering, hardly ever the punishment or penalty. It occurs upwards of a hundred times as 'sin-offering,' which seems to be its meaning here.

[3] 'The door'—the door of the paradise, in front of which they worshipped, and where the sin-offering slighted by Cain is pointed to as lying. 'The door of the tabernacle,' and 'the door of the temple,' were in after ages well-known expressions.

[4] The divine voice no doubt came from 'the excellent glory,' the Shekinah, the presence of the Lord, before which our first parents worshipped. 'Enough has been already said in the preceding volumes of this work to warrant the conclusion that the worship of the Israelites "was no other than patriarchism, by various additions and special institutions, adapted to the peculiar situation of a people which had been selected by Jehovah." There was therefore a special place where God was worshipped by sacrifice before the cherubim. Of the nature and character of the rites performed in this primitive worship it is difficult to speak with any precision; but it is evident that there must have been a person (in those days generally the father of the family) to offer the sacrifice; and in all probability there was, in the pure patriarchal period, some visible fire or glory representing the presence of Deity.'—SMITH'S *Sacred Annals*, vol. i. p. 9.

on the part of the rejected worshipper. He now *audibly* addresses him, just as he spoke afterwards to Abraham, and to Moses, and to Israel. The words spoken are in the form of a gentle *expostulation.* There is no wrath in them, as we might have expected. It is the voice of long-suffering and compassion. It is *grace* that is dealing with the sinner; grace like that which dealt with Judas when the 'sop' was given, the last token of friendly forbearance. 'Why hast thou become thus angry? and why has thy countenance fallen?' Art thou not acting most unreasonably as well as sinfully, showing anger against thy God,—anger without a cause? Am I to blame? May I not do what I will with mine own? Besides, hast thou not brought this upon thyself? Must I do as *thou* desirest? Must I show myself as loving and favourable to the man that regards my ordinances, as to the man that sets them at nought, and chooses ordinances of his own? If thou doest well, is there not acceptance for thee?[1] and if thou doest not well, there is a remedy; the sin-offering lieth at the door;[2] so that whatever has been thy past guilt and rejection of the way of approaching me, thou mayest yet enjoy my favour, and the birthright belonging to thee as the elder brother shall not be affected. To

[1] The 'doing well' here seems to refer to the offering, not to well-doing in general. If thou compliest with my ordinances, and bringest a lamb like thy brother, shall there not be acceptance (lifting up, favour, forgiveness) for thee? The expression is similar to that in Mic. vi. 8, 'He hath showed thee, O man, *what is good;*' the good thing; the thing in which God delights; the way of approaching Him by sacrifice.

[2] Lies or couches like an animal.

thee shall thy brother's desire still be; to thee he shall look up as his superior; and thou shalt still have the rule over him.[1]

This is God's last appeal to Cain regarding the birthright. As it was the threatened loss of this and its conveyance to Abel that had so troubled him, so God makes his appeal to turn upon this point. He is slow to anger and plenteous in mercy, and He shows this in His dealings with this sullen unbeliever. He will not cast off at once. He has long patience, and would fain bring the rebel to repentance. The birthright was Cain's as the eldest-born. Such was God's law; for the law of primogeniture is no mere human fiction nor modern invention. Nor will God depart from this law without a reason, whatever His own eternal purpose may be. Before transferring the prerogative to the younger brother, He will make manifest the righteousness of the alteration. Cain is rejected because he rejects God's appointed way of approach. To the last we see how God makes Cain's acceptance to turn upon this,—'Wilt thou take my way or thine own? If thou wilt take my way, then even yet all shall be well. Thy privileges shall not be taken from thee. Thy rights as the elder-born shall stand.' This is God's appeal to unbelief. How that unbelief met the appeal, the next verses show us. As Esau despised the birthright, so did Cain. It was the same

[1] תְּשׁוּקָתוֹ—desire or longing, occurs only three times. Chap. iii. 16, 'Thy desire shall be to thy husband.' Cant. vii. 10, 'His desire is toward me.' The verb signifies to run, run after, long for. See Gesenius; also Patrick on the passage.

unbelief in both; the same rejection of Messiah and of God's way of acceptance by His blood.

Ver. 8. '*And Cain talked with Abel his brother: and it came to pass, when they were in the field, that Cain rose up against Abel his brother, and slew him.*'[1]

Love is lost upon him. Kind words are in vain. God's appeal fails. It may be that the appeal recorded was made, not once, but many times; all without effect. He will not listen. His angry sullenness increases. He resolves to revenge himself both upon God and upon Abel. He cannot get at God directly, and therefore he takes his revenge on Him by slaying His beloved child, thus venting his impotent malignity against God. He hopes to frustrate God's purpose of love to Abel, and to prevent him enjoying the divine favour or the birthright. It is the same feeling as drew out the cry of after ages, 'This is the heir; come, let us kill him, and the inheritance shall be ours;' he hoped by this means to seize on the inheritance when Abel was gone. Blind revenge indeed, whether as regards God, or Abel, or himself! And not only revenge, but hatred of the good. Wherefore slew he him? asks the apostle. Because his own deeds were evil, and his brother's righteous. He was a hater, not a lover of the good.[2] Here is the enmity

[1] The Sept. read, 'And Cain said to Abel his brother, Let us go into the field.' The words according to the Hebrew run literally thus: 'And Cain spoke unto Abel his brother. And it (*or* this) was when they were in the field. And Cain rose against Abel,' etc.

[2] One of the characteristics of the last days is, that men are to be ἀφιλάγαθοι. Here we have the first trace of the sad feature,—'not lovers of good.'

of the seed of the serpent to the seed of the woman,—an enmity which nothing will satisfy but death. Hatred to Christ, hatred to the Father, hatred to the Church,—these are the world's deep and unchangeable feelings, modified or restrained by circumstances, but still unaltered. The root of all is hatred of Christ Himself; dissatisfaction with God's purpose of making him the one way, and his sacrifice the one ground of acceptance. It was thus that Cain's hatred was stirred up, and so is it in every son of Cain. 'If they have hated me, they will also hate you.' And then mark the *cunning* as well as the malignity of the serpent. By fair speeches Cain leads Abel away into a solitary field, and there murders him. He has forgotten the all-seeing Jehovah above, or is resolved to defy Him. All that he cares for is to be away from the eye of man. How near to the atheist he has come in his heart already, saying 'There is no God,' or at least God will not see!

Ver. 9. '*And the Lord said unto Cain, Where is Abel thy brother? And he said, I know not. Am I my brother's keeper?*'

God does not allow blood to be spilt like water on the earth, without inquiring after it. He 'makes inquisition for blood' (Ps. ix. 12), specially for 'innocent blood.' It is precious in His eyes (Ps. lxxii. 11).[1]

The murderer's conscience was not likely to be silent. It would burn like a furnace. It would sting like an

[1] In the day of Babylon's judgment, we find that it is 'the blood of the saints' that weighs her down and consummates her ruin. God comes and finds in her the blood of all His Abels (Rev. xviii. 24). She is the true Cain,—the murderer in full stature, grown old in wickedness.

adder. It is not, however, to this that our eyes are directed, but to something more awful,—to the Judge Himself; to Him 'whose eyes are as a flame of fire.' God comes down, as He had done in paradise to Adam after his sin. Probably it was soon after the event, at the next time of sacrifice, and to the usual place of offering that Jehovah came. Cain was there as usual, with his grapes and pomegranates. But Abel was awanting! A voice comes forth from 'the glory.' It is the voice of Jehovah. He speaks as one that missed a worshipper; nay, a favourite child; and He speaks to Cain as to the elder brother who ought to have care for the younger. 'Where is Abel thy brother?' A question fitted to go straight to the murderer's conscience, and no less fitted to rouse his wrathful jealousy, as showing how truly Abel was the beloved one. 'Where is Abel,—where is thy *brother*,—he who is bone of thy bone? I miss him, dost not *thou* miss him too?'

The question only draws from Cain a bold and reckless lie; sin leading on to sin,—murder, falsehood, effrontery, profanity. 'I know not,' he says to the All-seeing One. He can look up into the face of God and say, 'I know not.' As if he would add, '*You* may know, for he is your favourite, and you ought to look after him.' He is like the wicked one spoken of in the 10th Psalm, who says, 'God hath forgotten, He hideth His face; He will not see.'[1] Nay, more, he 'foams out his own shame' before

[1] Ps. x. 11. The whole tone and pleadings in this psalm carry us back to Cain and his brother. It sets forth very fully and awfully 'the way of Cain.'

God. He is not afraid to be insolent even to God. 'Am I my brother's keeper?' He rejects the natural claims of kindred and affection; even while afraid to own the dark deed, he is not afraid to speak as one who had cast off all natural affection. Strange inconsistency! He mocks God, he utters lies in His presence, he flings off the bonds of brotherhood, yet he will not own the murder! 'Thou canst not say I did it.' How unsearchable man's heart in its evil! 'It is deceitful above all things, and desperately wicked.' Cain will go on heaping sin upon sin, but his pride will not allow him to confess the charge. 'Am I my brother's keeper?' as if he would say, 'What have I to do with him? *Thou* art his keeper; he is Thy favourite; Thou shouldst know more about him than I; why ask such a question of me?' He speaks as one who would not allow himself to be questioned even by God; as one who denied God's right to question him, who was enraged at the suspicion thus cast upon him,—a suspicion to which his conscience at once responded, while his lips rejected it. What will man not do to God? Is there any length of pride, or deceit, or insolence to which he will not go? Many things may restrain him, yet he is ever ready to break loose, and to defy Jehovah. He will crouch to a poor mortal superior, but he will insult the God that made him.[1]

[1] The Chaldee paraphrast makes Cain to say, 'There is no justice, there is no judge, there is no world to come, there are no rewards for the just.' How applicable here the words of Ps. xxxvi. 1, 'The transgression of the wicked saith within my heart, There is no fear of God before his eyes.'

Ver. 10. '*And He said, What hast thou done? The voice of thy brother's blood crieth unto me from the ground.*'

The divine reply is calm, yet awfully piercing. There is no outburst of vengeance, nor sudden stroke of wrath. 'What is this dreadful deed which thou hast done, and which thou art trying to conceal from me? The voice of thy brother's blood cries to me from the ground.'[1] In the first part of the answer, God brings home the charge to the sinner's conscience, and makes him feel how vain was his attempt to evade it, or to conceal the deed. In the second part, He adduces *witnesses.* The voice of Abel's blood. That blood crieth *to me*, says Jehovah. It makes no vague or random sound, but appeals directly to me. Cain had shed that blood, and perhaps had hidden the body in the ground. The voice was silenced; there could be no witnesses; the murderer seemed safe. Who could accuse him? But from that very ground, in which

[1] The apostle's words (Heb. xii. 24) seem plainly to refer to this: 'The blood of sprinkling, which speaketh better things than that of Abel.' There seems no reason for referring this, as some do, to the blood of Abel's *sacrifice.* His blood cried for vengeance, Christ's for mercy. Abel's blood spoke of the curse, Christ's of the blessing. Abel's spoke of wrath, Christ's of grace. Abel's spoke of condemnation, Christ's of pardon. Abel's spoke of terror, Christ's of comfort and peace. Abel's spoke of death, Christ's of life. Abel's spoke of hatred, Christ's of love. Abel's spoke of earth become the dwelling-place of sin, Christ's was the pledge of earth yet to become the abode of holiness. It ought to be noticed here that the word 'blood' in the Hebrew is 'bloods,' and the verb 'crieth' is literally 'cry,' in the plural, agreeing not with 'voice,' but with 'bloods.' In the plural the word generally refers to murder. Ps. v. 7, 'Men of bloods.' The Targum gives a curious meaning: 'The voice of the bloods of the generations or multitudes of just men who should have proceeded from

he had buried the bleeding body, there came up a voice in the ears of God, accusing the murderer, and pleading for vengeance. Out of that very place of secrecy where he had hoped for ever to conceal his crime from every eye, the voice came up to God. The blood had made its appeal to Jehovah, and He had now come down to answer that appeal, and to show how precious was that blood in His sight. As yet there was no human judge to take cognizance of the crime. God Himself must do it.

Thus from the days of Abel has pleaded the blood of the saints:—'How long, O Lord, wilt Thou not judge and avenge our blood?' Thus the voice has been going up for ages from the ground, from the cell, from the cave, from the rock, from the glen, from the moorland, from the flood, from the flame, from the scaffold. What spot of Europe, not to take in more, is there from which this cry

thy brother,' etc. The reader will remember the well-known passage of Shakespeare—

> 'O my offence is rank, it smells to heaven,
> It hath the primal eldest curse upon't,
> A brother's murder.'

We ought to refer the reader to Dr. Kennicott's Dissertation on *The Oblations of Cain and Abel.* It is on some points strained and over-ingenious, but able and interesting. He thinks that 'I have gotten a man from the Lord' means, 'I have gotten a man according to the promise of the Lord' (p. 115). He thinks that Abel's name was given not at his birth, but afterwards, as expressive of his mother's feelings at his death (p. 117). He strongly and irresistibly argues out these two points: (1) that sacrifice was of divine institution; (2) that the Sabbath was observed by the patriarchs, and that it was on the Sabbath that the brothers brought their offerings.

is not ascending? From the plains of Italy, from the valleys of Piedmont, from the dungeons of Spain, from the streets of Paris, from the stones of Smithfield, from the fields of Ireland, from the moors of Scotland; from all these has been ascending for ages the cry, 'How long!' a cry unsilenced and unsatisfied; deepening and swelling as the ages roll on; a cry which will ere long be fully answered by the coming of Him who is the great avenger of blood and rewarder of His saints.

Ver. 11. '*And now art thou cursed from the earth* (Heb. *ground*), *which hath opened her mouth to receive thy brother's blood from thy hand.*'

This is the first *direct* curse on *man*. The serpent and the ground had been cursed before; but neither Adam nor Eve had been so. But now God, addressing a *man;* the son of a man; a creature of His own; says, 'Cursed art THOU.' Fearful words, coming straight from the lips of God into the very ear of man, standing in the presence of God. No lightning bursting on him from the clouds could be half so terrible. The blessing is revoked, and the curse goes forth. It is a curse because of *innocent blood*, as if foreshowing the curses which the shedding of innocent blood was yet to bring upon men. This curse is represented as coming up from the ground, as if the ground which had been moistened with the blood were to be the instrument of inflicting the curse.[1] In Ezekiel

[1] Why our translators in the previous verse rendered the word 'ground,' and here 'earth,' is not easy to say; perhaps for the same reason that the Sept. in the former verse renders מן by ἐκ, and in the

we read of the 'mountains devouring men' (xxxvi. 12–14), and elsewhere of the land 'spewing out' (Lev. xviii. 28, xx. 22); so here the very ground is impregnated with evil to Cain, and sends up its curses on him. The soil is to cast him off; the earth is to loathe him; inanimate nature, more tender-hearted than he (inasmuch as it drank in the blood), is to set its face against him. It had received the innocent blood into its bosom, and it was to send up unceasingly on the murderer an endless curse.[1]

Ver. 12. '*When thou tillest* (or *shalt till*) *the ground, it shall not henceforth yield unto thee her strength* (Heb. *it shall not add to give her strength to thee*). *A fugitive and a vagabond shalt thou be in the earth*' (Heb. *moving and wandering shalt thou be on the 'earth'—not 'the ground'*).

This curse is a twofold one; it was to affect the ground, and it was to affect himself. It was to inflict barrenness on the soil, so that it was not to continue to yield its strength as it had hitherto done to his tillage;[2] the

latter by ἀπό; both versionists seeming to understand the latter as if God meant to say, 'Thou art cursed, and driven out from the earth.' This idea, however, is afterwards (ver. 14) expressed by מֵעַל, 'from upon,' which the Sept. render ἐπί, and the Vulg. *super*, by which preposition they also render the passage before us. Patrick, however, makes 'cursed from the earth' to mean, 'thou art banished Eden.'

[1] Augustine dwells on the contrast between Cain and the ground, the one shedding the blood, the other receiving it into its bosom: 'Ille fudit sanguinem, non excepit. Ille fudit, alia terra excepit; et ab eâ terrâ quæ os aperuit et excepit, ille maledictus est.'

[2] The curse was specially suited to Cain as a 'tiller of the ground,' and as one who brought of the fruit of the ground as his offering to God. Now God rebukes both his tillage and his offering; marring the former, and drying up the source of the latter. His occupation

innocent blood had sterilized it. *Adam's* sin drew down on the soil the curse of fruitfulness in evil (chap. iii. 18); Cain's draws down on it the curse of barrenness in good. But the curse affected himself as well as the ground. It was to afford him no settled dwelling, as well as no return for his labour; sustenance and settlement were to be denied. He was to be rooted up from the soil and flung off, to be carried to and fro, like the withered leaf. Driven out from the presence of Jehovah, from the place where the glory dwelt, and where the altar was erected, he was to become a wanderer over earth; his sin, like a malignant demon, pursuing him, and allowing him no rest for the sole of his foot. As Israel, in after days, were made wanderers among the nations for the bloodshedding of the Lord of glory, so was Cain. Tortured within and cursed without, he was to bear the weight of a brother's blood whithersoever he went. Impelled by *envy*, he had murdered his holy brother, and now something more terrible and more unquenchable takes possession of him,—remorse of soul,—the undying sting of conscience. He had slain his brother to prevent his inheriting the birthright, and to secure the blessing for himself; and now he finds that he has called up against himself a curse which is to track his footsteps throughout earth, and render his very life a burden and a sorrow. Such is SIN! So terrible,

would thus become a perpetual witness against him; and hence, perhaps, it was, that he and his descendants betook themselves to the mechanical arts and city-building. Fruitfulness of soil being denied, they dug for gold, and silver, and iron. Thus was the memory of Cain's sin perpetuated.

so ruinous, so relentless, so armed with the curse of God. Such are the fruits of envy. Burden upon burden, stroke upon stroke, sorrow upon sorrow! From above, from beneath, and from around, the torment, and the terror, and the bitterness pour in. There is no peace to the wicked, no rest, no settlement. How sin uproots and unsettles, making a man to flee hither and thither, in order to get away from himself! How vain! O SIN, *sin!* what horrid things are all wrapt up even in its smallest indulgence! An unkind thought, a harsh word, an envious feeling, — then sullenness, anger, murder — a brother's murder! How little do we know sin, or reckon on its results, or calculate the fruits that come forth from its womb![1]

Vers. 13, 14. '*And Cain said unto the Lord, My punishment is greater than I can bear.*[2] 14. *Behold, Thou hast driven me this day from the face of the earth; and from Thy face shall I be hid; and I shall be a fugitive and a vagabond*[3] *in the earth: and it shall come to pass, that every one that findeth me shall slay me.*'

Up to this point the murderer has lifted up a bold front

[1] How like the curse on Cain has been that on Israel for ages! And both for the same crime,—a brother's blood! Israel is the true Cain, a wanderer among the nations; see Lev. xxvi. 36; Deut. xxviii. 25, 65. Augustine speaks thus of the Jewish nation, Com. on Ps. xl. and lix.; but he dwells fancifully on the *signs* which God has given to them that they shall not be destroyed, such as the sign of circumcision, unleavened bread, etc.

[2] The marginal rendering seems the true one here: 'Mine iniquity is greater than that it may be forgiven.' Hävernick remarks, 'The unbloody offering of Cain stands in a remarkable agreement with the expression, My sin is greater than can be taken away.'—*Introd. to the Pent.* p. 103.

[3] 'A fugitive and a vagabond.' The old English translations,

before Jehovah. But the sentence from God's own lips has overwhelmed him. It has smitten him like a thunderbolt. He can no longer defy God, nor brave His anger, nor trifle with His omniscience. He is not, indeed, humbled; repentance is far from him; but he is silenced, convicted, crushed. Like Ahab, in an after age, he bows before a power with which he can no longer trifle; but that is all. Like Judas, he is stung with remorse, as when the betrayer cried out, 'I have sinned, in that I have betrayed the innocent blood.' He now, for the first time, confesses sin; yet it is only *this* sin,—no more,—that he avows. In the sharp bitterness of remorse, he passes from callousness to despair. For there is no right sense of sin here, but the mere agony of blind remorse, arising from the reaction and revulsion of his furious passions, and the terrible thought that he is in the hands of an angry God. Transgressor, what does this avail? Remorse is not

Tyndale, Coverdale, and the 'Bishops,' give 'a vagabond and a runnagate;' the Vulgate, 'vagus et profugus;' Tremellius and Junius, 'vagus et infestus agitationibus.' How the Sept. got στενων και τρεμων, groaning and trembling, one hardly sees. Homer speaks of ἀλημονες ἄνδρες, 'wandering men.'—(*Odyssey*, Book xix. 74.) Horace uses the expression, 'fugitivus et erro.'—(*Sat.* Book ii. 7, line 113.) Byron, in his sad misanthropy, exclaims,

. . . . 'I am as a weed
Flung from the rock, on ocean's foam to sail,
Where'er the surge may sweep, the tempest's breath prevail.'
—*Childe Harold*, Canto III.

And Montgomery, even more beautifully, and in a far nobler strain, speaks of

. . . . 'Waifs in the universe, the last
Lorn links of kindred chains for ever sundered.'
—*Pelican Island*, Canto II.

repentance. Terror is not repentance. Despair is not repentance. The revenge which an outraged conscience takes on man for some dark deed is not repentance. These are but Cain's sullen ravings, or Ahab's alarm, or Judas' despair. There are outcries such as these in hell, with weeping and wailing, and gnashing of teeth; but where is godly sorrow, the tears of a broken heart?

Cain enumerates the causes of his despair. These are three,—the three articles of the sentence pronounced; and then he sums up with a conclusion of his own: 'It shall come to pass that every one that findeth me shall slay me.'

(1.) Behold, Thou hast cast me out this day from (or from upon) the face of the ground. *Thou* hast driven me! He sees it to be Jehovah's own doing. He who drove Adam out of paradise, now drives Cain out of Eden. Adam's sin brought expulsion from the inner circle, Cain's from the outer. He is to be cast out from the land where he had been born, where was his home; from the ground which he had tilled. He was now doubly banished; compelled to go forth into an unknown region, without a guide, or a promise, or a hope.

(2.) From Thy face I shall be hid. God's face means, doubtless, the Shekinah or manifested glory of Jehovah at the gate of Eden, where Adam and Eve, and their children, had worshipped; where God was seen by them, where He met them, and spake to them as from His mercy-seat. From this place of Jehovah's presence Cain was to go out. And this depresses him. Not that he really cared for the favour of God, as one 'in whose favour was life;' but still he could not afford to lose it, especially when others were left behind to enjoy it. And all his religious feelings, such as they were, were associated with that spot.

(3.) I shall be a fugitive and a vagabond in the earth.[1] Unchained from his primeval home, he was now to drift to and fro, he knew not whither. He was to be a leaf driven to and fro, a man without a settlement, and without a home. Poor, desolate sinner! And all this is thine own doing! Thy sin has found thee out. Thine own iniquities have taken thee, and thou art holden with the cords of thy sins (Prov. v. 22).

Cain now sums up all by drawing his own sad inference. He is sure to be slain by the first that meets him. There was nothing of this in the sentence; but a guilty conscience suggested it. He sees himself a marked man. Death surrounds him. What else can a murderer expect? What else can a murderer's conscience forbode?

Ver. 15. '*And the Lord said unto him, Therefore, whosoever slayeth Cain, vengeance shall be taken on him sevenfold. And the Lord set a mark upon Cain, lest any finding him should kill him.*'

Jehovah meets the murderer's despair with words and acts of grace. His sullen ravings draw forth no wrath. God has declared the punishment, and will not be provoked to exceed it. Nay, He takes measures to prevent its being exceeded. Not a drop more shall go into even

[1] 'A fugitive,' one 'moving' or flying from God and paradise. A 'vagabond,' a 'wanderer,' having no rest, even in the land to which he came.

Cain's cup than He Himself decrees.[1] And Cain must *know* this, and must be assured that nothing beyond the awarded penalty shall be permitted to come upon him. Grace meets the murderer, and gives him this assurance on the part of God. God will not allow any save Himself to deal with Cain. 'Vengeance is mine, I will recompense, saith Jehovah.' If any shall attempt to take his life, vengeance shall fall on him sevenfold. Of this God gives Cain a sign,[2]—a sign for himself, that he would be preserved safe from all attempts against his life, thus relieving his apprehensions, and in this respect delivering him from the terrors which surrounded him; terrors not confined to the time then present, but terrors of what might be in the ages which lay before him ere he returned to dust.[3]

[1] God's time had not yet come for the enactment, 'Whoso sheddeth man's blood, by man shall his blood be shed.' Till that enactment was made, no man had a right to slay even a murderer.

[2] Not 'set a mark upon,' but 'gave a sign to.' Dathe and Rosenmüller very decidedly adopt this as the true rendering, both remarking that שׂוּם is often used in the same sense as נָתַן; yet there must be some reason why the former word is used. The *nature* of the sign, or its position, required the use of 'placed,' not 'gave.' De Sola renders it, 'appointed a sign to Cain,' and shows that the preposition לְ does not mean *upon*, but *for* or *to*.—See also Hamilton's *Pentateuch and its Assailants*, p. 174. We may notice also, that the word אוֹת occurs seventy-six times in the Old Testament, and, save in the place before us, has always been translated a sign or token, not a mark.

[3] The world by this time (about 130) would be beginning to increase in population. But besides, Cain lived on for several generations, and needed to be assured that at no future time should vengeance be taken on him. Some may count it strange that in the first part of the verse God should provide for the possibility of his being killed, by appointing vengeance on the slayer, and in the latter should assure Cain that

But why is God so anxious to preserve Cain from death, and to give him the assurance of this security? Some reasons are obvious, besides those which run us up directly to the sovereignty of God. (1.) God's desire is to manifest the riches of His grace, and the extent of His forbearance, and that He has no pleasure in the death of the wicked, but wishes by His long-suffering to lead him to repentance. (2.) Death would not have answered God's end at all. It was needful that Cain should be preserved alive as an awful monument of sin, a warning against the shedding of man's blood. We find that this proved ineffectual; for in after ages we read that the earth was 'filled with violence,' which compelled God to interfere, with the Deluge; and we find also, that after the Deluge, God enacted the statute referred to above for the repression of murder, putting into man's hands the very power which before that He had kept wholly in His own. (3.) Cain was spared too, because of this partial repentance. God accepted Ahab's repentance (1 Kings xxi. 29); poor and hollow as it was, so does He Cain's; for He is gracious and merciful, looking for the first and faintest sign of a sinner's turning to Himself, willing to meet him at once without upbraiding, and putting the best possible construction on all he says and does. To what length is not the grace of our God able to go! Sin abounds, but grace superabounds. How desirous is Jehovah not to curse,

he should not be killed. But this is God's way of suiting Himself to man; as, for instance, when He speaks of the possibility of a saint falling away or being a castaway, and yet assures him that he shall not fall nor come short of the kingdom.

but to bless; not to smite, but to heal; not to destroy, but to save.

Ver. 16. '*And Cain went out from the presence of the Lord* (Heb. *from the face of Jehovah*), *and dwelt in the land of Nod, on the east of Eden.*'

He must tarry no longer within the bounds of Eden. Willing or unwilling, he must go. Like Judas from the presence of Jesus, so does Cain go out from the face of God, from the place where the visible glory of God, the Shekinah, had its abode. Partly troubled at his banishment, and partly relieved at getting away from the near presence of the Holy One, he goes forth, a banished criminal, whose foot must no longer be permitted to profane the sacred circle of Eden; an excommunicated man, who must no longer worship with the Church of God, round the primeval altar. He goes out, not like Abraham to the land of promise, the land flowing with milk and honey, but to the land of the threatening, the land where no divine presence was seen, and on which no glory shone, and where no bright cherubim foreshadowed redemption, and proclaimed restoration to paradise, and the tree of life. He goes out to an unknown and untrodden land; a land which, from his own character as 'the wanderer,' received in after days the name of Nod. He goes out, the flaming sword behind him, driving him out of his native seat, and forbidding his return.

A banished man, an excommunicated worshipper (the sentence of excommunication pronounced by God Himself)—one 'delivered over to Satan' (1 Tim. i. 20), he takes up his abode in the land of Nod. There he 'sits down,' not as if at rest, for what had *he* to do with rest? Can the cloud rest? Can the sea rest? Can the guilty conscience rest? He sits down in Nod, but not to rest, only to drown his restlessness in schemes of labour. He went towards the rising sun.[1] He and his posterity spread eastward, just as Seth and his posterity spread westward. The two great families separated, only to meet again in after ages, when overflowing wickedness had erased the line of separation, and a common ungodliness had made them one.[2]

'The way of Cain'—what is it? (Jude 11.) The apostle speaks of it as something terrible, and something which will be specially exhibited in the last days. 'Woe unto them, for they have gone in the way of Cain!' That way began in unbelief, in the rejection of God's way of 'salvation through the shedding of blood.'[3] It ended in utter worldliness and infidelity; in the unrestrained in-

[1] Montgomery thus paints the fugitive—

'Eastward ot Eden's early peopled plain,
Where Abel perished by the hand of Cain,
The murderer from his Judge's presence fled;
Thence to the rising sun his offspring spread.
But he, the fugitive of care and guilt,
Forsook the haunts he chose, the homes he built;
While filial nations hailed him sire and chief,
Empire nor honour brought his soul relief;
He found where'er he roamed, uncheer'd, unblest,
No pause from suffering, and from toil no rest.'
—*World before the Flood.*

[2] If this be the separation between the seed of the woman and the seed of the serpent, is Gen. vi. 2 the scene of their accomplished reunion? The sons of God and the daughters of men (as Israel and Moab) allying themselves together.

[3] See Mr. Faber's *Eight Dissertations*, vol. ii., appendix, for an article on Cain.

dulgence of the lust of the flesh, the eye, and the pride of life. It was a way very much marked by the Apostle Paul's characteristics of the perilous times of the last days (2 Tim. iii. 1). In it we find selfishness, envy, hatred, murder, hypocrisy, lying, pride, independence, rebelliousness, ambition, all coupled or covered over with the 'form of godliness.' Rejection of the woman's seed, and of God's way of acceptance through that seed—this is the main feature, that which influences all the rest. No Christ for him! No bruised heel for him! No shedding of blood for the remission of sins! No righteousness of a substitute in which he may stand before God! 'The *way* of Cain!' It still exists. It has not been ploughed up so as to become imperceptible. It is still visible, and it is coming more and more into admiration as man's conscience gets blunted, and as his proud self-sufficiency exhibits itself. No sacrifice, no substitute, no imputed righteousness, no blood-shedding, no 'religion of the shambles' for us!

And is such a way the way of holiness? Will such a religion lead men to love and gentleness, and brotherly kindness? Will such a faith make a happy kingdom and a blessed earth, introducing the reign of peace and gladness? So say its exulting votaries, emancipated, as they suppose, from the trammels of old creeds, and from the brutalizing influence of altars besmeared with blood. So says the philosophic theology of the day. So says the poetry of the age.[1]

[1] 'Christian Socialism,' as it is called, is, not less than the infidel's Socialism, 'the way of Cain.'

But look at Cain. That was *his* way. He rejected the expiatory blood, turning away from the 'religion of the shambles,' to the mild gentleness of a worship in which no life was taken, and no blood was spilt, and no suffering inflicted. Did this mild and genial religion of his lead to a loving, gentle life? No. He who had so many scruples about shedding the blood of an innocent lamb, has none about taking the life of a holy and unoffending brother. He who is too pure and refined in his ideas of religion to profane his altar by turning it into 'shambles,' is all the while busied in preparing 'shambles' of his own, where, for the gratification of malice, hatred, envy, and revenge, and every hellish passion, he may, with his own hand, butcher a brother for being more righteous than he.

Ver. 17. '*And Cain knew his wife; and she conceived, and bare Enoch: and he builded a city, and called the name of the city, after the name of his son, Enoch.*'

Cain had probably been married before his crime, yet had no family. His wife goes forth with him from Eden, and in the land of his banishment brings forth a son, who gets the name of Enoch; the same in *name* as the holy son of Seth in an after age, but in *character* unlike. Cain was himself born within the primeval region where Adam dwelt; but his children are not to be born there. Their native region is to be that of the banished wanderer, as if God, even in this thing, would draw the separating line between the seed of the woman and the seed of the serpent.

In his new country he had set himself to build a city,

and as his son was born while he was engaged in building it, he calls it by the name of his son. He does not call it by his own name. He deems it better that that should be hid, not published,—forgotten, not perpetuated. But he seeks to connect the city with a family name, though not with his own. How like the ungodly spoken of by David, 'They call their lands by their own names'! (Ps. xlix. 11.)[1] He is now settling down in worldliness, and trying to forget God amid stir, and movement, and pleasure. He is ambitious of being remembered in the earth. Posthumous fame is his desire. He is desirous to be not merely the founder of a family, but the builder of a city. He seeks thus to soothe his guilty conscience, to drown remorse, to bury out of sight and out of memory the dreadful past. He is the true picture of a sinner trying to flee from himself and to escape from God. But it cannot be! The void within still remains unfilled! Conscience still stings. The past, like a black spectre, frowns or moans behind him, and the future flings its cold shadow over him, pointing onwards to the endless sorrow. What can the sinner do? Return to God is his only 'chance,' as men speak; or, as the gospel tells him, his certain and joyful hope.

Ver. 18. '*And unto Enoch was born Irad: and Irad begat Mehujael: and Mehujael begat Methusael: and Methusael begat Lamech.*'

Thus son after son is born. The world runs on. Its

[1] The whole of this psalm is appropriate. It looks like a sketch of Cain and his children. It shows us the 'seed of the serpent' in their aspect of utter worldliness. See also Job xxi. 7–21.

families multiply: and name is added to name. Abel is forgotten, and the voice of his blood is silenced,—at least it ceases to disturb these generations of the prosperous sons of Cain. Enoch loses sight of his holy uncle's murder in the triumph of having a city called by his name. Cain's sin passes out of mind. God's curse upon the murderer is made light of. To lay aside the stranger's tent, and build the city for ages, as if they would dwell here for ever, is now the aim of these Cainites. The 'world' is now rapidly developing itself as 'the world.' There is 'eating and drinking, marrying and giving in marriage;' and the chorus of after ages begins to be adopted, 'To-morrow shall be as this day, and much more abundant.'

Ver. 19. '*And Lamech took unto him two wives: the name of the one was Adah, and the name of the other Zillah.*'

Here begins the brief story of Lamech the polygamist, —a story of lust, bloodshed, and defiant hardihood. He is the first to violate God's primeval law of marriage; and the violation of this soon leads to other sins. In Cain we have seen the man of *violence*. In Lamech we see the man of *lust*. From these two fountainheads of evil, what wickedness has flowed out upon earth! And, as in the last days we find men returning to 'the way of Cain,' so do we find them returning to the way of Lamech,— 'walking after the flesh, in the lust of uncleanness, and despising government, presumptuous, self-willed' (2 Pet. ii. 10). All the old world's sins repeated and intensified in the last generation, just before the arrival of Him of whom Enoch prophesied (Jude 14).

Vers. 20-22. '*And Adah bare Jabal: he was the father of such as dwell in tents, and of such as have cattle.* 21. *And his brother's name was Jubal: he was the father of all such as handle the harp and organ.* 22. *And Zillah, she also bare Tubal-cain, an instructor of every artificer in brass and iron: and the sister of Tubal-cain was Naamah.*'

Still the world goes on. God allows men to take their course. Forgetting Him in whom they live, they proceed onwards, each one in his own way and in the gratification of his own tastes. All kinds of professions, and occupations, and arts are introduced. The natural man is fertile in all things pertaining to this present evil world; and Satan, the god of this world, sharpens and quickens his ingenuity and skill.

1. *Pastoral pursuits* make progress. Jabal was the father of such as dwell in tents, and have cattle (ver. 20). Jabal takes the lead as the great shepherd of his day,—gentler, perhaps, and more peaceful in his nature,—more like Abel in his dispositions. The Spirit of God does not here cast censure on such employments, as if there were sin in them. He simply points out these children of Cain as sitting down contented with earth, and engrossed with its pursuits. It is the spirit of earnest and absorbing worldliness which is meant to be exhibited; the spirit that pursues lawful employments to such an extreme of engrossment, that by excess they become unlawful. These children of Cain seem to have shrunk from *tillage.* They would have had to till a cursed soil,—a soil cursed for

their father's sin (ver. 12). They would have had to labour on with their father's guilt overhanging them,—their sweating brow, and weary limbs, and baffled schemes, reminding them that they were labouring on under a double curse—the curse of Cain added to the curse of Adam; that they were tilling ground which Cain had sterilized with a brother's blood,—blood which was still crying from every clod and furrow. Hence they seem to have given up their father's original occupation, and become keepers of cattle, not tillers of the ground. The soil was too full of terror, as well as of toil, for them to attempt its tillage. How a man's sin finds him out! How it traces him out wherever he sets his foot! How it haunts his days and nights, standing in his way like the angel before Balaam, to turn him out of his road, and to compel him to seek other paths, and other occupations, where he may not be so perseveringly pursued by that dark shadow, or rather that living spectre!

2. *The Fine Arts.*—Jabal had a brother by name Jubal, who betakes himself to the harp and the organ.[1] Yes,—music,—the world must soothe its sorrows or drown its cares with music! The world must cheat its hours away with music! The world must set its lusts to music! The harp and the organ,—these must be employed to lull the conscience asleep, to minister to pleasure, to drown the sorrows of earth, to cheat the soul out of its eternal

[1] Without entering upon the inquiry what was the כִּנּוֹר, *Kinnor*, and what was the עוּגָב, *Ugab*, we may say that the former seems to comprehend all *stringed* instruments, the latter all *wind* instruments.

birthright! Thus Job describes these families of Cain:—'Their children dance: they take the timbrel and harp, and rejoice at the sound of the organ' (Job xxi. 12). Yet, sweet sounds are not unholy. There is no sin in the richest strains of music. And God, by bringing into His own temple all the varied instruments of melody, and employing them in His praises, showed this. But these Cainites make music of the siren kind. God is not in all their melodies. It is to shut Him out that they devise the harp and the organ. Yet these inventions He makes use of for Himself afterwards; employing these men as the hewers of wood and the drawers of water for His temple. They devise and fashion the instruments for their own pleasure and mirth; and God takes them out of their hands, and putting them into the hands of His servants, brings out of them divine music, for the service of His temple, and for the praise of His glory. When we are told, 'Thus all Israel brought up the ark of the covenant of the Lord with shouting, and with sound of the cornet, and with trumpets, and with cymbals, making a noise with psalteries and harps' (1 Chron. xv. 28), we are carried back to Jubal, and made to see how God can turn to His own ends the wisdom of this world, the natural skill and science which the men of earth pursue for the gratification of their own carnal desires.

3. *The Mechanical Arts.*—Zillah bare Tubal-cain to Lamech; and this Tubal-cain was an instructor of every artificer in brass and iron. The arts flourish under Cain's posterity. They can prosper without God, and among those in whose hearts His fear is not. God suffers them

to go on forgetting Himself, and occupying themselves with these engrossing employments. He permits them to put forth their skill and genius to the uttermost, fashioning for themselves all manner of curious or useful instruments for ornament, for tillage, for war, for all those various ends for which brass and iron are moulded by the artificers of ancient or of modern times. He does not interfere; and this not only because He is long-suffering, but because one of His great purposes is, that man shall have full scope to develope himself mentally, morally, and physically. Man has torn himself off from God; and God will let it be seen how the branch can unfold its leaves and fruit, or rather what kind of leaves and fruit it can put forth when thus severed from Himself. God will let the world roll on its own way, that it may be seen what a world it is. He will let sin come out in all its various manifestations, that its true character may be exhibited, as well as the true character of that fountainhead where it had now concentrated itself,—a human heart. There is no sin in working in brass and iron, or in attaining to the highest skill in so doing; but there is sin in the worldliness, the selfishness, the forgetfulness of God, springing out of the exercise of that skill in these Cainites.

Men are trying so to fit up and adorn the world, that they shall be able to do without God in it at all. The experiment is making, whether they may not be quite as comfortable and as safe in a world where God is not, as in a world where He is all in all. They till the soil; they clothe it with fair verdure in hill and dale; they cover it with the living creatures which God has made for it; and the cattle upon a thousand hills exhibit the life and the plenty with which they have made it to abound; they dig into its very bowels for the iron and the brass, out of which to construct instruments to fill its air with melody, or implements with which to cultivate its varied growth, or weapons with which to defend themselves against evil, or ornaments with which to beautify their dwelling; they call in the aid, too, of woman's attractions; for Naamah, Zillah's daughter, and Tubal-cain's sister, seems mentioned for the very purpose of suggesting this;[1] all that skill, and art, and ornament, and brilliancy, and harmony, and female grace can do to make earth a paradise is attempted. Poor man! What efforts he has made to undo the curse with which his own sin had smitten creation! What pains he has taken to render this world habitable and pleasant; to make himself and his children independent of God for happiness, or health, or safety, or blessing! But in vain; it will not do. The fashion of this world passeth away; its beauty fades, and its loveliest forms are but sunset-rainbows, brightening those vapours, that in an hour will vanish or grow dark.

What is earth without the God that made it, or the Christ by whom it is yet to be made new? What are the arts and sciences; music, painting, statuary? What are the wisdom, skill, energy, power, genius of the race, developed to the full? What are the mind's resources, the heart's fulness, the body's pliant power, man's strength

[1] *Naamah* seems to be the heathen *Venus;* as *Tubal-cain* is *Vulcan.*

or woman's beauty, youth's fervour or age's grey-haired wisdom? What are all these in a world from which its Creator has been banished; a world whose wisdom is not the knowledge of Christ, and whose sunshine is not the love of God?

Vers. 23, 24. '*And Lamech said unto his wives, Adah and Zillah, hear my voice; ye wives of Lamech, hearken unto my speech: for I have slain a man to my wounding, and a young man to my hurt:* 24. *If Cain shall be avenged sevenfold, truly Lamech seventy and sevenfold.*'

The substance of this abrupt and singular narrative may be set down as follows: Lamech had been engaged in some deed of blood,—to which, perhaps, his polygamy had led. From this murder his family apprehend the worst consequences to himself. To soothe their fears, he addresses his wives,—

'Adah and Zillah, hear my voice;
Ye wives of Lamech, hearken to my speech!
Surely I have slain a man to my wounding,
And a young man to my hurt.
Surely if Cain shall be avenged sevenfold,
Truly Lamech seventy and sevenfold.'

As if he had said, 'It is true that I have slain a man, but it was in self-defence, and in so doing I have been wounded; I have slain a young man, and in so doing have been bruised; but surely I have less cause to fear than Cain: if he was to be avenged sevenfold, then I may count upon being avenged seventy-sevenfold.'[1]

[1] Marbachius suggests that his wives were endeavouring to restrain his ferocity, especially representing the consequences of its indulgence,

Such was the argument by which Lamech sought to allay the alarms of his wives. And in this we see the man. We get a knowledge of his character, and no less so of the state of the times. It seems to have been an age of lust and bloodshed. Lamech is its type. It was the introduction to that darker time, when wickedness having swelled to its utmost, God was constrained to interpose and sweep the transgressors from the earth. The scene in Lamech's house was a specimen of the times,—times like those depicted in Psalms xi. and lii., or in Isaiah v. (especially ver. 18), like those predicted by Paul (2 Tim. iii. 1; 2 Pet. ii. 2, iii. 1, 2), and by Jude throughout his epistle. It is the dark picture of a dark time; men rushing headlong in the way of Cain, breaking asunder all ties of brotherhood, defying God, and making account of no interests save their own. It is a scene which shall yet be expanded to far larger dimensions in the last days, when evil shall cover the earth, and when 'the wicked one,' more cruel than Cain, viler than Lamech,

and that this speech is the answer to these remonstrances.—ERASMI MARBACHII, *Comm. in Pent.* vol. i. p. 63. The above is a brief but clear and shrewd commentary, of date 1597. Dr. Wells (also Julius Bates) renders the words interrogatively, 'Have I slain?' etc., thereby not involving Lamech in the crime of murder, but of *bigamy*. It is of this that he is thus supposed to speak; as if he would show that his marrying two wives was not so heinous a sin as Cain's murder of his brother (p. 40). This is forced, though כִּי might be used interrogatively, as in 1 Sam. xxiv. 20; 2 Kings xviii. 34, etc. On the whole passage, see Lowth's 4th Lecture on Hebrew Poetry. He takes the simple and natural view. His 'Annotators' are more ingenious than satisfying. Schlegel maintains from this passage that Lamech was the originator of human sacrifices.—*Phil. of Hist.*, Bohn's Ed., p. 201.

and more ambitious than Nimrod, shall shed man's blood in torrents, and impiously reckon on impunity at the hands of God.

But let us look more narrowly at Lamech. He stands before us in such aspects as the following :—

1. *As the first violator of God's primeval law of marriage.* —That law most strictly enjoined *one* wife; and doubtless had been observed till Lamech's time. *He* sets it at defiance. That law was the very foundation of society. It was the foundation of family peace, of true religion, of social order, of right government in the state. Take away this foundation, or place two instead of one, and the whole fabric shakes, the nation crumbles to pieces.[1] It is not merely the family hearth that is destroyed, but the throne of the King is undermined. Bonds the most sacred and needful Lamech breaks. The most ancient and venerable law of earth he tramples on. Lust has gotten the mastery in him. He is the true type of those 'filthy dreamers' who 'defile the flesh' (Jude 8); of those who in the last days are to 'walk after the flesh, in the lust of uncleanness, having eyes full of adultery' (2 Pet. ii.). And as Lamech's sin threw open the floodgates of lasciviousness, so may the sins of those who in our day are walking in his steps be

[1] In Mal. ii. 15, God tells us that His special reason for this law was, that thereby He might raise up a godly offspring. He had 'the residue of the Spirit,' and He might have produced not one Eve but many; yet He wisely ordered it otherwise. How much of godliness depends on unity and order in a household; and how much is it in the power ot the *woman* either to promote or to mar this unity! See on this whole subject, the Rev. Christopher Anderson's most admirable work upon the *Domestic Constitution.*

throwing open these same floodgates, and ripening the world for the judgment of the great day.

2. *As a murderer.*—Lust had led to adultery, and adultery had led to violence and murder. We are not told the name of him whom he slew.[1] It matters not. He is a murderer,—true follower of Cain,—true offspring of the serpent, of him who was 'a murderer from the beginning' (John viii. 44). Abhor Lamech's spirit as we would that of Satan. Flee anger, passion, revenge,—of all that would lead, however remotely, to bloodshedding. In Cain, it was envy; in Lamech, lust. Flee both.

3. *As a boaster of his evil deeds.*—He does the deed of blood, and he is not ashamed of it; nay, he glories in it, —nay, glories in it to his own wives. There is no confession of sin here, no repentance, not even Cain's partial humbling. Thus iniquity lifts up its head and waxes bold in countenance,[2] defying God and vaunting before men, as if the deed had been one of honour and not of shame. 'Boasters' are to rise up in the last days (2 Tim. iii. 2), specially boasters of evil, like Lamech. Men are to 'boast themselves in mischief' (Ps. lii. 7). The wicked is to 'boast of his heart's desire' (Ps. x. 3).

4. *As one taking refuge in the crimes of others.*—He makes Cain not a warning, but an example. He perverts God's purpose in sparing Cain, and takes courage in evil from Cain's example. He 'goes in the way of Cain' (Jude 11), and makes no account of God's awful monu-

[1] The Jews say it was Cain; others, his own son; others, a younger brother.

[2] *Frontemque a crimine sumit.*

ments of indignation against sin. He sins because Cain sinned! He thinks he has a *right* to sin, because Cain sinned! Oh, desperate perversity of man's heart! What will it not make an excuse for sinning? And yet it always tries to find an excuse or an example, as if afraid and ashamed to sin unless for some reason, or with some example before it!

5. *As one perverting God's forbearance.*—He trifles with sin, because God showed mercy to another.[1] He tramples on righteousness, because it is tempered with grace. He sets vengeance at nought, because God is long-suffering. Instead of saying, 'God is so loving that I dare not sin;' he says, 'God is so loving that I will go on in sin without limit.' Divine compassion has no effect in softening his obstinacy; but 'after his hardness and impenitent heart, he treasures up to himself wrath against the day of wrath and revelation of the righteous judgment of God' (Rom. ii. 5). Thus men still turn God's grace into lasciviousness, and make Christ the minister of sin!

6. *As a scoffer.*—He believes in no judgment, and makes light of sin's recompense. His words are evidently the words of a scoffer, and of one who believed in no wrath of God against the workers of iniquity. He speaks like the scoffers of the last days, 'Where is the promise of his coming? for since the fathers fell asleep, all things

[1] In the 52d Psalm, God meets this tendency of man to 'continue in sin because grace abounds,' and asks most touchingly and graciously, 'Why boastest thou thyself in mischief, O mighty man? The goodness of God endureth continually;' that is, 'Ought not this goodness to stop thy boastings and melt thy heart, and lead thee to repentance?'

continue as they were from the beginning of the creation' (2 Pet. iii. 1–3). Is not this the mocking that we hear on every side? No day of judgment, no righteous vengeance against sin, no condemnation of the transgressor! God has borne long with the world, He will bear longer with it still! He may do something to dry up the running sore of its *miseries;* but as for its *guilt,* He will make no account of that, for 'God is love'! But what then becomes of *law,* or of righteousness, or of the difference between good and evil? And what becomes of God's past proclamations of law, His manifestations of righteousness, His declarations of abhorrence of all sin? Was Adam's ejection from paradise the mere attempt to cure a disease, and not the condemnation of his guilt? Was the deluge the mere drying up of the world's running sore of wretchedness, that it might start healthy and vigorous on a new course, instead of being the expression of God's estimate of human *guilt,* and His determination to prevent men from imagining that He was indifferent to the evil of sin, and, as the God of love, that He could only treat it as a sad *misfortune,* but not as an infinite and unalterable *crime* against love, and majesty, and truth, and government, and holiness?

Ver. 25. '*And Adam knew his wife again; and she bare a son, and called his name Seth* (that is, *set or appointed*) : *for God, said she, hath appointed me another seed instead of Abel, whom Cain slew.*'

With Lamech's history ends the inspired record of the line of Cain. They pass away, and are seen no more. Their memory rots, and their names are forgotten. No man writes their story, or builds their monument. With Lamech's murderous vauntings, the sounds of their proud ungodliness die away in our ears. His voice is the last that we hear of the children of Cain. Cain the first, Lamech the last, are the representatives of the race,—its alpha and its omega. Brief but awful summary of the world's enmity to God, and rebellion against the promised seed! Enough to show us what the seed of the serpent is; what man's heart is; what the world is, with all its art, and science, and melody, and beauty. It has made evil its good; it has called darkness light; it has fashioned for its own worship its gods of the intellect, its gods of the flesh, to whom alone it bows down, disowning the true God, rejecting all allegiance to Him, banishing Him from earth, and seeking to make for itself a home on its surface without Him,—a circle for its joys to move in without His love.

But now the scene changes. A vision, bright though brief, passes before us, like a sudden burst of sunshine on a dark troubled sea. We get a glimpse of the holy family, the household of the redeemed and separated ones, who, in the midst of a world where evil is overflowing, are still faithful to God, and believers in the promised seed.

We are carried back to Abel and his bloody grave. He,—the Isaac of Adam's house, the hope of his father and the joy of his mother, in whom the promise of redemption seemed about to be fulfilled,—he was cut down, like a flower at dawn. It might seem as if, with him, his parents' hopes lay buried, and the prospects of the race blighted. It was not merely their feelings that were torn, but it was their faith, that, like Abraham's, was tried to the uttermost. Now, however, God is to visit them in tender love. He not only fills up the void in the family circle, and pours consolation into their wounded spirits, but He lifts up their drooping faith and gives it a new foundation to rest on. To Eve is born a third son; and he comes to them as the gift of love and the pledge of hope. Eve names him Seth, which means 'set' or 'placed' or 'appointed,' as being expressly given to her in room of Abel whom Cain slew. In this her faith shows itself again; for in the case of her three sons, it is she herself who gives the names, and in them displays her faith. In Cain, it was simple and triumphant faith, that had not yet entered into conflict, nor known what trials and crosses are. In Abel's, it was the utterance of hope deferred, making the heart sick, and realizing strangership on earth and 'vanity' in creation. And now, in Seth, it is faith reassured and comforted, brought to rest in God, as able to fulfil to the uttermost all that He had promised.

(1.) She recognises God in this. It is not the mere 'law of nature;' it is the Lord. It is in the fulfilment of his Sovereign purpose that He is doing this.

(2.) She gives a name expressive of her faith. She calls her infant the appointed one, the substituted one. She saw God making up her loss, filling up the void, providing a seed, through which the promised deliverer was to come.

(3.) She fondly calls to mind her martyred son. The way in which she does this, shows the yearning of her heart over him who was taken away, as if his place was one which needed to be supplied, as if there were a blank in her bosom which God only knew how to supply. She had learned, doubtless, that 'blessed are the dead that die in the Lord;' but still her heart went out fondly after the beloved child, and she could not be comforted till she had one like him to fill up his room. It is not sentimentalism; it is faith. It is not mere maternal love; it is faith, faith that clung to the memory of her holy son, as one not merely beloved of herself, but beloved of her God.

Ver. 26. '*And to Seth, to him also there was born a son; and he called his name Enos: then began men to call upon the name of the Lord.*'

We are yet to have another glimpse of the holy seed, the heavenly family, not merely passing onwards as strangers, but shining as lights in the world. God has reserved for Himself not one family, but many, in this age —and these are letting their light shine. God's witnesses seem not few, but many. To Seth a son is born, and though his name imports nothing great in so far as the flesh is concerned;[1] yet it seems that he was not only of the seed of the godly, but himself a man of faith; nay, a man mighty in word and deed for God. For in his days, and probably through his influence, a mighty and blessed work seems to have been accomplished, and men now publicly united together to worship *Jehovah*, gathering

[1] *Enos*,—weak mortal, or dying man, showing how truly believers were beginning to feel that 'all flesh is grass.'

round the primeval altar at the gate of paradise, and there, over the bleeding sacrifice, calling upon the name of the Lord.[1]

In Enos—the 'feeble mortal,' as his name imports, the bruised reed, the man who has no confidence in the flesh —we see a faithful witness for God,—one who gathers into one the scattered families of believers, and unites them in the worship of the living God.

Thus ebbs and flows the tide of heavenly life on earth.

[1] For the meaning of 'calling on the name of the Lord,' see Gen. xii. 8, xiii. 4, xxi. 33. It means generally the worship of the Lord, and the form of expression implies that it was public or general,—men gathering together in solemn assembly. This was the first gathering of the saints in the name of Jesus,—the anticipation of the Master's words, 'Where two or three are gathered in my name.' 'The Lord' or 'Jehovah' is properly Messiah's name: He who 'was, and is, and is to come,'—the I AM. Eve knew Him by this name (ch. iv. 1); Enoch also knew Him by this name (Jude 14). The Christology of the Old Testament, as centred in or clustering round that name, is worthy of being more thoroughly studied. Of late years, men *who wrest the Scriptures* have told us that we ought to meet 'under the Presidency of the Holy Ghost' instead of the name of Jesus; thus framing a profane phrase out of their own fancy, and setting aside the scriptural term 'the name of Jesus,' in which name all the saints have met from the beginning. That the Holy Ghost is PRESIDENT of a congregation, or gathering, or church, thus superseding Christ the head, is a fiction got up in order to form a new *sect*, which under professions of superior spirituality would get vent to its supercilious assumptions over other bodies, dividing Christians, splitting churches, compassing sea and land to make one proselyte, and doing what in them lies to grieve the Holy Spirit, to whom they have assigned the unscriptural designation of PRESIDENT of the Church. Such are the sayings and doings of the 'last days,' when men 'creep into houses,' lead captive the unwary, and beguile unstable souls, who have been running about from church to church, from minister to minister, finding no rest for their souls.

Thus has the cause of God been carried on,—not steadily progressing, but often cast back, and the saints reduced to a handful; then once more reviving, and believers added to the Church in numbers. Onwards from Seth's day the work has proceeded in this way, and is to do so till the Lord come. Let us not be discouraged; yet let us not seek great things for ourselves; but simply to do the Lord's work in our day, and to reach the reward.

CHAPTER V.

Vers. 1, 2. '*This is the book of the generations of Adam.*[1] *In the day that God created man, in the likeness of God made He him;* 2. *Male and female created He them; and blessed them, and called their name Adam, in the day when they were created.*'

THIS chapter stands by itself. It is one of names and dates; a chapter of genealogy, a page of early chronology. It does fill a larger space than we should have expected; yet of its importance we are not competent judges. The Holy Spirit has written it, and placed it in His volume, for all ages to read. It must therefore contain important truth, both for the world and for the Church, though we may not quite see or appreciate it. It has served mighty ends in ages past, for it has furnished history with the main stem of its chronological tree; and it may yet serve no less great ends in the ages to come; for in the world's *last* days men will be more thrown back upon its *first* days than they are willing to believe. We should have preferred a record of the sayings and doings of the patriarchs to such lists of names and years; and we may not be able to enter fully into

[1] De Sola renders this, 'This is the enumeration of the descendants of Adam;' and remarks that סֵפֶר, which is here used, signifies radically to count or number, and properly means enumeration. 'This is the list or catalogue' (POOLE). It is the same word that is translated 'register' in Neh. vii. 5.

God's reasons for giving us such barren verses, as we are apt to think them. But what we know not now we shall know hereafter. Bible history is written on the principle of abridgment and selection. God Himself is the abridger and selecter. He has written the story of His own world in His own way, and according to His own plan, keeping such things as these in view—(1) what would most glorify Himself; (2) what would most benefit the Church upon the whole; (3) what would mark distinctly the stages leading on to the Incarnation of His Son; (4) what would prove the true humanity of Messiah as the seed of the woman, and so the embodiment of the grace and truth wrapt up in the first promise to man. The first verse carries us back to the earlier chapters, and repeats the statement already given as to man's creation in the divine image. It is plain from it that God desires us to look at and ponder such things as these—(1) man's creation by God; (2) his creation in the likeness of God;[1] (3) his creation, male and female; (4) his being 'blessed' by God, and that he enters this world as a blessed being, not under the curse at all; (5) his receiving the name of Adam, or man, from God Himself, as if God specially claimed the right of nomenclature to Himself. How much importance must God attach to these

[1] While Luke traces Christ's genealogy to Adam (as Matthew does to Abraham), he traces Adam's parentage to God. How solemnly do his last words fall on our ears, 'Which was the son of God;' or, as it stands in its simplicity, just τοῦ Θεοῦ. 'Our generation,' says Philo, 'is from man, but him (the first man) God made' (ἐδημιουργησε). And again, 'But of him (Adam) no mortal was the father or cause, but God;' quoted in the Hellenistic Testament, on Luke iii. 38.

things when He thus repeats them at so brief an interval! He does not repeat in vain. Every word of God is 'pure,' and it is full of meaning, even though we may not now see it all. It is not a mere grain or atom; it is a seed,—a root.

Vers. 3-5. *'And Adam lived an hundred and thirty years, and begat a son in his own likeness, after his image; and called his name Seth.*[1] 4. *And the days of Adam, after he had begotten Seth, were eight hundred years; and he begat sons and daughters.* 5. *And all the days that Adam lived were nine hundred and thirty years: and he died.'*

This is the sum of Adam's life! He lived, he begat a son, he died! How brief and bare! Yet such is the outline of man's life as seen by the eye of God, and from that point of view which God occupies. Our memoirs of a man of threescore and ten fill volumes; God's memoirs of a man of nine hundred and thirty occupy but three verses. What desires have we to get some glimpse into Adam's life, to know something of his words and deeds! But not one is left on record!

In the third verse, we are told of Adam's age when he begat Seth,—one hundred and thirty years,—showing us how deliberately God proceeds in carrying out His promises. He does not 'make haste,' yet they are all sure. The woman's seed shall come forth in due time. Delay may occur, obstacles may intervene, Abel may be cut down, Seth may be long of coming; yet the promise shall not fail.[2]

[1] De Sola renders it, '*then* begat a son,' etc., making the meaning more definite.

[2] Adam is here said to give Seth his name, as elsewhere Eve is

But this son is in Adam's own likeness and image. Adam was made in God's image, Seth in Adam's; but Adam was no longer what he once was. It is the image of a fallen man, wrinkled and distorted with sin. 'That which is born of the flesh is flesh.' The thorn cannot produce the grape, nor the briar the fig; neither can a bitter fountain send forth sweet waters.

After Seth's birth, Adam lived 800 years, begetting sons and daughters; thus living on with all the patriarchs of the early age, till the 308th year of Enoch, and the 57th before his translation; almost to the very days of Noah; 930 years in all. Such was the long age of Adam,—an age which, though gradually diminished till it came to the threescore years and ten, is yet to be revived in millennial days, when, as it is written, 'the days of my people shall be as the days of a tree' (Isa. lxv. 22).

Then he died! He by whom death came in at last fell under it. He returned to dust. His sin found him out, after a long pursuit of 930 years, and laid him low. The first Adam dies! The tallest, goodliest palm-tree of the primeval paradise is laid low. The first Adam dies; neither in life nor in death transmitting to us aught of blessing. He dies as our forerunner; he who led the way to the tomb. The first Adam dies, and we die in him; but the second Adam dies, and we live in him! The first Adam's grave proclaims only death; the second Adam's grave announces life,—'I am the resurrection and the life.' We look into the grave of the one, and we see

said to have done (chap. iv. 25); both concurring in this, and expressing in it their common griefs and sympathies.

only darkness, corruption, and death; we look into the grave of the other, and we find there only light, incorruption, and life. We look into the grave of the one, and we find that he is still there, his dust still mingling with its fellow-dust about it; we look into the grave of the other, and find that He is not there, He is risen,—risen as our forerunner into the heavenly paradise, the home of the risen and redeemed. We look into the grave of the first Adam, and see in him the first-fruits of them that have died, the millions that have gone down to that prison-house whose gates he opened; we look into the tomb of the second Adam, and we see in Him the first-fruits of them that are to rise; the first-fruits of that bright multitude, that glorified band, who are to come forth from that cell, triumphing over death, and rising to the immortal life; not through the tree which grew in the earthly paradise, but through Him whom that tree prefigured—through Him who was dead and is alive, and who liveth for evermore, and who has the keys of hell and death.

Vers. 6-8. '*And Seth lived an hundred and five years, and begat Enos.* 7. *And Seth lived, after he begat Enos, eight hundred and seven years, and begat sons and daughters.* 8. *And all the days of Seth were nine hundred and twelve years: and he died.*'

The first link in the great chain of incarnation was Adam. The second link seemed at first to be Cain. At least so Eve thought; but it was soon seen that he was the first link of another chain,—the serpent's seed, whose last link is, not Christ, but Antichrist. Then it might seem as if the second link were to be Abel; but suddenly it was snapped asunder, and the promise looked as if ready to fail. But when thus the Lord had tried Adam's faith, as He did Abraham's, He stepped in and produced another link, which was neither to fail nor to be broken. Seth stands before us as the second great link of the wondrous chain. In him the promise was to be made sure. He was truly 'Seth'—*the substituted one*, brought in to supply a brother's place and to perform a brother's part, both to the smitten family and to the Church of God, whose hope seemed to be cut off. He was not, like Abel, suffered to be the victim of Cain's envy, but rose up to manhood, primeval manhood,—the manhood of an entire century. In his 105th year he begat Enos, thus making sure another link, and raising up another witness, besides being himself a noble witness for God. Thereafter he lived 807 years, and begat sons and daughters, of whom, however, we know nothing. They might be followers of their father, or they might be like their uncle Cain; we know not. God names but one, leaving the rest unheard of till the great day that shall give up all names. Seth lived altogether 912 years, —a shorter life by 18 than Adam, yet surviving him 112 years; nay, surviving Enoch, and perhaps witnessing his translation.

Then he died! He too, like Adam, paid the penalty, and gave up the forfeited life. It was not the debt of nature, as men idly speak, that he paid; it was the penalty of the righteous law. He died. The dust returned to dust, and the spirit to the God that gave it. He through whom the Prince of life was to come, died; and for now well-nigh 5000 years he has been resting in the tomb.

He, and Adam, and Abel have had a long sleeping time. Ours will be shorter; for the Lord is at hand; and, instead of 5000 years, it may be less than five. When Seth went down into the tomb, it had received few tenants; but now they are beyond number; and it is just when earth is overfilled, overcrowded with occupants, as if it could hold no more, that the gates of the grave burst open, and the ransomed ones arise.[1]

Vers. 9–11. '*And Enos lived ninety years, and begat Cainan.* 10. *And Enos lived, after he begat Cainan, eight hundred and fifteen years, and begat sons and daughters.* 11. *And all the days of Enos were nine hundred and five years: and he died.*'

Three verses contain the biography of Seth. God

[1] Suidas, upon the word *Seth*, has the following piece of information, derived from Jewish tradition :—'The men of that age called Seth a god, because he invented the Hebrew letters and the nomenclature of the stars ; and besides, they gave him the name of God in admiration of his great piety' (πολλὴν εὐσέβειαν αὐτοῦ θαυμάσαντες). He then, referring to Symmachus, affirms that the sons of Seth, Enos, and Enoch, were called by the name, 'Sons of God ;' and that afterwards these Sethites, or Sons of God, intermarried with the daughters of men, or Cainites (see *Lexicon*, vol. iii. pp. 305, 306). The Popish fabulists, however, have a much more wonderful story than the Jewish rabbis. One of their historians, Joannes Gerbrandus, thus relates it :—'In the year 1374, when the Christians and Saracens were digging in the valley of Jehoshaphat, they found a tumulus of bricks ; and opening it, they found a body of wonderful size, entire, with flowing beard and long hair, wrapped in sheep-skins, and above his head this inscription, carved in Hebrew—I am Seth, the third son of Adam ; I believe in Jesus Christ the Son of God, and in Mary the Virgin, His mother, who are to come out of my loins.' No wonder that the old author who quotes this, though a Romanist, should add, 'fides penes auctorem sit' (*Adagia ex Sanctorum Patrum Monumentis prompta, etc.*, p. 377, by Aloysius Novarinus—a folio, full of curious extracts, A.D. 1637).

counts this enough, and passes on. Enos comes next, and other three verses sum up his life. He is the *third* link of the wondrous chain through which the promise descends. He is a sinful man, like the rest; nay, as his name signifies, a weak, poor, mortal man; yet still one of the blessed succession through whom the Sinless One was to come; God showing thereby that He still reserves to Himself to bring the clean thing out of the unclean. Enos lives ninety years, and begets Cainan. thus fastening another link of the glorious chain. Afterwards he lives 815 years, begetting children; in all, 905; thus passing into Noah's days, and approaching towards the flood. Then dust returns to dust. He is seen to be not 'the Living One,' but an heir of mortality, a true child of him through whom death came into the world. How true is God to His threatenings! Not a jot of one of them shall fail. The oft-repeated phrase in this chapter, 'and he died,' is the testimony to God's truthfulness in His sentence upon Adam, and the proclamation of Satan's falsehood, when he said, 'Ye shall not surely die.'[1] 'And he died' is the solemn toll of the patriarchal funeral bell. How it makes us long for the 'trump of God,' when all this shall be reversed, and it shall be said of each, 'he liveth,' to die no more! What a contrast between this chapter and the 15th of First Corinthians! In the one, it is death swallowing up life; in the other,

[1] See *Pererius Valentinus*, vol. i. p. 775. He takes up the question why 'he died' occurs so often, but says little to the point, save showing that God thus manifested His own veracity, and the shortness of life, in comparison with the eternity that lies beyond.

it is life swallowing up death ; nay, it is death swallowed up of victory. Genesis is truly the book of DEATH.

Vers. 12–20. '*And Cainan lived seventy years, and begat Mahalaleel.*
13. *And Cainan lived, after he begat Mahalaleel, eight hundred and forty years, and begat sons and daughters.* 14. *And all the days of Cainan were nine hundred and ten years: and he died.* 15. *And Mahalaleel lived sixty and five years, and begat Jared.* 16. *And Mahalaleel lived, after he begat Jared, eight hundred and thirty years, and begat sons and daughters.* 17. *And all the days of Mahalaleel were eight hundred ninety and five years: and he died.* 18. *And Jared lived an hundred sixty and two years, and he begat Enoch.*
19. *And Jared lived, after he begat Enoch, eight hundred years, and begat sons and daughters.* 20. *And all the days of Jared were nine hundred sixty and two years: and he died.*'

The *fourth* link of the mighty chain is Cainan. His seems to have been an earlier manhood than the others, for at 70 he begat Mahalaleel. Thereafter he lived 840 years ; in all, 910. Then he returned to dust, and went to the grave of his fathers. The sentence still remained in force. Death still prevailed, even over those through whom the Prince of life was to come.

The *fifth* link is Mahalaleel. His is yet an earlier ripened manhood. At 65 he begets Jared, thereafter living 830 years ; in all, 895 ; then, like his fathers, he died. The patriarchal bell has tolled again ; yet he had lived far on into Noah's days ; a witness, doubtless, against the increasing ungodliness of the world, and a protester against the intermixture of the heavenly and the earthly, the sons of God and the daughters of men.

The *sixth* link is Jared. He ripens not so soon, yet the result of his late maturity is a wondrous birth. At the age of 162 he begets Enoch. Perhaps his faith was tried, like Abraham's; it was so long before this son of the promise came; yet, when he came, what an Isaac was he! What a child of gladness! And how must his father have rejoiced in such a son,—rejoiced even when bidding him farewell, as he went up to a home above, through the first opening that had been made in these heavens to admit ascending man.[1] Yet, after a long life,—962,—the second longest on record, 'he died.' Again the bell tolls, and again God's truth is proved against the lie of the devil. The sentence takes its due course, and he, the father of one who was not to taste of death, himself must die.

Vers. 21-24. '*And Enoch lived sixty and five years, and begat Methuselah.* 22. *And Enoch walked with God, after he begat Methuselah, three hundred years, and begat sons and daughters.* 23. *And all the days of Enoch were three hundred sixty and five years.* 24. *And Enoch walked with God; and he was not: for God took him.*'

Enoch's manhood is an early one, as if the early ripe are the early taken. He begets Methuselah when 65. This singularly holy man has sons and daughters, as if to show us that there is no special sanctity in the unmarried state. 'Forbidding to marry' was unknown in Enoch's days. He 'walked with God' as a husband and a father. He 'walked with God' as one loved and loving; as one who knew Jehovah, and who had got so intimate with Him, that he is described as 'the man that walked with God.' It was faith, as the apostle tells us

[1] He survived Enoch's translation 435 years. It must have seemed a marvellous thing to him, that his son should be singled out for going upwards, when all others were going downwards.

(Heb. xi. 5, 6), that began this walk, and it was faith that maintained it. It was this that first brought him nigh, and that afterwards kept him nigh. It was thus that his close, confidential, happy intercourse with God was commenced and carried on. For 300 years he thus walked with God, as husband and father, before his family, setting an example to his children; an example to the age.

He pleased God. God delighted in him. He was among the patriarchs what Daniel was among the prophets, and what John was among the disciples. He was the greatly-beloved one. And God had made no secret of His delight in him. He had, in some way not told, given clear indications of this, for 'before his translation he had this testimony, that he pleased God' (Heb. xi. 5).

God took him. At the age of 365 he went up to be with his God, not tasting that death which was laying low all around him. He did not wither down like the rest of those primeval trees. He was at once transplanted from the desert below to the paradise above. He had lived and worshipped within sight of the paradise below, and he is caught up at once into the better paradise. And there he has been for nearly 5000 years already. Not merely in soul, like other saints, but in body; glorified and incorruptible, like the children of the resurrection, or like those who shall be alive when the Lord returns. Such was God's love to Enoch; such was His desire to take him out of a world of sin, to snatch him away from the evil to come; such His desire to reward and bless him with the nearer vision of his glory; such His desire to have him near Himself, as if He could not bear his absence any longer, nor wait the appointed period of death; but carried him off in His fatherly arms, to be with Him in His glory.

Thus God showed that, while death was the law, still He could make exceptions; and these exceptions indicated the nature and extent of the deliverance which God was preparing for man. It would not rest till it had glorified even man's body, and given him a home above, an inheritance in the heavens, something better and more glorious than the earthly Eden. Hitherto man had looked up from earth to heaven; he was taught that ere long he should look down from heaven to earth. The link between him and his native earth was not to be broken, but to be established on a new footing, according to the distinction afterwards brought more fully out, between the earthly and the heavenly, the 'things terrestrial' and the 'things celestial.'

Other patriarchs are taken away by death from the evil to come, and 'hidden in the grave,' while wrath is passing over earth; but he is lifted up, and hidden in Jehovah's own pavilion. Even Noah, who also 'walked with God,' is but *carried through* the storm, sheltered in the ark, where he hears its violence beating on every side; but Enoch is caught up out of it,—transfigured and translated,—type of those who shall be caught up out of the fiery judgments of the last days, and brought into the royal chambers, there to consummate their espousals with the Lamb; and thence to issue forth, 'when the Lord comes WITH ten thousand of His saints to execute vengeance' on an ungodly world. For it is remarkable that Enoch's prediction, as preserved for us by Jude, is not of the Lord's coming *for* His saints, but of His coming *with* them. Enoch speaks in the name of those who have been caught up by him already, and who come along with Him to 'judge angels,' to 'judge the world,' to share the awful honour of accomplishing the Father's purpose of righteous recompense upon a world that has disowned His Son, and set at nought His grace (Ps. cxlix. 9).

Yet in Enoch's removal there is nothing said to indicate that it was striking or terrible to the world. No token was given,—no trumpet summoned the world to witness his ascent. 'He was not;' 'he was not found.' This is all we learn. He disappeared from among the children of men. He walked with God for three centuries; and in the midst of this calm walk he passed upward, as by an invisible ladder, into the presence of his God! How blessed, how congenial, this termination of a lifetime's walk with God! How natural the transition from the fellowship below to the nearer communion above! As in the case of Elijah, they might seek him, but 'he was not found.' Without a sick-bed, or a death-bed; without the pains or weaknesses of decaying age, in the full maturity of primeval manhood, he went up to the inheritance above. Such shall be the blessed lot of the waiting saints when the Lord returns. Let us watch with girded loins. Let our life be Enoch's walk with God.

Vers. 25-27. '*And Methuselah lived an hundred eighty and seven years, and begat Lamech.* 26. *And Methuselah lived, after he begat Lamech, seven hundred eighty and two years, and begat sons and daughters.* 27. *And all the days of Methuselah were nine hundred sixty and nine years: and he died.'*

The *eighth* link of the chain is Methuselah. His manhood ripens slowly, and he lives long. It was not till he was 187 that he begat Lamech. Sprung of a parent that had passed into the skies, and himself the longest liver upon earth, he is certainly no common man. Yet, though Enoch is his father, and though he resists death till the age of 969, still he yields at last. The last enemy conquers. The man of a thousand years dies. He seems given us as the type of the race in millennial times, when their 'days shall be as the days of a tree' (Isa. lxv. 22), as his father is the type of the glorified Church. The two classes are separate, yet closely connected together; the one, as it were, the offspring of the other,—the earthly the offspring of the heavenly.

Vers. 28–32. '*And Lamech lived an hundred eighty and two years, and begat a son;* 29. *And he called his name Noah,*[1] *saying, This same shall comfort us concerning* (or '*for*' or '*from*') *our work and toil of our hands, because of* (or '*from*') *the ground which the Lord hath cursed.* 30. *And Lamech lived, after he begat Noah, five hundred ninety and five years, and begat sons and daughters.* 31. *And all the days of Lamech were seven hundred seventy and seven years: and he died.* 32. *And Noah was five hundred years old: and Noah begat Shem, Ham, and Japheth.*'

The *ninth* link is Lamech. He begets Noah at the

[1] Noah signifies 'rest.' The word is not unlike נָחַם, to comfort, and seems used because of its expressive similarity. 'Work' denotes the lighter labour; 'toil' the heavier and more painful. This toil arose *from* the curse; and 'from' comes nearer the Hebrew than 'because of.'

age of 182, but lives a shorter life than most of the others,—only 777. Then he died. The sentence took its course on him. Dust returned to dust. It would seem that the original curse upon the ground began to be felt heavier. The population increased, and the means of subsistence grew more difficult to men, who knew but little about the tillage of the ground, and who probably shrank from such tillage of an accursed soil, laying out their labour the more on pastoral employments. Besides, probably, they had been, age after age, expecting the Deliverer, and He had not come. Hope deferred had made their heart sick, and their toil sorer. Enoch's prophecy, too, of the coming Deliverer would rouse up their sinking hope, and make them sanguine that the day of rest from their labour was at hand. Hence Lamech, in full expectation that such was the case, called his son Noah,—anticipating rest in his day, if not from him, as the expected seed of the woman. He did not read the signs of the times aright. He did not see that evil, and not good, was at the door. He was disappointed. Yet still we see in him the man of faith, looking for rest, and realizing it as coming in some way or other from the woman's seed. How much man felt his need of rest and comfort! How deeply did he sympathize with the groans of a travailing creation! How earnestly did he long for deliverance from the heavy curse! That deliverance came not in his day, yet he did not wait and hope in vain. And though the Lord should not come in our day, yet if we look for Him, we shall not lose our reward.

Just five years before the flood Lamech dies. He must have been a fellow-preacher of righteousness along with his son,—a fellow-witness during the 120 years of testimony,—a fellow-builder of the ark; father and son fighting the battles of the Lord together, and encouraging each other in their toil and suffering,—and then the aged saint is taken away from the evil to come, after having seen the ark all ready, and heard the assurances given by God to his son, that all should be well with him, though the looked-for rest was not to come in his day.

The *tenth* link is Noah. Of him we learn nothing at present, save that he was 500 years old ere he begat his three sons. What befell him and them we shall learn subsequently. This last verse of the chapter seems a sort of introduction to what follows in the next.

Such are the ten antediluvian links in the great chain, whose last link is the Son of God. Such are the ten early witnesses for God. They lived, and testified, and died. A single chapter contains ten biographies. Such is God's estimate of man, and man's importance! How unlike man's estimate of himself! How unlike are the biographies contained in this chapter to those volumes of biography over which are spread the story of a single life! Is not this man-worship, hero-worship? And was it not to prevent this that God has hid from us the details of primitive history,—everything that would magnify man and man's doings? Just as He has taken pains to prevent the grosser idolatries of sun-worship and star-worship, by exhibiting these orbs in the first chapter as His own handiwork; so in this fifth chapter He has sought to anticipate and prevent the more refined idolatry not only of past ages, when man openly and grossly deified man, but of these last days, when man is worshipping man in the most subtle of all ways, and multiplying the stories of man's wisdom, or prowess, or goodness, so as to hide God from our eyes, and give to man an independent position and importance, from which God has been so careful to exclude him. We might say, too, that this chapter is God's protest against that special development of hero-worship, which is to be exhibited in the last Antichrist, when God shall be set aside, and man be set up as all.

The importance attached to these recorded names is just this, that they belong to the line of the woman's seed. It was this that made them worthy of memory. The chain to which some precious jewel is attached, is chiefly noticeable because of the gem that it suspends. The steps which led up to the temple were mainly important because of the temple to which they led. So it was the connection of these ten worthies of the world's first age with the great Coming One, that gave them their importance. Standing where we now do, far down the ages, and looking back on the men of early days, we are like one tracing some great river back to its distant source amid the lonely hills. The varied beauties of its banks, however great, yet derive their chief attraction and interest from the mighty city reared upon its margin, at some turn of its far downward course, and from the mighty ones which that city has given birth to. It is Bethlehem that gives all its interest to the river whose beginnings this chapter traces; or rather, it is He who was there born of a woman,—Jesus the son of Abraham, the son of Adam. Save in their bearing upon Him, how unmeaning do these names appear! It is not in sacrifices alone, or promises, or types, that we are to look for Jesus, but even in such bare genealogies as those before us. It is He who gives fulness and interest to them all. It is from Him that they derive all that brightness which, to the natural eye, is quite invisible. And from them we rejoice to learn, that Jesus of Bethlehem is as truly the Son of Adam as He is the Son of God.

These all died. They *died.* And death has been passing upon all men since, godly or ungodly. We are carried to the same house to which the patriarchs, one after the other, descended. We are laid side by side with Adam, and Seth, and Lamech, and Noah. But our hope burns brighter now. We shall not have so long to sleep as they have had. They were laid to sleep just when the night was falling, and they have had to sleep through the whole hours of darkness. But the morn is near. The day will soon break. We shall not have long to sleep. It may be that some of us shall scarcely have laid down our wearied heads and limbs, till the voice of the archangel shall awake us. Then it shall not be written of us, 'he died;' but of each of us, as we awake, it shall be said, 'he rose again.'

CHAPTER VI.

Vers. 1, 2.[1] '*And it came to pass, when men began to multiply on* (or *over*) *the face of the earth* (Heb. *the ground* or *soil*), *and daughters were born unto them,* 2. *That the sons of God saw the daughters of men that they were fair; and they took them wives of all which they chose.*'

THE original law of increase is still in force. Sin has not cancelled nor weakened it. The sentence of death against man does not interfere with it; nay, rather seems to give it new impulse,—as if creation, threatened with death, urged forward all the processes

[1] The Septuagint makes this chapter to begin with the last verse of the preceding, as if the statement respecting Noah and his sons (ver. 32) were the introduction to what follows. The ו here, like the Greek καί, is not so much a link with what goes before as an introduction to what follows, and corresponds with our particle 'now.' The expression, 'on the face of the earth,' might be more literally rendered 'over (עַל) the surface of the ground,'—alluding to the population *spreading itself out* as well as *increasing*. We ought to notice, too, that the word translated *men* is singular, yet it is said 'born to *them*.' The passage might run thus:—'Now it came to pass that men began to multiply over the ground, and daughters were born to them.' There ought to be a period at this verse. Hävernick remarks,—'We must pass over the genealogies in chap. v., which interrupt the history, and join the passage with iv. 26. Here it is the progeny of Seth that is spoken of, and the worship of Jehovah which they practised; by which the narrator has evidently made sufficient preparation for "sons of God," especially when, in ver. 25, they are designated as a whole, a seed (comp. Deut. xiv. 1; Ex. iv. 22).'

of life to prevent its own extinction; or rather, as if God, who loves not to see His works destroyed, and who has a glorious purpose in view, were hastening on the different steps, that so the days of evil may be shortened.

Men multiply over the earth, though, perhaps, at a slower rate than now. The whole race now has become evil, so that the name 'man' has become, as the word 'world' did in later days, an expression for the ungodly. Earth is becoming what David afterwards felt it to be, when he saw the faithful failing 'from among *the children of men*' (Ps. xii. 1), so that there were hardly any left on earth save 'the children of men;' or when, seeing himself surrounded with an evil generation, he said, 'How great is Thy goodness, which Thou hast laid up for them that fear Thee; which Thou hast wrought for them that trust in Thee *before the sons of men!*' (Ps. xxxi. 19); or when he speaks of 'the works of *men*' (Ps. xvii. 4); or when he speaks of his 'soul being among lions, even among *the sons of men*' (Ps. lvii. 4). Thus we find (even in this chapter) that the words 'man,' and 'flesh,' and 'world,' which are not in themselves names of evil, are becoming synonymous with ungodliness.

To 'men' daughters are born. Sons, of course, as well as daughters are born; but daughters are specially mentioned, because of the part they act in the scene that follows. It is a scene which is the natural summing up and result of what began in Lamech, when woman's beauty took the lead in seducing man from God. It is in the region of the beautiful that Satan lays his most subtle snares. He combines in one the lust of the flesh and the lust of the eye. It is the comeliness of woman that gives new impulse to the ungodliness of earth.

The earth is a scene of gaiety and lust. 'Man' and his daughters overspread it. To the eye of the flesh, it is a bright display of earth's perfection. The song and the dance, and the fair attire, and the rich gem, and the ringing mirth,—these make up the sum of this 'magic of bliss,' in which the world was revelling.[1]

The fame of these 'daughters of beauty' spreads. Eyes are attracted to them that should not have looked on them; and hearts are beguiled by them that should have repelled their advances. But as it was the beauty of the daughters of Moab that ensnared Israel, and led on to wickedness which drew down God's stroke of judgment, so did the attractions of these daughters of men entangle those who stood, in reference to God before the flood, as Israel did in later days.

For there were still some that 'dwelt alone,' and were not mingled with the ungodly. They were few, but age after age they held fast to the early faith. Adam was their head; for long did he dwell among them; and he was known as the son of God (Luke iii. 38).[2] Seth and Enos, and the band of patriarchs, were

[1] See Milton's description of the time and the scene in *Paradise Lost*, book xi. 581–592—

> 'A bevy of fair women richly gay,
> In gems and wanton dress.'

[2] If Luke drew his catalogue from the regular and legal genealogical tables, as doubtless he did, then it is plain that Adam's name had been entered in these tables as 'son of God.'

called by Adam's name; and even after his death they and their children clung to Adam's faith, and worshipped Adam's God. When Cain and his posterity spread over the earth, Adam and Seth, and their offspring, still clustered round the primeval home, and worshipped at the gate of paradise, within sight of the flaming sword and the cherubim within. This region was to them what Canaan was to Israel; and as Israel in after days got the name of sons of God, so did these in the earlier age; for the name of the redeemed has been one throughout—'sons of God.' Identified with Him who is the Son of God, and washed in His blood, they get His name.[1]

These sons of God, though for ages dwelling alone, at length came into contact with the ungodly. The

[1] It is said that in the Old Testament none but angels are called 'sons of God.' In proof of this, Job i. 6 and ii. 1 are adduced; but these are at least doubtful. The only apparently undoubted one is Job xxxviii. 7, 'The sons of God shouted for joy;' where, however, we may notice that the article is awanting in the Hebrew before 'God,' so that this passage stands alone. But admitting that angels are called sons of God, we do not need to concede that men may not be called the same. In Luke iii. 38, Adam is called the son of God. In Ex. iv. 22, 23, God calls Israel His 'son;' and that this is not in any inferior sense, is proved by Hos. xi. 1, which, referring originally to Israel, is applied by Matthew to Christ. In Isa. xlv. 11, God calls them His 'sons;' and in Jer. xxxi. 21, He calls Ephraim His 'dear son;' and in the same chapter, at the ninth verse, God says, 'I am a father unto Israel, and Ephraim is my first-born,'—the very words which are used in reference to Messiah, Ps. lxxxix. 27. See also Hos. i. 10, 'Ye are the sons of the living God;' Deut. xiv. 1, 'Ye are the sons of Jehovah, your God.' And one of the apostle's objects in the 3d and 4th of Galatians is to show that we are brought into the participation ot sonship, such as Abraham had, long before the law

tide of the world's population gradually swelled till it reached the confines of Eden, and there it flung ashore its glittering gems, which soon attracted the eyes of the inhabitants of the sacred region. They picked them up, adorned themselves with them, and soon the separating line between the two regions disappeared. The sons of God were captivated with the beauty of these daughters of men, and entered into marriage affinity with them.[1] Thus the godly are entangled and corrupted. Thus the ungodly became more ungodly still. The barrier is quite broken down between the seed of the woman and the seed of the serpent. Thus is not merely an individual ruined, as in the case of Samson; not merely a nation, as in the case of Israel; but a whole world is destroyed. Such are the evils flowing from

was given by faith in Christ,—'Ye are all the sons of God (υἱοὶ Θεοῦ—just as the patriarchs were) by faith in Christ Jesus' (Gal. iii. 26). The Church's privilege is to be brought into that standing and relationship towards God which Abraham had enjoyed, and which had been known from the beginning, but which the introduction of the law had narrowed or curtailed. The verse above cited means, 'Ye all, who believe in Jesus Christ, Abraham's true seed, are placed on Abraham's footing, and get Abraham's name, υἱὸς Θεοῦ,'—a name which appears to have been much better known in patriarchal times than we imagine. Philo writes: 'Ye who have knowledge are rightfully addressed as the sons of the one God, as Moses says, "Ye are the sons of Jehovah, your God."'—(*De Confusione Linguarum*, sec. 28.)

[1] There is no proof of unlawful violence here. The expression is a common one to intimate the lawful marriage union—'they took themselves wives;' as the Lord expressed it, 'they married and were given in marriage.' The words, however, probably intimate that, like Lamech and the Cainites, they took as many wives as they pleased. Mark the contrast between the words 'whom *they chose*,' and 'a prudent wife is *from the Lord*.'

the lust of the flesh and of the eye! We have seen it in Lamech's case; we see it in the case before us on a larger scale; we see it in after ages in Sodom, in Israel, in Samson, in David, in Solomon. What endless evils have flowed from impure desires! What corruption of piety; what strifes, and hatred, and wars! One of the marks of the last days is 'incontinence;' and both Peter and Jude have left warnings for the Church as to these special sins. Let us mark, too, the danger of unequal marriages. 'Only in the Lord' is the apostle's rule; and when this is wilfully neglected,—when beauty and wealth, instead of piety, are preferred,—then what sin is there, what peril, to the individual soul, to the family, to the Church, to the land! See Gen. xxxvi. 35; 1 Kings xi. 1–6; Ezra ix. 12; Neh. xiii. 23–28; Mal. ii. 11; 1 Cor. vii. 39; 2 Cor. vi. 14.[1]

Ver. 3. '*And the Lord said, My Spirit shall not always strive with man, for that he also is flesh: yet his days shall be an hundred and twenty years.*'

Perhaps these words were spoken by the lips of Noah. It was thus that, as God's preacher of righteousness, he condemned the world (Heb. xi. 11), speaking to that generation, in the name of Jehovah, both of grace and righteousness, both of His long-suffering to the sinner, and of His hatred of the sin. It is of the Holy Spirit

[1] How expressive these words of the prophet Malachi, 'Judah hath married the daughter of a strange god;' Judah, of whom, in the previous verse, he had called God the father,—distinguishing him thereby from the heathen, as if Judah only could be called the son of God!

that he speaks; of Him who 'moved upon the face of the waters' at the first, and who now is seen moving upon the more turbid waters of the ungodly world. It is He whom God calls here, as elsewhere (Prov. i. 23; Isa. xlii. 1; Ezek. xxxix. 29; Joel ii. 28; Hag. ii. 5; Zech. iv. 6; Matt. xii. 18), 'My Spirit;'—*mine*, in opposition to man's spirit, to Satan, to the flesh. The 'striving' here spoken of implies conflict between God and the sinner, nay 'judgment' also, as the word seems to indicate,—God contending with man in righteous love,—sitting in judgment on his sins, yet seeking to win himself. But all this love is vain. The striving fails. Man, like Israel, resists and vexes the Holy Ghost. He refuses to be won. He accomplishes this awful victory over God,—the victory, of which the trophy is his own perdition. God's name for man's corruption is 'flesh,'—that 'flesh' in which 'dwelleth no good thing.' The words 'man,' and 'world,' and 'flesh,' have originally no bad meaning. But when overflowing ungodliness has filled man, and the world, and the flesh, with sin, then these words become synonymous with pure and unmixed evil. God's Spirit had been striving long with man; but there must be a limit to this; and when man has reached this limit,—when he has become a mass of utter sin,—then God's Spirit withdraws, and he is given up to a reprobate mind. Yet in resolving to let man alone, that he may ripen for judgment, God gives a time of respite,—an hundred and twenty years. A long day of grace indeed! God will not take advantage of man in any way. He gives him full time to turn. He is long-suffering to the uttermost. How vast His compassions! How great is His unwillingness to smite! How infinite His patient love!

Ver. 4. '*There were giants in the earth in those days* (Heb. *the Nepheelim were on the earth in those days*); *and also after that, when the sons of God came in unto the daughters of men, and they bare children to them, the same became mighty men which were of old, men of renown.*'[1]

Earth's wickedness had long been on the increase. There had been mighty men (like Lamech before, and like Nimrod afterwards) on the earth; but this sad union gives a fresh impulse to the ungodliness, and raises up a new race of giant-sinners. The union between the Church and the world led to physical improvement; to a higher perfection in all things pertaining to the flesh, bodily strength, natural accomplishments, and everything that man calls 'progress.' But it made the flood of evil to swell the more rapidly, when thus the windows of heaven and the fountains of the great deep mingled their mighty stores, as if in prefigurement of the coming flood of waters, and the two sources of its overflow, the one from above, the other from beneath. That which 'letted' did 'let,' until it was taken out of the way; and when that which divided the waters

[1] The origin of the word 'Nepheelim' is hard to settle; but the meaning of it is sufficiently well expressed by 'giants,'—mighty men of prowess and stature. See Num. xiii. 33, the only other place where the word occurs. The latter clause of the verse is more literally rendered by the Septuagint: *ἐκεῖνοι ἦσαν οἱ γιγαντες οἱ ἀπ' αἰῶνος, οἱ ἄνθρωποι οἱ ὄνομαστοι*—'these were (*or* are) the giants who were of old, men of name.'

above from the waters beneath was removed, then the tides mingled, the flood of sin swelled up, 'the wicked one' was revealed, whom the Lord swept away with the stroke of His overwhelming sword, leaving righteous Noah lord of the earth in room of those who had so long usurped the sway.[1]

Ver. 5. '*And God saw that the wickedness of man was great in the earth, and that every imagination of the thoughts of his heart was only evil continually.*'

This scene is represented as coming specially under the eye of God. He looked down from heaven, and saw! (Gen. xviii. 21; Ps. xiv. 2.) What further need of witnesses? Here is one better than a thousand human witnesses. He saw, and could not be mistaken. He saw, and would not misrepresent. Five chapters before, we are told that God saw that all was good; now He sees that all is evil. Nothing but evil meets His eye, in the outer or the inner world of man. He had made this world not fifteen hundred years before; it was then holy and blessed, fit dwelling for Himself and all holy beings. Now not a trace of its excellency remains. All is evil. There was 'wickedness:' it was 'in the earth,' His own earth; it was the wickedness of 'man,' the very being whom He had formed in His own image; it was 'great.' And surely that which God calls 'great

[1] This is only one of the many points in which the days of Noah resemble the day of the Son of man. One of the best books on this subject, though it does not bring out the above parallel, is the volume of Mr. Maitland, *Discourses on the History of Noah's Day.*

wickedness' must be great indeed. But it is not the outer world alone that is evil. The inner world is worse. The fountain has become thoroughly polluted. Man's 'heart is evil;' the 'thoughts' of his heart are evil; the 'imaginations' of the thoughts of his heart are evil; nay, 'every imagination' of the thoughts of his heart is evil; nay, 'only evil,' and that 'continually.' Such is God's picture of a human heart! What difference now between a man and a devil? Is earth now any fairer than hell? Such is the race of man when ripe for judgment. Is not, then, that judgment righteous? Is it strange that God should sweep such a race away? Nay, is it not strange that He should bear with it so long, and be so unwilling to destroy it, as to suspend His stroke for a hundred and twenty years, and all this while deal with it in patient pity, yearning over it with unquenched love?

Ver. 6. '*And it repented the Lord that He had made man on the earth, and it grieved Him at His heart.*'

While thus describing man's guilt, God still owns him as His handiwork. We here read, not that man 'had been made,' but that 'He had made man.' God does not keep out of view the fact, that the being who had become so thoroughly evil was the very man whom He had made. There is no hiding of this apparent failure of His plans. It is said that He 'repented' that He had made man; and though in one sense God cannot 'repent' (Num. xxiii. 19), yet in another He does repent; nor does He hesitate to speak of His 'repentings'

(Hos. xi. 8).[1] For though He is unchangeable, yet that unchangeableness is no arbitrary or unreasonable thing, as if no altered circumstances could lead God to change His mind. That would be the unchangeableness of folly, not of wisdom. Besides, let us remember that it is unchangeableness of purpose that we ascribe to God as His perfection, not unchangeableness of procedure. Nay, it is through the very variation of His procedure that He carries out His unchangeable purpose. But it is added, 'it grieved Him at His heart.' The expression is so strong as to be startling. It makes us ask, Is it right to speak thus of God? Is it right to speak so; for it is God who thus speaks of Himself. And how deep the insight which He thus gives us into His heart; how marvellous the discovery which He thus makes to us of His yearnings over rebellious man! It is the same word that He uses in Ps. lxxviii. 40, when He speaks of Israel 'grieving Him in the desert;' and in Isa. lxiii. 10, when He speaks of their vexing His Holy Spirit. Only it is stronger than these, for it is, 'it grieved (or afflicted) Him at His heart.'

[1] The word נָחַם is, as Robertson gives the meaning in this place, 'to express deep sorrow, to repent.' It occurs frequently, sometimes in reference to God, and sometimes in reference to man. For the former, see Ex. xxxii. 14; Deut. xxxii. 36; Judg. ii. 18; Ps. cvi. 45; Joel ii. 13; Jonah iii. 10; in all which passages, while it is true that God speaks after the manner of men, yet He also shows us this, that change of mind, when circumstances change, is not inconsistent with His unchangeable character; as, for example, when the sinner is brought to repent, then God changes His mind and procedure towards him. The pardon of the sinner is the result of this change on the part of God.

It was not that an *unexpected* crisis had arisen. It was not that God's purpose was frustrated. It was not that God is subject to like passions as we. It was not that He had at length ceased to care for the works of His hands, and to wish that they had never been. But God is here speaking after the manner of men. He is looking at facts simply as they are, without reference to past or future. He isolates or separates them, and looking at them as they stand alone, He declares what He thinks and feels. Nor do God's eternal purposes alter His estimate of events. It was God's purpose that Christ should be delivered up and slain; yet that did not alter God's estimate of the crime. Each action of man is in one aspect a necessary link in God's mighty purpose, yet each must be weighed and measured by itself. God is looking at the scene just as a man would look at it, and expressing Himself in language such as man would have done in such circumstances. He sees all the present misery and ruin which the scene presents, and they truly affect Him according to their nature; and as they affect Him, so does He speak in the words of man. The scene affects God just as it would have affected a wise and just but most tender-hearted parent; and His words correspond to this. The feelings implanted in man must, to some extent, be the same as those existing in God. For man was made in God's image in respect to his feelings as truly as in respect to his intellect. The human heart is the counterpart of the divine. Hence it is that God so often uses the language of human feeling when referring to Himself. God's love, hatred, wrath, pity, grief, are all *real;* and they correspond to those feelings which He has implanted in man; with only this difference, that in God there is no admixture of sin.

Yes, God is 'grieved at His heart.' These are His own words. Let us not explain them away. He is grieved at the change which sin has made in the works of His hands. He is grieved at the dishonour thus brought upon Himself. He is grieved at man's misery and ruin,—so fearful, so eternal! He is grieved because He must Himself be the pronouncer of man's sentence, the inflicter of man's doom. How unutterably gracious must this God be with whom we have to do! How unwilling to destroy, how willing to bless and to save! With what a yearning love does He bend over rebellious man!

Ver. 7. '*And the Lord said, I will destroy man, whom I have created, from the face of the earth; both man and beast, and the creeping thing, and the fowls of the air: for it repenteth me that I have made them.*'[1]

Probably these words were spoken to Noah, 'the preacher of righteousness,' or to some of the other of the righteous patriarchs then on the earth, that they might proclaim the message of judgment. Not without special meaning are the commencing words, 'And Jehovah said.' He lifts up His voice and makes public declaration of His purpose of judgment, that man may be fully warned; that

[1] 'I will destroy man,—even that very man whom I created, not regarding the work of my hands,—from that very earth which I made for him,—man and all these living creatures which I made for his benefit.' Thus the words may be paraphrased. The reader may remember Ovid's words: 'Perdendum mortale genus.'—*Metam.* i. 188.

he may know when ruin comes that it is no sudden outburst of vengeance, but the coming forth or carrying out of a calm and deliberate purpose.[1]

God's declaration is, 'I will destroy man!' He has purposed, and who shall gainsay Him, or disannul His purpose? He will 'blot out' man,—He will sweep him away as men do what they loathe.[2] When He 'blots out' our sins, on our believing the record of His grace, He blots them out entirely, removing them from us as far as the east is from the west; so He will 'destroy' man as completely as He will remove sin; He will 'blot out' these *sinners* of an unbelieving world as thoroughly as He 'blots out' the *sins* of believing Noah and his children.

It is *the* man whom He has created that He is thus to 'blot out.' As He blots out the sin that He has *not* made, so He blots out the sinner whom He has made. He spares not the work of His own hands. Words of deep dread, truly! 'I will destroy man whom I have created.' Solemn warning and rebuke to those who flippantly taunt us with believing in the eternal doom of the ungodly, and say, 'Oh! God did not make man to destroy him.' True, He did not make him to destroy him; but He will do it! He did not make him for the dark-

[1] 'Before weird (doom) there's word,' says the Northern proverb.

[2] The word is מָחָה, the same as is used for the washing away of filth. Deut. xxix. 20; Ps. li. 1; Isa. xliv. 22. Sept. ἀπαλείψω; Vulg. *delebo*. The word translated 'destroy' in the 13th verse is שָׁחַת, the same word as 'corrupted,' ver. 12: as if God would say, 'They have *corrupted* themselves; I will *corrupt* them; I will make them reap the fruit of what they have sown.' The Septuagint gives καταφθείρω; the Vulgate, *disperdam*.

ness, but for the light; yet the everlasting darkness shall be his lot. He desires not the death of the sinner, yet he shall die. He did not make man for hell, nor hell for man, yet the wicked shall be turned into hell. 'I will destroy man whom I have created.' He will do it Himself; with His own hands will He destroy His own workmanship. He will not leave him to fall to pieces himself, nor merely make his own conscience his tormentor, as some men speak; He will execute judgment Himself. And all this because He is the 'righteous God that loveth righteousness.'

He will destroy him 'from the face of the earth.' The earth is not to be destroyed in this ruin. It is not to receive any further curse on account of man's sin; nay, it is to be delivered from a burden, an intolerable load of defilement that had been accumulating for fifteen centuries. Though God had cursed the earth, yet He always makes it appear that it is for man's sake, not its own. 'The creation was made subject to vanity, not willingly' (Rom. viii. 20). Nay, we might say that here there is a purpose of *grace* intimated respecting the earth, when judgment is proclaimed against its dwellers. God's object by the flood of waters was to *cleanse* the earth of its pollution, just as hereafter He shall purge it by fire, removing on that day not merely the incumbent wickedness, but *burning out* the curse from its veins. Water can do the former; but fire is needed for the latter.

But though the earth itself is not to share man's ruin, the beasts and fowls and creeping things must be swept away along with him. They must share his doom, as being more closely linked to him than the material earth. What, then, must sin be in the sight of the Holy One, when it draws after it such boundless ruin? Whatever is most intimately connected with man, the sinner, must perish with him. Man's first sin introduced the curse, but it did not destroy the creatures; now, however, sin has so swelled, so risen and overflowed creation, that God's righteousness insists upon execution being done even upon the unintelligent creation, that He might thus publish before the universe, by the voice of an all-devouring flood, how terribly He hated that which man had done.

Then the statement of the sixth verse is repeated: 'For it repenteth me that I have made them.' How solemnly does this *reiteration* of God's mind fall upon our ears! How deeply does He feel the sin, the wrong, the dishonour that man had done! How profound the compassion for those very sinners whom, in His righteousness, He was thus compelled to sweep away![1] How awful must have been the scene presented to His view, when, after surveying it, He was constrained to say, in reference to the creatures which He had made, 'It repenteth me that I have made them'! Can any ignorance—can any madness exceed theirs who would make light of sin, who would treat it as a mere transient disease, which is in the course of ages working itself out of the system, and will soon pass away? Terrible will be thy position, O man, when God comes to say this of thee! It will be terrible

[1] Ovid's verse is very striking, as if borrowed from this:

> 'Quæ Pater ut summa vidit Saturnius arce,
> Ingemit.'—*Metam.* i. 163.

enough when thou art brought to feel, 'Oh that I had never been made!' but it will be more overwhelming still when God comes and says, 'Oh that I had never created thee!'[1]

[1] The Fathers speculated much and often on the nature and feelings of God, raising all manner of questions as to His anger, love, hatred, repentance, etc. There is much more, however, of philosophy than of Scripture in their disquisitions; and Cicero, Plato, etc., are oftener quoted than Paul or John. Minucius Felix has some good remarks in his *Octavius*, p. 144, Ouzel's edition. Lactantius, besides many general references to the subject, has a long discourse, *De ira Dei*, in which there are good statements and well-pointed arguments; but a woful lack of Scripture. He quotes Plato's remark, 'Nemo prudens punit quia peccatum est, sed ne peccetur,' ἵνα μη αὖθις ἀδικηση; a remark which, though lauded in our day, is but a one-sided axiom, which, if accepted as the whole truth, would set aside moral guilt, and do away with all necessity for a *judgment*. His treatise throws no light upon the subject. It merely affirms the truth, that if anger be denied to God, so must love, etc.—'si non ira est in eo nec gratia est,' sec. 4. It is curious to notice the opposite sentiments of the ancients on this point. Ovid, referring to the world's wretchedness, speaks of the great Father as 'groaning,' *ingemens;* whereas Epicurus is represented as saying, respecting the nature of God—

'Semota a nostris rebus, sejunctaque longe,
Nam privata dolore omni, privata periclis,
Ipsa suis pollens opibus, nil indiga nostri
Nec bene promeritis capitur, nec tangitur ira.'

Augustine's remarks are more satisfactory: 'The anger of God is no perturbation of His mind, but a judgment assigning sin its punishment. His revolving and re-revolving (Augustine follows the Sept. ἐνεθυμηθη, "He pondered") is but the unchangeable ordering of changeable things ("Mutandarum rerum immutabilis ratio"). For God repents not of what He does, like a man; for His opinion ("sententia") of everything is as fixed as His foreknowledge is certain. But Scripture without such expressions cannot insinuate itself familiarly into all kinds of men. . . . This it could not do if it did not bend itself towards us, nay stoop to us sometimes, when lying prostrate.'—*De Civ. Dei*, book xv. chap. 25.

Ver. 8. '*But Noah found grace in the eyes of the Lord.*'

There is one exception. The race is not to be wholly swept away. There is a remnant according to the election of grace. God has mercy on whom He will have mercy (Rom. ix. 15). God's purpose shall stand, in spite of the world's sin. Not by nature above the level of an unbelieving world, Noah by grace stands fast. 'Not of works, but of Him that calleth.' He rises when others fall. He rises higher, the lower the rest sink. For Jehovah has laid hold on him; and Jehovah upholds him. Nor was it because he was better than the rest that God's choice fell on him; but he was made better in consequence of that choice. And where is the believing man that cannot trace his faith, his love, his whole change, to the same eternal fountainhead?

God's description of a saint, then, is *one that has found favour in His sight.* And this is the saint's own account of himself—'Then was I in His eyes as one that found favour' (Cant. viii. 10). This is all he can say for himself,—all the account he can give of the origin of his sonship, the cause of his spiritual change. How blessed to be able thus simply to trace all that is good in us directly to the sovereign will and love of Jehovah!

Ver. 9. '*These are the generations*[1] *of Noah: Noah was a just man, and perfect in his generations, and Noah walked with God.*'

The general testimony to Noah was, that he 'had found

[1] 'Generations.' This word occurs about forty times in the Old Testament, and is always translated in our version by the same word:

favour with God.' The fuller and particular testimony now follows. It is God's own opinion of His saint. It takes up three features.

1. He was a *just* man,—a man whom God accounted righteous. It seems to be with reference to this expression that the apostle calls him 'an heir of the righteousness which is by faith' (Heb. xi. 7). There is righteousness *on* him and *in* him; and God recognises both. The surety-righteousness of the Son of God places him in the *state* of a just man; and the inward righteousness of the Spirit gives him the *character* of a just man. He stands out before us, holy in a generation of the unholy, justified in a world of the condemned.

2. He was *perfect* in his age.[1] He stood out 'complete' as a man of God, in all the various features which constitute that character; as the apostle speaks when he tells of the fitness of the divine word to make 'the man of

Gen. v. 7, xi. 10, xxxvi. 1, etc. Calvin, followed by Rosenmüller, Dathe, etc., extends its meaning, and gives as its signification, 'Tota vitæ historia.' Paulus Fagius renders it, 'These are the things which befell Noah and his family.' Our version in this same verse gives generation as the sense of דוֹר, which occurs about 150 times; and almost always in the sense of age, or men of a particular age: Ps. xcv. 10; Eccles. i. 4. The Septuagint translates the former word by γένεσις, the latter by γένεα. Calvin remarks that the plural (generations) is used to show that it was not in one age, but several, that he kept his integrity.

[1] The words are literally, 'Noah, a just man, was perfect in his time.' The word means whole, complete—'a full year' (Lev. xxv. 30); 'a *whole* day' (Josh. x. 13). It occurs about fifty times in the sense of 'without blemish' as applied to sacrifices. Noah is 'without spot,'—a complete sacrifice,—body, soul, and spirit,—and so accepted of the Lord. Gesenius makes it refer simply to moral integrity. Scripture connects it with sacrifice and priesthood.

God perfect, thoroughly furnished unto all good works' (2 Tim. iii. 17). He was not a man without sin; for 'there is not a just man upon earth, that doeth good and sinneth not' (1 Kings viii. 46; 2 Chron. vi. 36; Eccles. vii. 20); but he was perfect as pertaining to the conscience, and in all the parts of his character and life he bore the stamp of righteousness,—as is written of Zacharias and Elizabeth, 'They were both righteous before God, walking in all the commandments and ordinances of God blameless' (Luke i. 6). Yes, he was 'perfect in his generation.' He stood alone; yet he *stood.* He held aloof from the evil around. He had taken on nothing of the pollution which abounded. He held fast in an age of matchless sin, when he had none to side with him but God.

3. He walked with God. The word is strong and peculiar, denoting the repetition and energy of the act. He walked and walked; yea, walked with fervent and untiring energy.[1] Through centuries he lived on, walking with God, as Enoch had done before him; nay, during part of the time, with Enoch at his side; for only of these two is the expression used. It is as if

[1] Both in this verse and in chap. v. 23, 24, it is the *Hithpael* that is used; in the former the Hithpael preterite, in the latter the Hithpael future (with the ו conversive). It is this that makes it so expressive. See Job i. 7; Zech. i. 10, vi. 7; Ezek. i. 13. The Septuagint makes it εὐηρέστησε τῷ Θεῷ. Rungius has some excellent remarks on Noah's standing alone, and preserving a testimony to the 'woman's seed,' also on the reproaches he must have endured from these 'giants.' He calls him the martyr of martyrs: 'Vere fuit martyr martyrum Noah,' p. 295.

God had come down to earth and walked through it, with Enoch on one side, and Noah on the other. Of Abraham it is said, 'Walk *before* me, and be thou perfect;' but it would almost seem as if this walk of Enoch and Noah were something nearer and more blessed than this.

Ver. 10. '*And Noah begat three sons, Shem, Ham, and Japheth.*'

This holy man is a husband and a father. For the marriage bond is holy, nay, 'honourable in all' (Heb. xiii. 2), and the paternal relationship excellent and blessed. To the members of Noah's family the whole human race was ere long to be reduced. Such is the narrow isthmus between the old world and the new; such is the remnant to which the Church of God is brought. How will Satan triumph at the prospect of cutting off the seed of the woman; nay, of compelling God (let the expression be pardoned) to cut off that seed Himself, and so to break His first promise, as well as destroy the world's one hope! The seed of the woman was fast becoming extinct. The promise hung upon a thread. The Church's hope was narrowed to a single saint. Thus God lets matters go to a crisis,—an extremity,—that His own wisdom and power may be brought out, and pride hidden from man. It is all of God.

Shem is named *first* in this list, though Japheth was the elder (x. 21). Like Judah, he was to have the preeminence,—the birthright; and this not by any natural right, but solely by the choice of God. How often does God teach us in His word that all honour is of Him, and that the highest pre-eminence which He could confer on a man was to make him a link in Messiah's line. Connection with Christ, even before He came, was God's badge of nobility—His star of honour. It is so still. Connection with Christ, through belief of the Father's testimony to Him, is man's truest, highest honour, either now on earth or hereafter in the kingdom.

Vers. 11, 12. '*The earth also* (Heb. *And*, or *Now, the earth*) *was corrupt before God; and the earth was filled with violence.* 12. *And God looked upon the earth, and, behold, it was corrupt: for all flesh had corrupted his way upon the earth.*'

It was 'corrupt.'[1] It had become a decaying and abominable carcase; defiled and hateful; the very opposite of that which God had made it. For though it was not made, like the future inheritance, 'incorruptible,' still it was 'incorrupt.' There was no blemish on it; no sin; no taint; no stain.

It was corrupt 'before God.' Full in His sight and under His eye, it revelled in its vileness. Its wickedness was daring, and dark in its defiance of God. He declares this not as one relating a thing from report, but narrating what had come under His own eye. Yes, He looked on it. He hated the sin; yet He bore long with it. Such are His compassions!

'The earth was filled with violence.' Injustice, cruelty, rapine, wrong,—these formed the sum of its story. Like

[1] The Jews refer this specially to licentiousness, and to the strange intermarriages previously spoken of.

a mighty sea, violence had swelled up, till every plain and valley were overflowed. It was drenched in sin ere it was drowned in water.[1]

Such was earth! Transformed from paradise into worse than a wilderness; from being the seat of God to be like Babylon, the abode of devils, giants, murderers, and all unclean and hateful things. What has sin done! What can it not do! How quickly can it empty a soul or a world, of all good, and fill them with all evil! The frosts of winter do not so destroy the tender plant as sin does the soul or the world into which it finds its way.

But the awful description is repeated in the next verse, and God Himself is declared to be the witness of the evil. *God looked at the earth.* He surveyed it, so that there might be no mistake; and that no man might say that He judged hastily or untruly. He will not misjudge His creatures; nor will He allow them to suppose that He is doing so. *Behold, it was corrupt.* There could be no mistake. The divine eye could not be deceived. *All*

[1] Montgomery thus describes the scene :—

'But as they multiplied from clime to clime,
Embolden'd by their elder brother's crime,
They spurn'd obedience to the patriarch's yoke;
The bonds of nature's fellowship they broke;
The weak became the victims of the strong,
And earth was fill'd with violence and wrong.'
—*World before the Flood*, canto i.

Du Bartas thus describes the scene :—

'From these profane, proud, cursed kisses sprung
A cruel brood, feeding on blood and wrong;
Fell giants strange, of haughty hand and mind,
Plagues of the world, and scourges of mankind.'

flesh had corrupted its way upon the earth.[1] The whole race had gone astray, and become vile. Outwardly as well as inwardly all was evil. Thus sin spreads and widens, as well as deepens. It has no end. It never dies out, nor loses its hatefulness. God bears long with it. He allows evil as well as good to ripen. He will not pluck the unripe evil, any more than the unripe good. It is not till 'the grapes are fully ripe' that the clusters of earth's vine are gathered (Rev. xiv. 18). Every sin is rendering earth riper for the last vengeance, and preparing it for the flood of fire.[2]

Ver. 13. '*And God said unto Noah, The end of all flesh is come before me; for the earth is filled with violence through them: and, behold, I will destroy them with the earth.*'[3]

It is to Noah, face to face, that God now speaks. The

[1] We may just notice here the use of *his*, where we should have *its*. Attention to this will help to clear up several difficulties in Scripture.

[2] It may be worth while to throw together in a note some of the classical allusions to the events recorded in this chapter. It would be impossible to cite Hesiod, as, both in his *Works and Days* and *Theogony*, the passages are too long and too numerous to come within our limits. But their resemblance to the divine narrative is striking. Homer has several allusions to the early giants, ὑπερθύμοισι γιγάντεσσι (*Odyss.* vii. 59); and Sophocles speaks of the γηγενὴς στρατὸς γιγάντων. Virgil refers to their 'immania corpora' (*Æneid*, vi. 582); and Ovid to the 'gigantas, immania monstra' (*Fast.* v. 35). Describing the wickedness of this age of giants, Ovid writes,—

> 'Tertia post illas successit ahenea proles
> Sævior ingeniis et ad horrida promptior arma.'—*Metam.* i. 126.

And again—

> 'Sed et illa propago
> Contemptrix superum sævæque avidissima cædis,
> Et violenta fuit; scires e sanguine natos.'—*Metam.* i. 160.

[3] The LXX. give καιρός as the rendering of קֵץ; while Aquila,

preceding utterances, though probably spoken through Him, were general proclamations, meant for all. He tells him that now at length His long-suffering is exhausted, and that the end of all flesh has come up before him. It had been long delayed, but it comes at last;—the end of all flesh;—the end of their day on earth; and with the end of that day, the end of grace, the end of hope, the beginning of wrath and everlasting woe! How simply, but how solemnly, God speaks! Not in anger, yet with awful decision! Such shall be the judgment of the great day.

God does not judge hastily, or in a spirit of revenge,

more correctly, gives τέλος, and Symmachus πέρας. The following passages will show that our translators have rendered it correctly by 'an end:'—Gen. viii. 6, xli. 1; Jer. li. 13; Lam. iv. 8; Ezek. vii. 2; Amos viii. 2. The last of these passages resembles the one before us clearly—'The *end* is come upon my people.' 'All flesh,' a very universal term, including man and beast. See chap. viii. 17; Num. xviii. 15. Most critics interpret the clause thus: 'The end (or destruction) of all flesh has been determined by me' (see Gesenius, Rosenmüller, Dathe, etc.); and perhaps this is substantially correct. But may it not be as if God were looking on the earth (ver. 12), and after each scene, from the first to the last, has presented itself to His view, He speaks—'I see the end of all flesh'? Philo has a curious passage of mysticism on the clause, understanding the words of the Sept. as if they had meant, 'The time of mankind has come against me' (ἐναντίον). See his *Questions and Solutions*. 'Through them'—*lit.* Heb. before their face, *i.e.* coming forth from them; see Ex. viii. 24, 'the land was corrupted by reason of' (Heb. from the face of) 'the swarm of flies;' Judg. vi. 6, 'by reason of;' Heb. 'from the face of;' Jer. xv. 17; Ezek. xiv. 15. We may notice that the word פָּנִים occurs above 2200 times in various applications. 'With the earth.' That this is the proper rendering of את is evident from chap. ix. 11, where the destruction of the *earth* is spoken of. That this is a literal meaning is plain from chap. xxxvii. 2, xliii. 16; Judg. i. 16; Jer. li. 59. The Sept. has καὶ τὴν γῆν, which is the same meaning. Is it not to this that the Apostle Peter alludes (2 Pet. iii. 6), ὁ κόσμος ἀπώλετο?

against poor sinning man. He has reasons for what He does, and they are worthy of Himself. No stroke comes at random. All is calmly spoken, and calmly done. And will not this, O sinner, be the aggravation of your endless sorrow? You cannot soothe yourself with the idea that you are suffering unjustly, or are the victim of a hasty sentence. The wisdom and the justice of the proceeding will be clear even to yourself. This, too, makes your case so hopeless. Were the reasons for your condemnation weak or partial, you might hope for a reversal of the decision; but they are so wise, so good, so holy, that reversal is eternally impossible. In the case before us, God's reasons are man's total corruption of his ways, and his filling the earth with violence. He has not only let in evil, but he has made it overflow; he has *filled* the earth with it. 'The earth is defiled under the inhabitants thereof' (Isa. xxiv. 5). It is not *one* sin that brings down the judgment; no, nor many. It is the persisting in sin till others are corrupted, and the earth polluted, and the Spirit grieved away. God hates even *one* sin; but He is slow to punish. Not till sin has become an overflowing flood, does He smite. But when He does judge, how terrible the stroke! Thus God waits now in His patient love. Earth is full of sin, but He waits. He will not cast it into the winepress of His wrath till its grapes be fully ripe (Rev. xiv. 18). The flood of waters waited till iniquity had filled the earth. So is it with the flood of fire; it waits till the wickedness of the last days has reached its height. Then the *judgment* sits; and it is seen that sin was no mere disease which needed healing, but *guilt*, which could only be dealt with at a seat of justice by the great Judge of all. For the inflicter of the sentence is God Himself: 'I will destroy them with the earth.' They have corrupted the earth; I will corrupt them with that earth which they have corrupted. They and their earth shall be destroyed together; for the sentence comes forth against both.[1] This destruction does not infer the annihilation of either man or the earth. Nor does the Apostle Peter, when he speaks of the old world 'perishing,' mean annihilation. So, when this earth is spoken of as consumed by fire, we are not to understand *annihilation*. It passes through fire, only in order to be purified; and thus, purged from its dross by the Refiner's fire, it comes forth a more glorious world than before.

Vers. 14–16. '*Make thee an ark of gopher-wood; rooms shalt thou make in the ark, and shalt pitch it within and without with pitch.* 15. *And this is the fashion which thou shalt make it of; the length of the ark shall be three hundred cubits, the breadth of it fifty cubits, and the height of it thirty cubits.* 16. *A window shalt thou make to the ark, and in a cubit shalt thou finish it above; and the door of the ark shalt thou set in the side thereof; with lower, second, and third storeys shalt thou make it.*'[2]

'How shall any escape?' would be Noah's feeling, on hearing God's sentence against the world. Without

[1] The word in the original is the same in both clauses: 'They have corrupted the earth; I will corrupt them,' etc. The Sept. has preserved the identity of phrase. Trapp paraphrases it, 'I will punish them in kind, pay them in their own coin.'

[2] There is no need for minute criticism on the words of these three verses. Gesenius, Robertson's *Clavis*, and Moses Stuart's *Chrestomathy* (p. 153), will give the radical meanings and common uses of

delay, God reveals the provision to be made for the deliverance of the few. That deliverance *was to be of God* as directly as was the destruction. Yet *man* was to make the vessel of deliverance. 'Make for thyself,' is the express and urgent command. Deliverance was secured and provided by God, yet everything was made to depend on man's using the appointed means, just as in the case of Paul's deliverance from shipwreck.

The ark was well planned, well proportioned; admirably adapted for its end; not for sailing, but floating, not for ornament, but safety. God knows how to deliver His own, yet He does so by means, though these means are sometimes apparently slender enough. His providing means, and placing them at our disposal, implies the promise that in using them we shall attain what they

the terms, which our translators have rendered with sufficient accuracy. The word used for 'ark' occurs only in connection with Noah's vessel and Moses' basket,—a proof that the word is a general term applied to any sort of chest, great or small, made to float on the water. The word is not the same as that used for the 'ark of the covenant.' Gopher-wood, a resinous tree, such as the pine or cypress, probably the latter, from the likeness of the letters,—*κυπάρισσος*. The word translated pitch (both noun and verb) means properly 'cover'—'cover inside and outside with a covering;' the word nowhere else means pitch. It always means 'covering,' or 'ransom,' or 'atonement,' save in Canticles, where it is translated 'camphire' (chap. i. 14, iv. 14). We ought to add, that in 1 Sam. vi. 18 it means village, giving origin to *Caper*naum, or *Capher*naum, and similar prefixes. The ark was divided into *chambers*, or *nests*, or *rooms* (see Num. xxiv. 21; Job xxix. 18; Hab. ii. 9). It had a *window*, or *transparency*, or *clear light*. It was finished or sloped to a cubit above. Its door was in the side. It had a threefold division (which the Fathers greatly loved to mystify). It was 300 cubits long, 50 broad, 30 high; a measurement in which Augustine finds profound signification.

were meant to lead to. God does not mock us. He does not place a ladder up to heaven, without meaning us to ascend. He does not provide a Saviour merely to tantalize or mock. He provides an Ark, and He opens a door in it, that we may go in and be saved. He provides comfort as well as safety; light in this Ark, that we may not go blindfold to heaven, or in the dark; not merely safely lodged, but carried through with comfort and gladness. And just as the Church's deliverance is sure, so is the destruction of the world. The flood of fire will spare none. Yet the open door of our Ark bids welcome to all. And we know that our Ark is as sufficient as it is suitable. Christ is just such a deliverer as we need. And we must receive Him as such, not fashioning an ark of our own, or making a Christ of our own; but taking just the very Christ whom the Father here provides.[1]

Ver. 17. '*And, behold, I, even I, do bring* (or *am bringing*) *a flood of waters upon the earth, to destroy all flesh, wherein is the breath of life, from under heaven; and every thing that is in the earth shall die.*'

Now, for the first time, the *nature* of the coming destruction is announced. It is to be a flood of waters;

[1] The references to the ark in the Fathers would furnish matter for a long *Excursus*, which might be curious, but certainly would not be profitable, more especially as they make the ark a type not of Christ, but of the Church. It was to them a favourite and prolific subject for allegory.—See Origen in his *Homilies on Genesis.* Irenæus has a few brief allusions to the subject. Ambrose, *de Noe et Arca.* Chrysostom, *Homilies on Genesis.* Augustine, *De Civit. Dei*, book xv. chap. 26 and 27, in which that Father gives full vent to his fancy. Lactantius merely gives the narrative, *De Orig. Erroris*, book ii.

and it is to be no accidental outburst, but brought upon the earth by God Himself. He Himself is to be the doer of the whole. His object is to destroy all flesh wherein is the breath of life,[1] 'from under heaven,' that these blue heavens may no longer bend over such a mass of wickedness, and that sun no longer look down on such crimes. And then, to show how terribly complete this destruction is to be, it is said, 'Every thing on the earth shall perish.' What a sweep of judgment God makes when He begins! How like these words to those announcing the terror of the last day, 'They shall not escape!' (1 Thess. v. 3; Jer. xi. 11.) Noah's day, and the day of the Son of man, are like each other not merely in their suddenness, but in the fierceness of the judgment.

sec. 13. The same may be said of Prosper, *De Vocat. Gent.* book ii. chap. 13 and 14. Jerome, *Adversus Jovinianum*, etc., chap. 9; more largely *Adversus Luciferianos*, chap. 8; *Commentary on Ezekiel*, chap. 42. Athanasius makes a fine use of the subject, in his brief tract against those who judged of truth by the multitude of adherents: 'Prefer, if you please, the multitude drowned by the flood to Noah saved; yet allow me to betake myself to the ark which contained the few'—ἐμοὶ δὲ συγχώρησον τῇ τοὺς ὀλίγους ἐχούσῃ κιβωτῷ πρόσδραμεῖν. Gregory Nazianzen, on referring to the ark, speaks of Noah 'preserving the seeds of the second world in a small vessel of wood'—κόσμου δευτέρου σπέρματα. Twentieth Oration. Fulgentius, *De Trin.* chap. xii.; *De Remiss. Peccat.* chap. xx. We might multiply such citations, but these are sufficient.—See *Pererius Valentinus*, vol. ii. book x., where, however, the references are not full or complete. See also *Glossæ Literales in Genesim*, by the Jesuit Del-Rio (p. 158), A.D. 1608. Christopher Ness, however, while equally ingenious, is more satisfactory than these ancient mystics. See his *History and Mystery of the Old and New Testament*, chap. ix. pp. 99–129.

[1] The clause might be rendered more emphatically, 'To destroy all flesh which is in it (the earth); and to destroy the breath of life from under the heavens; everything that is in the earth shall perish.'

It is written, 'The flood came and destroyed them all' (Luke xvii. 27); and again, 'Even thus shall it be in the day when the Son of man is revealed' (Luke xvii. 30). Increasing ungodliness ended by overflowing judgment in both.

Vers. 18–21. '*But with thee will I establish my covenant: and thou shalt come into the ark, thou, and thy sons, and thy wife, and thy sons' wives with thee.* 19. *And of every living thing of all flesh, two of every sort shalt thou bring into the ark, to keep them alive with thee; they shall be male and female.* 20. *Of fowls after their kind, and of cattle after their kind, of every creeping thing of the earth after his kind; two of every sort shall come unto thee, to keep them alive.* 21. *And take thou unto thee of all food that is eaten, and thou shalt gather it to thee; and it shall be food for thee, and for them.*'

There is an exception to this destruction; Noah, and all those whom God was to treat as one with him, and to spare for his sake. This exception is to be made on the footing of a covenant, or rather *the* covenant.[1] The reference seems to be to a previous covenant, well known and recognised. This covenant had 'fallen down,' and seemed as if about wholly to fail. If all flesh is to be cut off, how is the covenant to be carried out? God sets apart Noah, making him the link by which the chain is to be kept unbroken. All the previous promises are to be centred in him. Through him the race of man is to be perpetuated, that in this way 'the Seed of the

[1] 'With thee I will establish my covenant,' or *set up* my covenant. It is the same word as in Gen. xvii. 7; Ex. vi. 4, xxvi. 30; Deut. xxvii. 2; 1 Sam. ii. 35; Ezek. xvi. 60. 'And I will raise up that which is fallen down.' That such is its sense in the Hiphil, see Gesenius, who gives as instances, Deut. xxii. 4, Job iv. 4, Ps. xli. 61.

woman' may at length come. Though the covenant thus 'set up' with Noah is in substance the old promise made to Adam, yet it comes before us in a new aspect, and with new appendages. It connects Noah personally with itself, and his preservation with its ultimate accomplishment. It is cast as the life-preserver to Noah in the midst of the rushing flood. It is made to encircle the ark with its sure girdle, that so the assurance may be given that all shall yet be well, in spite of man's desperate ungodliness. Evil may abound, hatred may assail the chosen one, the waters may compass him about, the fire may wrap him round, but the covenant holds him fast—surer than any anchor. He *cannot* sink or drift away, or be destroyed, for God's everlasting purpose has taken up its abode in him, and that purpose must fail ere he can be overthrown.

The covenant provides not only that there shall be an ark, but that some shall enter it; nay, it fixes on those who are to enter it. So, in regard to Christ and His salvation, love planned a covenant, love provided an ark; but love did more than this—it secured the entrance of at least some. It saw that none would enter if left to themselves, and it laid hold of some and drew them in.

God provides for the beasts of the field and the fowls of the air. They are to be saved; and, in order to this, they are to be made to enter. In the one verse it is said, 'Thou shalt bring,' and in another, 'They shall enter,' showing Noah's part and God's part in the matter. Noah makes ready the ark; God inclines them to go in. But more,—God must have all these *fed* as well as *sheltered;*

and Noah is instructed to take provisions with him for man and beast. God overlooks nothing. He cares for all His work; He clothes the lilies, He feeds the rivers, He watches the falling sparrow, He counts the hairs of our head. Truth and grace are with Him. His tender mercies are over all His works. What a gospel does the ark preach to us!—glad tidings of grace, the reception of which at once links us to the God of all grace.

Thus has Jehovah His time and His way for inflicting His judgment, as well as His time and His way for providing deliverance. He is altogether sovereign in His dealings with earth and its dwellers; sovereign in grace, sovereign in judgment. He establishes His covenant with whomsoever it pleases Him; blessing Noah in His free love, and for his sake saving his family; nay, saving the brute creation and sparing the earth, which had, for well-nigh sixteen centuries, been polluted with the crimes of man.

Ver. 22. '*Thus did Noah; according to all that God commanded him, so did he.*'

He listened to God and obeyed in faith, overlooking nothing, just as we read of Moses in regard to the tabernacle (Ex. xl. 16). He staggered not through unbelief, but gave God the credit for knowing what was to be done far better than he. Faith leads to obedience; the simpler faith is, the more prompt and implicit the obedience. Much as faith is needed in our time, surely obedience is no less so. Ours is the day of *disobedience* as well as of *unbelief;* of *selfwill*, no less than of *enmity* and *mistrust.*

NOTES.

I.

THE SABBATH.

GOD, at the very outset of the world's history, draws the distinction between *work* and *rest*. Even in regard to Himself, this difference is to be noticed. Work is not rest, and rest is not work, even to Omnipotence.

In both His own work and His own rest He is glorified, though each has its own kind of glory. He expects both kinds from us; and hence He set us the example at the beginning. In working we glorify Him, and in resting we glorify Him; but still the glory which He gets from our work is one thing, and the glory which He gets from our rest is another.

Nor must these two things be confounded. They are distinct in themselves, and distinct in their bearings upon our deportment and service here in this dispensation.

There are some that confound these two things, and overlook not only their *separableness* in themselves, but their actual and explicit *separation* by God. These joiners together of what God has sundered do not deny that we ought to glorify God whether working or resting; but they mix up together the working and the resting, and think that what God wants is a sort of mingled glory rising out of both these conjoined, and fused into one, instead of a distinct and separate glory from each; a glory which cannot be thus mingled without being injured and stript of that definite and clear character which He desires that it should possess. His purpose is, that He should get a certain glory from working, and another glory from resting; and who are we that we should, by any theories of our own, seek to thwart the purpose of Jehovah, or rob Him of the twofold glory which He is looking for at our hands?

It was not for nothing that He laid down so expressly, in the beginning of His volume, His own twofold line or method of action, if we may so speak; the active and the passive, the work and the cessation from work. Nor was it without a purpose that, when in the course of ages the distinction might be undergoing a process of obliteration, He took it up and proclaimed it to Israel. For what He did, both in paradise and in the wilderness, was not merely to give forth an arbitrary appointment as to a certain day; but it was to bring out a mighty distinction, on which very much was to depend in after ages, both as to His own glory and man's proper service.

If this be the case, then it is plain that the distinction between the six days and the seventh day lies much deeper than we generally conceive. It is not a distinction founded upon *the* seventh day or *the* first day of the week. The actual day is of comparatively small importance, and only comes before us in its connection with the past events to which it is linked by way of memorial, or in connection with future events, to which it is linked by way of type or earnest. It is a distinction founded on the difference between working and resting, and upon the peculiar glory which God is to obtain from the one and from the other. Whether we can fully comprehend the reason of this distinction, it matters not. There it is. There are the original facts in the very forefront of the Bible. There are God's own actings, and there are His declarations and injunctions as to the manner in which He expects us to act; in which He expects every one to act who, with the Bible in his hands, believes that 'God created the heavens and the earth,' and that 'on the seventh day He rested from all His works which He had created and made.'

Among those who look upon the Sabbath as a mere limitation of man's liberty, an abridgment of his pleasures, we cannot expect to find any sympathy with the above distinction. They deny the Sabbath because it is a weariness, and because the Lord of the Sabbath is not their Lord.

But there is another class with whom we may expect some sympathy, even though they have rejected the Sabbath as a divine ordinance. There is a class which holds that every day should be a Sabbath, and that, therefore, there ought to be no such diversity as we hold to be obligatory. They differ from the others in this respect. These others get rid of the Sabbath by lowering it to the level of every other day; whereas *they* set it aside by raising every day to the level of a Sabbath. Now, even granting that this latter were possible,—which, according to the present construction of God's world, it is not,—it would not be carrying out God's original intention. It looks very well; it sounds very lofty; it bears the stamp of superior spirituality; so that when we hear a man say, 'Oh, I make every day a Sabbath!' we may be led to think him a very holy man, and his life a very angelic one, and his whole system a very elevated and enlarged one.

But what if this very holy man gets all his holiness from being wiser than God? This is a serious question.

God knows what is best for us. He knew what was best for *unfallen* man, and He did not tell him that every day should be a Sabbath. If Adam had reasoned as many do in our day, and resolved to make every day a Sabbath, would not God have condemned this piece of will-worship? and would Adam, in devising it, have been less guilty of a disregard to the divine purpose, than if he had rejected the Sabbath altogether? God knew what is best for *fallen* man, and nowhere, from Genesis to Revelation, does He hint at the desirableness, or propriety, or profit of making every day a Sabbath.

In thus trying to be wiser than God, and striking out a more elevated walk than He has pointed out, we are sure to fall into an *unhealthy* religion; not necessarily a religion of gloom, but certainly, if not one of gloom, at least one of sentiment, and sickliness, and unmanly bearing. No religion can be healthy or vigorous which departs from the divine arrangements, and tries to elevate itself by altering the proportions of time which God has established. What has Romanism gained by its endless saints' days, or High Churchmen by their 'Christian year'? Attempts, whether made by Protestant or Papist, to raise our week-days into Sabbaths can only end, as they have always done, in subverting the Sabbath, and defeating God's gracious design in giving it.

The original distinction, made by God Himself, and founded both upon His nature and ours, between *working* and *resting*, must be kept in mind; and we must not attempt to confound these, or suppose that, provided we try to glorify God in *everything*, it matters little whether we set the two different things distinctly before us; viz. the glory which we are to give Him in working, and the glory which we are to give Him in resting. In trying to make every day a Sabbath, we are doing what we can to efface this divine distinction. And can it be effaced without sin, without injury to the soul, without harm both to the Church and to the world, both to Jew and Gentile? It cannot; for thus God does not get the glory which He desires. He does not get the separate glories of which we have been speaking, but a mere human compound of both,—vague, indefinite, diluted,—something that neither glorifies Him nor benefits His saints, nor bears witness to the world.

When God entered on His rest, He erected a memorial of it; a memorial both of His work and of His rest, for *rest* was to be a memorial of work. This memorial, suitable even to unfallen man, was especially needful to fallen man in a fallen world. God erected this pillar of testimony; nor has He taken it down. It was first set up in paradise, then in the wilderness, then transplanted to Calvary, and there it remaineth to this day.

In one thing only was there a difference. The seventh day having become a blank, by the Son of God lying, during it, under the power of death, its special glory passed on to the next, so that the first day of the week, while retaining all earlier meanings, is presented to us as a more complete memorial of the past,—creation-work and creation-rest,—and at the same time a more perfect prefiguration of resurrection-work and resurrection-rest.

Thus much we can say as to the general principles on which the Sabbath-Institute is founded. Let us look at the question a little more minutely; for, if these principles are correct, the subject is one of deep moment.

No one thinks of denying that the law of the Sabbath is written broadly and legibly enough in the Old Testament; so that up to the coming of Christ it could not be disputed. God laid His hand upon the seventh portion of man's time, and claimed it as His own. It was provided that, in one day out of seven, the sun should go forth to shine upon a world at rest; memorial of what it was intended to be; relic of what it once had been; type of what it is yet to be hereafter, when all things are made new.

Now, there has been no repeal of this law. The fourth commandment was carefully inserted in the Decalogue by God's own finger, and it behoved to be as distinctly taken out and erased by the same finger that placed it there. Has it been so? Have the commandments been reduced from ten to nine? Did Christ come to destroy, not to fulfil the law? Those who deny the authority of the Sabbath now must undertake to prove the following things:—

1. *That the Decalogue, or law, is no longer binding;* or at least that one out of the Ten Commandments is no longer binding. And if one man cancels the fourth, has not another,—viz. the Romanist,—a right to cancel the second? If this man is at liberty to erase this jot or tittle, another man may do the same with another, till the whole has been abrogated,—abrogated by man, not by God,—abrogated simply because its observance was an inconvenience and a weariness.

2. *That Christ came to diminish our store of blessings during the present dispensation;*—that He has narrowed instead of enlarging our privileges: as if He had made the announcement, 'Israel was blessed with a Sabbath, but I cancel that blessing; Israel had Sabbath privileges and Sabbath joys, I blot them out; Israel was called on to give the seventh of his time to God, but I set you free from all such restraint, to do with your time just as you please.' Thus we have, according to these men, fewer privileges, fewer blessings than Israel. And is this what Christ came to do? Was it for this that the Son of God took flesh and died?

3. *If they shrink from this, then they must maintain that the Sabbath is not a blessing;*—that it is an unwholesome, unnatural, intolerable restraint;—a weariness, a bondage, a curse. And, indeed, this is the basis and drift of their reasonings, if they have any meaning at all. These men evidently have the secret feeling, that the Sabbath is not a blessing, that it is a restraint, —a restraint upon their worldliness, their follies, their gains, their business. Hence their eagerness to prove its non-existence, its abolition. The wish is father to the thought, the desire is father to the conclusion. They wish no Sabbath, and, with daring blasphemy, they ascribe its abolition to Him who came not to destroy the law, but to fulfil it. So that one of the chief benefits, according to them, which Christianity has conferred on our race is, that it has effaced the Sabbath. It did virtually eighteen hundred years ago exactly what the French Revolution did eighty years ago,—it effaced the Sabbath. Thus the chief thing for which the world has to praise the Saviour is, that He first struck off its Sabbath chains, and bid it go free from Sabbath obligations;—nay, perhaps the only thing for which some of these men think they have to thank the Lord of the Sabbath is, that He abolished it! Will they maintain this? Yet this they must, if they will honestly and consistently carry out their argument. To what extremity will not the hatred of the Sabbath drive a man?

4. *That the Sabbath was a Jewish institution exclusively, and therefore fell when Judaism fell.* Now, that there were several Jewish observances connected with the Sabbath in Israel, we do not doubt. But when these fell, did the Sabbath fall with them? Did their passing away bring the Sabbath to the ground? No. When the veil was rent, and Judaism crumbled to pieces, the Sabbath stood erect and untouched amid these ruins. It had not risen with Judaism, and it did not fall with Judaism. It was made for *man*, not for the *Jew*. It was an ordinance as old as creation, and therefore, strictly speaking, had nothing to do with Judaism. It was an ordinance evidently known to Israel before proclaimed from Sinai; for as soon as they had entered the wilderness, and long ere they reached Sinai, the manna fell, and thus the Lord spake

to them: 'To-morrow is the rest of the holy Sabbath unto the Lord. Six days ye shall gather it; but on the seventh day, which is the Sabbath, in it there shall be none' (Ex. xvi. 23, 26). From which it is plain that Israel knew the Sabbath well before its proclamation from Sinai, and that when called on to 'remember' it, they were called to remember something which they and their fathers knew; something older than Moses, older than Abraham, older than Noah, as old as Adam and paradise.

5. *That every day should be a Sabbath, and that, therefore, there is no need of a Sabbath.* When this argument comes from the lips of a worldly man;—a man who never spent an hour upon his knees, and who knows nothing of communion with the Father and the Son, it is profanity;—it is hypocrisy. But even when it comes from the lips of one who seems to be living above the world, and to prize fellowship with God, we confess it appears strange and suspicious. Should not every day have been a Sabbath to Adam? Yet he was commanded even in paradise to keep a Sabbath to the Lord. Was not every day a Sabbath to the Lord Jesus when on earth? Yet He kept the Sabbath, and always made known His reverence for it by vindicating Himself from the charge of Sabbath-breaking, and showing that works of mercy might be done upon that day. But, apart from this, we dislike and suspect this sentiment even from the lips of religious men. They profess to bring up every day to the level of a Sabbath; but it is invariably found that, in reality, they bring down the Sabbath to the level of every day. We have heard of individuals, some years ago devout and spiritual. They were placed in the midst of worldliness, exposed to Sabbath gaiety, Sabbath parties, Sabbath dinners, Sabbath pleasure, from week to week. Their souls were burdened, and each Sabbath evening they retired to rest with a wounded conscience and a heavy heart. After a while they ceased to be thus vexed in spirit, and were quite at ease. Had they got quit of their worldly company? No. Had they boldly testified for Christ and for His Sabbath in the midst of them? No. They had been led to see that 'to a Christian every day should be a Sabbath.' Therefore their

conscience no longer smote them, even when mixing all day long in the society of the world. Alas! they were deluding themselves with the dogma that every day should be a Sabbath. Yet they had not brought up each day to the elevation of a Sabbath. Nay, they had evidently brought down the Sabbath to the level of the day of commonest worldliness and folly.

6. *That the reasons for the observance of a Sabbath no longer exist.* These reasons are: (1) Man's need of *rest.* Is this reason gone? Does man need rest no longer? Is the world now so calm a scene, and earth so serene a region, that no seventh day's rest is needed? If not, if the reason still exist, must not the day still remain? Can the institution be erased when the reason for it still remains, not only as strong as ever, but stronger than ever, in these days of earnest worldliness, and excitement, and hurrying to and fro? (2) Time for unhindered fellowship with God. Is there no longer need for this? Is there not more than ever, in this age of business and enterprise? Adam in paradise, Israel in the wilderness, when there was no bustle, no tempting world around, needed a Sabbath for fellowship and worship. And do we not in these busy days? And if the reason remains, the ordinance must. (3) A memorial of creation. For four thousand years God kept up this memorial of creation as a thing that was needed; and where is His declaration that creation needs no memorial now? Ah! do we not feel how needful it is to uphold the Sabbath in these days, when men are undertaking to prove from science that the world created itself? Ought we not to prize the Sabbath as God's standing testimony against atheism, —God's own loving voice proclaiming, 'I created all this out of nothing,'—God's appointed witness to a universe created by Himself, against the atheistic theory of a self-creating universe? (4) A memorial of resurrection. The Sabbath has now become a double memorial, viz. of creation and resurrection. If, then, it was sacred before, it is doubly sacred now. And to say that the Sabbath has ceased because Christianity has risen, is just saying this, that so long as we had but one reason for this memorial, we kept it up; but now that we have two, we must level and efface it. (5) A type of the rest or Sabbath which

remaineth for the people of God. Now a type must stand till it be succeeded by the antitype. That antitype, that rest, has not yet come. And till it arrive, the Sabbath must be maintained. So that, whether you look backward to the old creation or forward to the new,—backward to resurrection, or forward to the restitution of all things,—you see how entirely untouched, nay, how thoroughly immoveable, are the reasons for its sacredness and perpetuity. Till these reasons be swept away, the Sabbath must stand. Unless you can say that man has no need for rest, no need for communion with God,—unless you can sweep away creation, resurrection, and the hope of the coming rest, you cannot cancel the Sabbath, nor dispose of its obligation and authority.

The character of a cause is generally known by the character of its friends and its enemies. No one will deny that the great mass of the religious-minded men is in favour of the Sabbath, and the great mass of the ungodly against it. Popery is an enemy to the Sabbath; and wherever Popery flourishes, there the Sabbath goes down. Infidelity is an enemy to the Sabbath; and wherever infidelity flourishes, there the Sabbath goes down. Popish Spain has no Sabbaths, infidel France has no Sabbaths; Protestant England, Protestant America, and Protestant Scotland, have their Sabbaths still. And may we not conclude favourably of that cause against which Popery and infidelity are confederated as one man? May we not conclude well of that ordinance which takes root deepest, and spreads its branches widest, in the most religious and God-fearing nations of the earth?

They who oppose the Sabbath are standing in the position of men who are enemies to one of the brightest blessings and best birthrights that a nation can possess. They need not wonder that we should feel strongly the robbery which they are seeking to perpetrate. They are robbing us and our children of that which is worth more than a kingdom's riches, and which we will not part with without a struggle. And they themselves, were they men in earnest, should feel the seriousness of the position they assume. If they are in earnest, it must have cost them much pain before they could bring themselves to the conclusion that there is no Sabbath. In arguing with the atheist, who denies a God, we can appeal to him and say, If you are in earnest, it must have been with the profoundest grief that you have come to the conclusion that there is no God, no infinite good, no being of infinite love. In reasoning with the infidel, who sets aside the Scriptures, we can say, If you be in earnest, it must have cost you unutterable pain to come to the conclusion, there is no Bible, no book of divine wisdom and truth. And you, of all others, ought to be serious, solemn men, weighed down with the conviction of such an infinite blank. And so, in reasoning with the opposers of the Sabbath, we appeal to them, and say, If you are men in earnest, it must have been with bitterest grief that you have brought yourself to the conclusion that there is no Sabbath,—no day of holy rest, no day of fellowship with God, no memorial of creation, no pledge of coming glory. You must have weighed the evidence well before coming to so sad a conclusion, and you must be most willing to hear evidence in favour of that which, if we can prove it, should be good and grateful news. Would you but listen in such a spirit to our reasonings, would you but believe us when we tell you how much your own temporal comforts, your own immortal interests, are bound up in the observance of this day,—a day that of itself preaches to you the glad tidings of Him who died, and rose, and ascended, and lives, and intercedes, and will come again in glory,—you would hesitate before you tried to obliterate the most ancient of all distinctions between day and day; you would try rather to preserve and perpetuate its testimony to creation, to redemption, to resurrection, to the glory of the Kingdom, and the security of the rest which remaineth for the people of God.[1]

[1] An old critic thinks that the number *seven* was called ἑπτάς, or more anciently σεπτάς, from σέβεσθαι, to worship,—the worshipping day.

II.

SATAN.

OF Satan's creation we know nothing. That he was created holy we cannot doubt, for God is not the author of unholiness, but of holiness.

Of the time when he was created nothing is revealed; nor of how long he stood; nor of how he fell. For aught that we know, he might not have stood longer than Adam, or he might have done so for ages. This only would we say, that it seems impossible for a creature, standing alone, simply in creature strength, to stand any length of time, however short.

What led to his fall we know not. He 'kept not his first estate, but left his own habitation.' This is all that we are told,—as if he had become dissatisfied with that estate, and gone in quest of another habitation.

How he came to be connected with this earth is wholly unrevealed. Whether this were his 'first estate,'—his realm,—and he had become dissatisfied with it, or whether some other planet were his kingdom, and he having become dissatisfied with it, had come in quest of another abode to this earth,—these are questions which we may ask, but cannot answer. Certainly his connection with our world is a mysterious fact. How he should be found here,—and found here just at the time of man's creation,—is quite inexplicable. We are so accustomed to consider him as connected with earth and its history, that we lose sight of the mystery of the *commencement* of this connection. Why, out of all the millions of stars, should this be the place where he appears? How did he find his way to this orb if he were not here before? What brought him to it? Was it solely as a tempter that God allowed him to come? or is he wandering about like a dethroned monarch, seeking to regain his lost sceptre, and once more to be sovereign of this his lost planet?

We are not concerned to account for his sudden appearance

on this globe at the time of man's creation, nor to answer any of the above questions. We are satisfied to take the simple facts of Scripture, and to learn from them his character and actings.

He is brought before us under several characters, or rather, we might say, his character is brought before us under several aspects,—all of them dark, repulsive, horrid. There is nothing in any of them of that grandeur and nobleness which Milton has ascribed to him. He tells us that

> 'His form had not yet lost
> All her original brightness, nor appeared
> Less than archangel ruined, and the excess
> Of glory obscured.'

Scripture attributes to him nothing save evil,—unmingled evil, enmity to God and man, special enmity to Christ and to His Church.

We find him set forth to us under such names or aspects as the following :—

1. *The Tempter* (1 Thess. iii. 5).—It is under this character that he first appears before us in paradise,—tempting the woman, and persuading her to disbelieve, to distrust, and to rebel.

2. *The Deceiver* (1 Tim. ii. 14; Rev. xx. 3, 8, 10).—He is not merely a tempter, but a deceiver. He beguiled Eve with his subtlety, and his object has been, ever since, to practise deceits upon the children of men,—nay, to transform himself into an angel of light,—and by his cunning to deceive, if it were possible, the very elect.

3. *A Liar* (John viii. 44).—He tempted Eve by a *lie;* he deceived her by a lie; he carries on his temptations and deceptions still by a lie! He has lied from the beginning; he lieth still; he is a liar; he is the father of lies, and with his lies is he seeking to cover the whole earth.

4. *A Murderer* (John viii. 44).—His whole aim from the beginning has been to slay men, both soul and body. He has delighted to torment men's bodies, as we see in the case of Job, and in the case of the demoniacs in the time of our

Lord. He bears deadly malice against the whole race, and specially against the woman's seed, which he has been carrying out in persecution and murder, age after age; so that his name is truly Abaddon, or Apollyon, 'the destroyer.' It is he who has so often unsheathed the sword against the godly, and shed the blood of saints. It was he who entered into Judas, and led him to hand over his Master to His murderers. It is to be he who is to muster the great Armageddon host, to fight against Jehovah in the last days.

5. *An Executioner* (Heb. ii. 14).—He is said to have the 'power of death,' as if he were God's executioner; as if it were through him that disease smites us, and death is at last inflicted. He is the angel of death! Terrible name! How he came to have the power of death, or when the sword of death was put into his hands, we know not. But there he stands, executing that very sentence which he so cunningly declared to the woman would not take place,—'Ye shall not surely die.' At the time he uttered the words he had the sword in his hand; he stood waiting for his prey, ready to seize his victim as soon as, by disobedience, she should put herself into his power.

6. *An Adversary* (1 Pet. v. 8).—He is the Church's great enemy, watching to destroy, like a beast of prey prowling round the fold in order to seize his victims. This enmity is what the first promise predicts: enmity between the seed of the woman and the seed of the serpent; yet limited enmity, enmity which God restrains, and which can go no further than the heel, either in the case of Christ or His Church.

7. *He is an Accuser* (Rev. xii. 10).—His name, devil or διάβολος, signifies this, just as Satan signifies adversary. No doubt, after deceiving our first parents, he went straight and accused them to God, which he seems always to have had the power of doing, and hence he is called 'the accuser of the brethren.' Awfully true to his name has he proved himself to be! What evil reports has he not set on foot against the saints! what lies has he not invented! what slanders has he not heaped upon them! Both before God and man he has proved the truth of his name, 'the accuser of the brethren.'

8. *He is the god of this world* (2 Cor. iv. 4).—This name seems to correspond with that which our Lord gives him, 'the prince of this world' (John xiv. 30), and to that which the apostle gives to the principalities and powers, 'the rulers of the darkness of this world.' He has got dominion over the earth. The world obeys him. He has covered it with darkness, and that darkness he rules or wields at pleasure. And hereafter he will induce the whole world to wonder after his representative, 'the beast;' nay, to have its name stamped upon their forehead; nay, to fall down and worship it.

Other similar names he has, such as Beelzebub, that old serpent, the dragon, the wicked one. All these indicate the same characteristics of utter wickedness and rebellion against God and His Christ.

These characteristics have been exemplified in each age and clime of this world. To trace his workings in the earth, would lead us into a larger field than we can at present occupy; this, however, we may say, that he has, without cessation, been working in our world from the beginning hitherto. By his legions of evil angels he carries on his schemes in every kingdom and in every heart. He leaves no place unassailed, no heart untempted, in so far as he is permitted of Jehovah. For let us remember that he is not omnipotent, nor is he at liberty to do all he desires or plans, unrestrained. But in so far as this divine permission allows him, he works without ceasing everywhere.

Nor does he work at random. He has evidently had a regular and consistent plan all along to carry out. Possessed of vast wisdom, he does not fling away his efforts uselessly. He works out a consistent and considered scheme. He does not allow wrath to blind or malice to mislead him. He plans and he executes with all the superhuman skill with which he is gifted, as originally an angel of light, excelling in wisdom as in strength. All error comes from him, all apostasy, all idolatry, all denial of Christ. He is ever on the watch to ensnare and lead captive the unwary.

His greatest device is that of Antichrist. This he has been building up and maturing during past centuries; and this he is still occupied with in these last days. This is his main central scheme, on which he expends his utmost cunning and strength. And for a time he succeeds. He has led men into the entanglements and abominations of Popery; and he is yet to have more universal success in other ways, when he deceives the whole world, and makes it to wonder after and to worship the beast. (See Rev. xiii.)

Instead of losing, he gains ground in the course of ages. He comes down, having great wrath, because he knows he has but a short time. He persecutes the saints; he slays the witnesses; he makes war with the Lamb; he sets Antichrist upon the throne, and brings all the world to worship him. For just as he tempted Christ by offering Him all the world's kingdoms, so does he tempt Antichrist, and prevail. Antichrist worships him, and he in turn brings the whole world to worship Antichrist. Up to the last he is seen maintaining his old characteristics. He is the deceiver, the liar, the murderer, the god of this world, and the prince of the air, to the very last. His enmity to the seed of the woman has lost none of its intensity or ferocity. His warfare continues as unrelenting and murderous as when he stirred up Cain to slay his brother. The battle of Armageddon is wholly of his organization. And the following passages describe his last act of enmity, Rev. xvii. 14, xix. 19.

And what follows this last outburst of Satanic rage against the Lamb and His followers? Does he muster his routed forces for another conflict, and come forth for a second and more terrible Armageddon! No; the 20th chapter gives the result. He is not merely overpowered and his legions scattered, but he is seized and bound. A mighty angel descends, and his reign is over; the spoiler is spoiled; the destroyer is destroyed; he that led into captivity has gone into captivity; the imprisoner of the saints is led to prison, and bound in chains too strong for all hell to break.

And what follows this binding of Satan? The saints take their seats upon their long-promised thrones; the righteous reign of Christ begins; the earth is swept clean of its long pollution; the times of the restitution of all things now run their course; the 'darkness of this world' is exchanged for the light of the world to come; for the ruler of the long darkness has been expelled from his seat, and the glory of the Son of God takes possession of that air where Satan had dwelt, and where he had exercised his power on earth.

And what is the great event which ends the reign of Satan and begins the reign of the saints? The coming of the Lord! In proof of this, we have only to look at the concluding part of the preceding chapter. At the 11th verse a new scene unfolds itself. The saints have been caught up to the clouds to meet their Lord, and the marriage-supper of the Lamb is described as then taking place. Then the heaven opens; the Lord Himself appears. The beast is taken, and the false prophet, and cast into the lake of fire. Then follows the scene in the 20th chapter, of Satan's binding, and the reign of the saints during the period of his binding.

It is plain that, up till this period, Satan has had dominion on the earth. During that dominion there could be no millennium. To end this dominion of the Evil One, by destroying the beast whom Satan had set up, and binding Satan himself, the Lord comes in person. And now the glory is manifested. There can be no millennium before Christ comes. Immediately on His coming it commences.

Into the momentous question of Satan's *power* we have not entered. It is one which demands our most solemn attention, and it is one which will necessarily force itself upon the notice of the Church as the last days draw on. It must be evident to every reader of Scripture, that he has far greater power than we have usually ascribed to him, at least of late years. Our forefathers came much nearer the truth on this point than we do. Modern *enlightenment* has exploded the ancient ideas of Satanic operation. How far this enlightenment can claim to be scriptural, we do not now say.

A recently published work of Mr. Smith takes up the subject in a way such as few historians have ventured to do. The work is entitled *The Gentile Nations*, published some years ago, and forms the conclusion of his *Sacred Annals*. We cannot better conclude our remarks than by giving a few extracts, which may help our readers to pursue the subject at greater length.

The origin of idolatry is thus traced to Satan by Mr. Smith :—

'The origin of idolatry will never be understood while the investigation is confined to the character of the human mind or the history of the human race, without a distinct recognition of man's exposure to Satanic influence and aggression. It might as reasonably be attempted to write a history of England whilst ignoring the Norman Conquest, or a system of physics without reference to gravitation, as to give a consistent and rational account of the origin of idolatry in the absence of all reference to Satan, its real author and object. It may be said, "This is unscientific and unphilosophical." But is it not in perfect accordance with the purest science, and the soundest philosophy, to apply all truth to useful purposes, and by the judicious adaptation of ascertained principles to cognate subjects, to solve apparent mysteries, unravel difficulties, and make that clear and plain which was before confused and obscure? Why, then, should this mode of proceeding be prohibited in respect of the truths of the Holy Scriptures by those who admit their divine origin? Sceptics and infidels may decline such a method: it is their consistent habit so to do. But why should those who make the undoubted verity of God's Holy Word the basis of their highest hopes and dearest interests, hesitate to apply its teaching to the great problems presented by all the aspects of the world's religion?

'In the investigation of the origin and character of idolatry, this aid is essential. The moment we enter on this study, we are met by such questions as these: "What were the origin and design of bloody sacrifices? Why were they universal, when the most profound sages were ignorant of their origin and object? Why was the form of the serpent, above every other, consecrated to supreme elevation and honour?" These and many other queries cannot be solved by any study of human nature or human history. No recondite researches into ancient mythology, no laboured exploration into the poetry or religion of the primitive nations, will afford a satisfactory answer. To understand the origin, object, and character of idolatry, we must pass beyond the twilight of mere human intelligence and induction, and, standing in the full glory of revealed truth, contemplate the primitive condition and early history of mankind. Here we learn our glorious origin, and the mighty agencies with which our nature, in the outset of its career, was brought into contact; mark the fearful change wrought in man's moral nature, and watch its terrible results until we see him turn away from the God of his life, and bow in profane adoration before the most filthy impersonations of his foul destroyer.

'In this light we see that the relentless foe of God and man did not quit his prey, when covered with guilt, and involved in condemnation. It may be fairly questioned whether any crisis in the affairs of the human race stands invested with more terrible grandeur than this. Here we see, that as divine mercy interposed the scheme of redemption for the salvation of man, the arch-foe not only opposed its principles and its progress by a wide range of malignant effort; but, in a manner at once daring and insidious, he devised idolatry, and succeeded in introducing it into the world, as a means of wresting the spiritual dominion of mankind from the Mediator-Deity, and establishing himself as "the god of this world." This was the agency under which idolatry was introduced, and rose into influence and power; and throughout its almost infinite range of development, the evil and debasing character of its author is legibly imprinted upon all its numerous deities, doctrines, rites, and religious observances.'

The origination of idolatry, in the *perversion of divine truth* by Satan, is thus stated:—

'Having thus ascertained by undoubted induction, confirmed as it is by Scripture proof, the period and place whence idolatry originated, we may proceed another step, and elicit from the great and common principles of all heathen mythology some notion of the ruling elements of unhallowed feeling and corrupt imagination, which generated the evil of which we speak. In this effort it will be of consequence for us to recognise the important fact, that in all ages Satanic error has been most successful when presented to the human mind as *a perversion of truth.* Faber justly observes, "The human mind rarely tolerates any great changes if they be violent and sudden, particularly in matters of religion. It seems natural to suppose that this great apostasy was not a violent and abrupt setting aside of true religion; that it was not a sudden plunge from the worship of Jehovah into the grossness of rank idolatry. I should rather apprehend, that it must have commenced with a specious perversion of sound doctrine, and with an affectedly devout adoption of authorized rites, and ceremonies, and phraseology." This judgment of an experienced and learned writer, who had carefully investigated the subject, may be safely admitted as a sound principle, of important use in the prosecution of this inquiry.'

Satan's object in these idolatrous systems—to defeat God's scheme of redemption—is then briefly noticed, along with the general overlooking of this awful fact in studying heathen mythology. Our youth are taught mythology, but not as they ought to be. They are not taught to look on it with abhorrence, as Satan's scheme for opposing redemption; they are rather made to regard it as a beautiful and wonderful exhibition of human intellect!

Then Satan's efforts to get *himself* worshipped under the form of a serpent, are thus sketched :—

'That the malign foe should repeat his assault on human happiness after the promise of redemption, is not wonderful. That he should have persevered in his aggression, might be inferred from his subtlety and malice. But it will scarcely be believed, that even Satan should not only have aimed so high as to supplant the adorable and eternal God as the object of human worship, but should also have aspired to put himself forth as the object of supreme worship, and challenge the adoration of the world under the precise form in which he had succeeded in effecting the ruin of the race. Yet so it was. The serpent form has in all probability approached nearer to universal adoration than any other.

'A learned author, who has investigated this subject with

great labour and research, assures us that he has "traced the worship of the serpent from Babylonia, east and west, through Persia, Hindustan, China, Mexico, Britain, Scandinavia, Italy, Illyricum, Thrace, Greece, Asia Minor, and Phœnicia. Again, we have observed the same idolatry prevailing north and south, through Scythia on the one hand, and Africa on the other. THE WORSHIP OF THE SERPENT WAS THEREFORE UNIVERSAL. For not only did the sacred serpent enter into the symbolical and ritual service of every religion which recognised THE SUN, but we even find him in countries where solar worship was altogether unknown, as in Sarmatia, Scandinavia, and in the Gold Coast of Africa. In every known country of the ancient world, the serpent formed a prominent feature in the ordinary worship, and made no inconsiderable figure in their Hagiographa, entering alike into legendary and astronomical mythology.

'"Whence, then, did this ONLY UNIVERSAL idolatry originate? That it preceded polytheism, is indicated by the attribution of the title OPS, and the consecration of the symbolical serpent, to so many of the heathen deities. The title OPS was conferred upon Terra, Vesta, Rhea, Cybele, Juno, Diana; and even Vulcan is called by Cicero, *Opas.*

'"In Grecian mythology, the symbolical serpent was sacred to Saturn, Jupiter, Apollo, Bacchus, Mars, Æsculapius, Rhea, Juno, Minerva, Diana, Ceres, and Proserpine; that is, the serpent was a sacred emblem *of nearly all the gods and goddesses.*

'"The same remark may be extended to the theogonies of Egypt, Hindustan, and Mexico, in all of which we find the serpent emblematic, not of *one* deity, but of *many.*

'"What, then, is the inference? *That the serpent was the most ancient of the* heathen gods."'

How curiously this serpent-worship, or rather, Satan-worship, was developed in different places, is thus adverted to :—

'So the great and terrible truth stands clearly attested, not only by the Word of God, but by authentic records of every ancient nation, that the old serpent the devil, who seduced our first parents from their allegiance, succeeded in establishing himself, under the very figure in which he wrought his first fatal triumph, as the almost universal object of human worship —"the god of this world." Yes, and as the corrupt fancy and bewildered speculations diversified modes of worship, and multiplied forms and objects of adoration, this malign spirit, as if to assert his universal supremacy, and perpetuate his name and influence over the wide world of human nature, stamped the serpent name on every deity, and the serpent form on every ritual. To use the eloquent language of the author already cited, "The mystic serpent entered into the mythology of every nation; consecrated almost every temple; symbolized almost every deity; was imagined in the heavens, stamped upon the earth, and ruled in the realms of everlasting sorrow. His *subtlety* raised him into an emblem of *wisdom;* he was therefore pictured upon the ægis of Minerva, and crowned her helmet. *The knowledge of futurity* which he displayed in paradise exalted him into a symbol of vaticination; he was therefore oracular, and reigned at Delphi. The '*opening of the eyes*' of our deluded first parents obtained him an altar in the temple of the god of *healing;* he is therefore the constant companion of Æsculapius. In the distribution of his qualities, the genius of mythology did not even gloss over his malignant attributes. The fascination with which he intoxicated the souls of the first sinners, depriving them at once of purity and immortality, of the image of God and of the life of angels, was symbolically remembered and fatally celebrated in the orgies of Bacchus, where serpents crowned the heads of the Bacchantes, and the *poculum boni dæmonis* circulated under the auspices of the ophite hierogram, chased upon the rim. But the most remarkable remembrance of the paradisaical serpent is displayed in the position which he retains in Tartarus. A cunodracontic Cerberus guards the gates; serpents are coiled about the chariot wheels of Proserpine; serpents pave the abyss of torment; and even serpents constitute the caduceus of Mercury, the talisman which he holds when he conveys the soul to Tartarus. The image of the serpent is stamped upon every mythological fable connected with the realms of Pluto."

'To such a fearful extent is the presence and image of Satan the destroyer impressed on the wide range of idolatry! Nor is the character with which he has imbued it less dubious than the symbolism under which it is exhibited to the world. The genius of heathen idolatry is throughout diabolical.'

In a subsequent page he comes to the question of how far Satan was really at work in the heathen oracles, and how far he was permitted to communicate supernatural knowledge to mankind:—

'The important question is then suggested, What was the real character of these oracles? Were they the result of combined fraud and ingenious contrivance? Or did they in any measure emanate from, and were sustained by, Satanic influence? In the solution of this question, the learned of our own as well as of other countries are much at variance with each other. Bishop Sherlock is so confident of the Satanic character of the heathen oracles, that he does not hesitate to state that he regards those who deny that *the devil* gave out the oracles to the heathen world, as evincing a "degree of unbelief" which deprives them of all right to debate questions of this kind; while, on the other hand, Dr. Middleton pleads guilty of this degree of unbelief, and maintains that these oracles were "all mere impostures, wholly invented and supported by human craft, without any supernatural aid or interposition whatever." When such divines stand thus opposed to each other, nothing can be hoped for in respect of authority. Our only resource is, therefore, to investigate the subject for ourselves, under the guidance of such aids as its nature affords.

'It may be observed, *in limine*, that an objection has been taken to supernatural interposition in respect of oracles, which appears to be most unsound and unreasonable. It has been asserted that numerous proofs exist of fraud, deceit, and corruption, in the agency by which they were administered: and hence it is argued, that they could not have emanated from diabolical influence. It is difficult to conceive of a more inconsequential conclusion. If it had been alleged that these oracles were the result of divine prescience, then the proof of positive guile and wickedness in the agents might be held sufficient to disprove the claim. But surely there is no such obvious antagonism between Satanic influence, and fraud, guile, and wickedness, that the presence of the one must necessarily prove the absence of the other. On the other hand, I am free to confess, that this asserted guile and fraud, instead of disproving the presence of Satanic influence, rather inclines me to infer the operation of such agency.'

Mr. Smith next comes to historical examples confirmatory of his statements. He adduces the following from Scripture :—

'Passing by other and more doubtful cases, I call attention here to a clear and indubitable instance of the communication of superhuman knowledge by diabolical agency. The case I refer to has been noticed for another purpose in a note; it is that of the Pythoness of Philippi. We have here (Acts xvi. 16–19) an unquestionable proof of such a communication of superhuman knowledge. It may be first observed, that the term used by the sacred writer to describe this woman's occupation, μαντεύομαι, and which our translators have rendered "soothsaying," signifies "to *foretell, divine, prophesy,* DELIVER AN ORACLE." It is precisely the same word which is used by Herodotus when referring to the divination of the Scythians, and which is also employed by him when speaking of the famous oracle at Delphi. The case is therefore strictly in point.

'In this instance, then, it is clear that an evil spirit gave to the woman the power of making superhuman, or *oracular* communications. The presence and power of this spirit were absolutely necessary to the production of these results: for when the demon was expelled, her masters "saw that the hope of their gains was gone," and their chagrin and rage led to a fierce persecution. It is vain to urge that this was a mere mercenary affair, and that it is not to be supposed that Satanic influence would be permitted in such a case. The Holy Ghost has declared it to be a fact. Whatever fraud or wickedness might have been employed in connection with this business, it is therefore an acknowledged truth by every believer in revelation, that oracular answers communicating superhuman knowledge were in this case given by diabolical agency.'

He then treats specially of the heathen oracles, taking up the question as to possibility of fraud and imposture :—

'It is important to consider the fact, that these oracles were sustained in high credit, and trusted with implicit confidence, by the wisest statesmen and sovereigns of the nations of antiquity most celebrated for their high state of civilisation. Not only did this continue under particular circumstances, and for a season or an age, but it lasted throughout successive centuries. This is an argument which all candid minds have felt. Hence the learned Banier asks, "Is it then credible, that if the oracles had been nothing but the offspring of priest-craft, whatever artful methods they may be thought to have used, and however successful in pumping out the secrets and schemes of those who came to consult them ; is it credible, I say, that those oracles would have lasted so long, and supported themselves with so much splendour and reputation, had they been merely owing to the forgery of the priests? Imposture betrays itself, falsehood never holds out. Besides, there were too many witnesses, too many curious spies, too many people whose interest it was not to be deluded. One may put a cheat for a time upon a few private persons, who are overrun with credulity, but by no means upon whole nations for several ages. Some princes who had been played upon by ambiguous responses,—a trick once discovered,—the bare curiosity of a freethinker,—any of these, in short, was sufficient to blow up the whole mystery, and at once to make the credit of the oracles fall to the ground. How many people, deluded by hateful responses, were concerned to examine, if it was really the priests by whom they were seduced! But why? Was it so hard a matter to find one of the priests themselves, capable of being bribed to betray the cause of his accomplices, by the fair promises and more substantial gifts of those who omitted no means of being thoroughly informed in a subject of such concern?"

'Lemprière echoes the same argument, and says, "Imposture and forgery cannot long flourish, and falsehood becomes its own destroyer." Yet it is an undeniable fact that, "during the best period of their history, the Greeks, generally speaking, had undoubtedly a sincere faith in the oracle, its counsels and directions." Hence Lucan, who wrote his *Pharsalia* scarcely thirty years after our Lord's crucifixion, laments, as one of the greatest evils of the age, that the Delphic oracle was become silent. From the general credit which the oracles maintained in an enlightened age, and during a very lengthened period, it is extremely improbable that they should have been nothing more than the base results of fraud and fiction.'

The following instance from heathen history is given as illustrative of the author's statements :—

'I refer to the case of Crœsus, king of Lydia, and the Pythian oracle. Herodotus informs us that this sovereign, alarmed at the growing power of Cyrus, king of Persia, and meditating an attack on his dominions, was anxious first to consult the most celebrated oracles as to the issue of such an important enterprise, before he committed himself to it. Prior, however, to his submitting to the oracle the important question upon which his fate depended, he was determined to propound one which should enable him, as he thought, to test the prescience of the oracle. He accordingly sent messengers to Delphi; and having carefully considered the period required for the journey, and allowed them ample time, he commanded them at the appointed hour to present themselves before the Pythoness, and propose this question : "What is Crœsus, son of Alyattes, now doing?" They were to write the answer carefully down, and send it to him. The answer was to this effect :—

> "I count the sand, I measure out the sea ;
> The silent and the dumb are heard by me.
> E'en now the odours to my sense that rise,
> A tortoise boiling with a lamb supplies,
> Where brass below and brass above it lies."

'The fact was, that Crœsus, determined to be occupied in the most unlikely and unkingly manner, was engaged at that time in boiling the flesh of a tortoise and a lamb together in a covered vessel of brass.'

The following conclusions are then deduced from the preceding statements. They are worth pondering :—

'First, then, it cannot be denied that the first answer, which referred to the strange occupation of Crœsus at the time, exhibits remarkable accuracy. We may think ourselves very wise in dismissing such a case with the cry of "jugglery and cheating;" but it is doubtful whether by such conduct we do not evince great folly. The king of Lydia was a man of great energy and intellectual power: he was therefore competent to judge of the chances of imposition, and to guard against them, much better than we can now imagine. Yet he, by the presentation of gifts to the value of nearly one million sterling, gave ample proof that he regarded the whole as a *bonâ fide* transaction. Is it not, then, reasonable to ask, "By what means could the Pythoness have given such a reply? By what means could the priestess at Delphi have ascertained what the king of Lydia was doing at a given hour, in his palace at Sardis, hundreds of miles away, when he had determined to exercise his utmost care and ingenuity in order to test her ability?" Neither captious querulousness nor unmeaning sneering will meet the case. Here is an undoubted historical incident, which, I am bold to say, admits of no satisfactory solution, except on the principle of diabolical agency. But on this principle all is plain: the difficulty, otherwise insurmountable, immediately vanishes.

'But then it is asked in the most triumphant tone, "Why were not all the responses given in language equally distinct and intelligible? Why the double meaning and equivocation of the other replies?" It is truly astonishing to see the confidence with which this objection is urged, when it is open to a very simple and rational solution. It is easy to conceive that diabolical agency might enable the Pythoness to give a clear and distinct answer as to what was transpiring at the moment in a distant place, which to all merely human intelligence would have been wholly inscrutable. But it is far from certain that this agency could unravel the mystery of future contingent events. This is the exclusive attribute of Jehovah: He challenges this power to Himself alone: "I am God, and there is none else; I am God, and there is none like me, declaring the end from the beginning" (Isa. xlvi. 9, 10); whilst to the idols and their worshippers He says, "Produce your cause, saith the Lord; bring forth your strong reasons, saith the King of Jacob. Let them bring them forth, and show us what shall happen: let them show the former things what they be, that we may consider them, and know the latter end of them; or declare us things for to come. Show the things that are to come hereafter, that we may know that ye are gods" (Isa. xli. 21-23). Diabolical aid, therefore, although it might give superhuman knowledge in respect of passing events, and afford a means of conjecture beyond all human wisdom as to the future, could not communicate the power of foretelling future contingencies. Obscure, conjectural, and enigmatical expressions, in the communication of oracles, would consequently be as necessary under this agency as without it.

'The result of our inquiry then is,—

'1. That we find the heathen oracles maintaining a high character and general confidence, to an extent, and for a period, beyond that which would be likely to result from continued and unaided human fraud and falsehood.

'2. The accredited declarations of these oracles exhibit a measure of knowledge respecting passing events, and a sagacity in respect of futurity, far above all that merely human ingenuity or contrivance could produce.

'3. Yet all this is found in such combined operation with wickedness, fraud, and corruption, as clearly to prove that if superhuman knowledge was connected with the oracles, it must have been diabolical.

'It is a certain fact, based on the authority of New Testament revelation, that diabolical agency was used in ancient times, for the purpose of giving forth superhuman oracular responses.

'From all these premises we conclude that the sagacity and general credit of heathen oracles was in some instances owing to diabolical agency.'

The whole subject of the personality and agency of Satan demands our most solemn study. It has been far too much overlooked,—in many cases evaded and denied. The Church's prospects in these last days call on her to weigh the matter. There is far more in it that concerns her than she seems aware of. Individually, we have a *superhuman* adversary to face; and so, collectively, has the Church. Let us know what God has revealed concerning his craft and power, that we may know with what weapons to contend, and in what strength we are to overcome.

The tendency of the age is to ignore the supernatural. The wisdom of this world rejects the idea of another race of beings, either good or evil, by which things are done for man and man's world, which man could not have done for himself or by his own power. This desire to throw out of the circle of agency all beings save man himself, and all laws save those of nature, is very startling. To centralize all action in himself, and all power of action in the visible and tangible instrumentalities which science has revealed,—this is man's aim. Thus God is shut out as a direct power, and all invisible beings are set aside as agents. Of these, and such as these, man refuses to know anything. In his wisdom, he is fast becoming either an atheist or a Sadducee, or both. Most imperative, then, is the duty, most urgent the necessity, for giving emphatic prominence to the revelations of Scripture concerning the beings and agencies belonging to that outer circle, which, surrounding man on every side and touching him at every point, do operate most influentially, though unseen and unheard, upon his physical constitution and his spiritual life. The Bible recognises, with awful explicitness, him who is 'the prince of the power of the air;' and it does indicate most sadly the self-sufficiency, the vain philosophy, the hardihood, the flippant Sadduceeism of the age, to scorn, or even to overlook, the revelations which God has made regarding the personality and the actings of a being whose malignant enmity against the Church is only equalled by his mysterious power; and whose strange proximity and presence in the midst of us render him the most successful of seducers, no less than the most dangerous of foes.[1]

[1] Is it in allusion to Satan, as 'Prince of the power of the air,' that Shakespeare writes?—

'Some airy devil hovers in the sky,
And pours down mischief.'—*King John.*

The annals of our world are the records of sin and its manifold developments. Our earth is not, in its spiritual aspects, like the sun, all over luminous, with a few dark spots, but rather a body all over dark, with a few broken streaks of light here and there.

But in this dark story there is a twofoldness, a duality throughout, which strikes us with a strange awe. It is not *two sins* or *two sinners* that are presented to us, but two kinds of sin and two kinds of sinners; one visible, the other invisible; one human, the other superhuman; the two acting mysteriously together, yet without open compact; the invisible and the superhuman operating upon the visible and the human, and both together working against God.

It would seem to be God's purpose to bring out the whole evil of sin in these two ways, and to develope it from these two centres,—to unroll the dark web of evil from these two instrumentalities, thereby indicating to us that without such a duality and such a combination or alliance, the whole frailty and corruptibility of creaturehood could not be brought out. For God's purpose during the present dispensation evidently is to evolve and exhibit, once for all, creature-impotency for good, creature-potency for evil. He takes the two orders of intelligent creaturehood, first successively and then conjunctly, and places them in circumstances in which all the goodness and power and stability that are in them may be allowed full scope for development; and in which, on the other hand, also all the evil and feebleness and instability may be brought out.

The angels are created and placed in a condition the likeliest of all to draw out and to maintain all the good that was in them, and that their finite nature could contain. They kept not their first estate, but left their own habitation, and that which should have been a manifestation of goodness became an unfolding of evil; not simply of non-goodness, but of positive evil, transgression, rebellion, hatred of God.

Man was next created and set here in a holy paradise, in circumstances best fitted to evolve and to mature all the excellences which had been deposited in his finite nature, with the fewest possible temptations, and the greatest amount of strength which his being was capable of. He let go his hold of God and His love, falling from his perfection, and bringing forth evil—only evil, from that hour to this;—evil which has deluged earth with crimes and horrors for six thousand years, and is to fill hell for eternity with weeping and wailing and woe.

But these two forms of creaturehood (and we know no *third*) successively and singly could not exhibit all the exceeding sinfulness of sin, and the power of the creature for evil. They must be brought together and permitted to work in combination. And it is this confederacy of evil, and revolt, and lawlessness, and enmity to the Creator, that has been exhibiting itself on earth during the whole period of its dark history. Not single evil, but double; not the evil of one sinner, but of millions; not the evil of millions merely, but the evil of two classes of sinners in alliance; each of these composed of millions; each bringing out the peculiar evil proper to his class and kind; yet also the still worse evil produced by their combination. This, all this, has been exhibited in the world's past history, and is to be exhibited yet more terribly in the closing scenes of its career of wickedness, when the alliance of the two classes will yet be closer and more intimate, and the fruits of that alliance, the darkest form or forms of evil that creaturehood has yet exhibited, or the world ever seen.

At the head of what I may call invisible or immaterial creaturehood is *Satan*, and behind him a host of fallen spirits, all of them ministers of evil. Scripture speaks of them as 'Satan and his angels.' It is chiefly, however, of Satan himself that we have now to speak. And first of all let us read his names as they are written in the word of God.

1. *Satan* (Job i. 6; 1 Chron. xxi. 1; Zech. iii. 1; Matt. iv. 10, xii. 26). This means the Adversary. It is a name no doubt given by God; for who could name him rightly but God. It is as the adversary of man and God that he first appears.

2. *The Devil* (Matt. iv. 1, xxv. 41; Jude 9). The Greek word signifies accuser, and it is as such that he acts out his character.

3. *Abaddon* (Rev. ix. 11). The Destroyer. In the Hebrew

it is Abaddon; in the Greek Apollyon, but having the same meaning. He is the destroyer, the slaughterer of the race, the persecutor of the Church.

4. *The Old Serpent* (2 Cor. xi. 3; Rev. xii. 9, xx. 2). That he is signified by the old serpent, is evident from the words of the last two passages, 'that old serpent, which is the devil and Satan.' And this name connects him with the first temptation of man in paradise.

5. *The Dragon* (Rev. xii. 7, xx. 2). This was some monstrous, mystic animal of the serpent kind, supposed by the ancients to be endued with destructive power. Thus the serpent and the dragon are distinguished; the former the emblem of cunning, the latter of power.

6. *Belial* (2 Cor. vi. 15). This means worthlessness and malignity, but it came to be used as a name of Satan, as in the above passage, from his being the personification of all evil.

7. *Beelzebub* (Matt. xii. 24). The name of a heathen god, but applied by the Jews to Satan, and recognised by our Lord as one of his names, when He asks, How can Satan cast out Satan?

8. *The god of this world* (2 Cor. iv. 4). He whom this present world (age) worships and obeys; believing his temptation and his promise, 'All these things will I give Thee if Thou wilt fall down and worship me.'

9. *Ruler of the darkness of this world* (Eph. vi. 12). He who inhabits the darkness; who produces the darkness; who sits as king over it; ruling it for his own ends, in opposition to Him who is the light of the world.

10. *Prince of the power of the air* (Eph. ii. 2). He is the dweller in high places, and as such he is the prince who has authority in the air, and who, from that seat of authority, works upon the inhabitants of earth.

11. *The prince of this world* (John xiv. 30). He who rules over this world (κόσμος), and is acknowledged by it as prince, in opposition to Him who is Prince of the kings of the earth, King of kings.

In addition to these great outstanding names, he is designated 'the wicked one' (Matt. xiii. 38); a 'murderer' (John

viii. 44); a 'liar,' the 'father of lies;' a persecutor, for it is written, 'The devil shall cast some of you into prison' (Rev. ii. 10); a tempter; a deceiver; an accuser; the inflicter of disease (Job ii. 7; Luke iv. 6); he who has the power of death (Heb. ii. 14). We read, too, of the seat or throne of Satan; the 'synagogue of Satan;' the dwelling of Satan; the 'depths of Satan' (Rev. ii. 24); the 'wiles of the devil' (Eph. vi. 11); the 'snare of the devil' (2 Tim. ii. 26); 'the works of the devil' (1 John iii. 8).[1]

These various names and designations show the following things:—

1. *His personality.* He is no mere ideal of sin, nor principle of evil, nor figure of human wickedness; as when we sometimes, for effect in writing or speaking, personify sin, or lust, or pride. He is thoroughly real and personal; as much so as we are. Men may scoff at him, and take their jest out of his doings, or point their oaths with his name, or mock at his hell, but he is real in spite of all their mockery.

2. *His malignity against God, and Christ, and the saints.* He hates these utterly, and takes revenge upon them. He bruises the woman's seed in the heel, and he is doing the same to all the saints. For cruelty he has no equal.

3. *His cunning.* He is the serpent, the liar, the tempter, the deceiver; and as such, with his angels, he is doing his daily work amongst the sons of men. He is the master of all spells and wiles. There are no snares like his for subtlety and success.

How fearful is the battle of the Church; with such power, such malignity, such cunning, arrayed against her! What strength, what wisdom, what watchfulness do we need!—strength, wisdom, watchfulness, beyond what we ourselves

[1] The word devil occurs thirty-eight times in the New Testament. In all these cases, with three exceptions, it is synonymous with Satan. The three exceptions are striking: 2 Tim. iii. 3, 'Men shall be truce-breakers, *false accusers* (devils), incontinent;' Tit. ii. 3, 'The aged women, that they be not *false accusers*' (devils); 1 Tim. iii. 11, 'Their wives be grave, not *slanderers*' (devils).

possess. For we are but human, he superhuman; and how can feeble, fallen humanity do battle with the superhuman, the invisible; with angelic power and wisdom; save by the possession of that which is beyond the human and the superhuman,—beyond the angelic and the created,—the uncreated and the divine? 'Be strong in the Lord, and in the power of His might.' 'Be filled with the Spirit.'

But let us proceed now more directly to his history.

What he was originally, where his first habitation was, when and how he fell, we do not know. All that is revealed concerning these points is contained in the following passages:—'He abode not in the truth' (John viii. 44), implying that he once stood in the truth (vers. 32 and 36); 'the angels which kept not their first estate (or principality, lordship, ἀρχή), but left their own (proper or original) habitation' (Jude 6); 'God spared not the angels that sinned' (2 Pet. ii. 4), or when they sinned, though what their sin was is not said. These passages refer (1) to an originally perfect state, both for Satan and these angels; (2) to a time when they fell; (3) to their fall as being from a rejection of 'the truth;' (4) to their loss of dignity and power—*i.e.* of that which constituted them the principalities and powers in heavenly places; (5) to their being cast down to hell (literally, Tartarus), in chains and darkness.

It has been supposed by some that there are two classes of fallen angels; the one headed by Satan, roaming widely over the earth and peopling the air; the other bound in chains, in the darkness of Tartarus. But though there is nothing positively adverse to this opinion in Scripture, it does not seem borne out by the passages cited in support of it. They may be chained, or restrained, in comparison with the former liberty of their unfallen estate, and yet go to and fro on the earth; or the words may mean not reserved *in* (present) chains, but for future chains,—the chains or chain spoken of in the 20th of Revelation; and the darkness referred to may be the future darkness of the bottomless pit, or it may be that alluded to by the apostle when he speaks of 'the ruler of the darkness of this world.' We do not take up the question of there being two classes; but certainly, as to the opinion that one of these sections is referred to in the 6th of Genesis as 'the sons of God,' we may say this, that while on the one hand it is quite *unproved*, on the other it is connected with very great improbabilities.

In connection with Satan's early history we read the story of the temptation in paradise. We ask naturally, How came Satan to be there at all? and how came he to be there at the very time that man was created? We should not wonder at a good angel being there, sent on some errand of goodness to the new-created dweller; but Satan's presence is not so easily accounted for. We ask, with musing wonder, Was this Satan's world once? Was he its guardian angel or its sovereign? And do we find him, like Marius, sitting among the ruins of his former palace, or, like a beast of prey, prowling round the habitation of its new possessor? Is it because of his original connection with our earth that he is still prince of the power of the air; disenthroned, dispossessed, yet still allowed to work and plot here against God, against His Christ,—the second Adam,—against His Church, and to ally himself with man for carrying out his purposes of evil? Is it to him that reference is made in that marvellous and mysterious prediction of Ezekiel concerning Tyre, and 'the prince of Tyre,' 'the king of Tyre'? for certainly the personage here spoken of seems more than mortal; looks like a spirit or fallen angel, of which Tyre was the incarnation and habitation. The allusions in that passage to 'wisdom' indicates that he who is spoken of is the genius, or spirit, or possessor of all earthly wisdom; he who tempted man with the bait of proffered wisdom, with the hope of being wise as God; he who took possession of the serpent as the wisest or most subtle of creatures. 'Say unto the prince of Tyrus, Thou art wiser than Daniel: . . . With thy wisdom thou hast gotten thee riches. . . . Thou hast set thine heart as the heart of God. . . . Thou sealest up the sum, full of wisdom, and perfect in beauty. Thou hast been in Eden, the garden of God; every precious stone was thy covering: the sardius, topaz, and the diamond, the beryl, the onyx, and the jasper, the sapphire, the emerald, the carbuncle, and gold. . . . Thou art the anointed cherub that covereth; and I have set thee so: thou wast upon the holy mountain of God; thou hast walked up and down in the midst of the stones of fire. Thou wast perfect in thy ways from the day that thou wast created, till iniquity was found in thee' (Ezek. xxviii., where the visible Tyre and some invisible being are mixed up together).

But whatever may be the cause of Satan's presence in paradise, or the link of his connection with Eden, we find him there at man's creation. He is there to plot against man. To act upon man, he requires to take possession of some fleshly being whose organs he can use in addressing man. He enters into the serpent as the wisest and most subtle of all the beasts of the field; and through him he commences his terrible work, as the murderer, the liar, the deceiver, the slanderer. He baits the hook of hell with 'wisdom,' and he succeeds. Ye shall be as 'God,' he says to man, and man believes him. He had begun by shaking his confidence in the goodness and truthfulness of God; and having succeeded in this, the rest followed inevitably. The promise of knowledge,—knowledge like God's,—was irresistible. For what will not man give for knowledge? Power, empire, fame, military glory, pomp, gold, lust, the beauty and love of woman, —all these have been the objects which man has coveted, and for which he has flung away the favour of God. But, beyond all these, *knowledge* has been his ambition—the ambition of his ambitions! What has he not given, what has he not ventured, what has he not flung away, in order to win knowledge? What mountain has he not climbed; into what cavern has he not penetrated; to the bottom of what sea has he not dived, in order to win knowledge? Through toil, through danger, through sin, and braving hell itself, he has pursued it. And it is the knowledge of *evil* as well as *good* on which he has set his heart. The range and region of evil is to him strangely attractive, partly because it is so various and boundless, and partly because it is forbidden. To know beyond what man knows, or ought to know; what God knows; and, in pursuit of this, to beat down the barriers of goodness, or law, or benevolence, this has been his aim. To stand upon the highest pinnacle of earth, and gaze around on the boundlessness of the universe, this has been his ambition. The poison of the tree of knowledge is still in his veins, impelling him restlessly onward in the pursuit of knowledge, knowledge without God.

> 'The wish to know, that endless thirst,
> Which even by quenching is awaked,
> And which becomes or blest or cursed
> As is the fount whereat 'tis slaked,
> Still urged me onward, with desire
> Insatiate to explore, inquire
> Whate'er the wondrous things might be
> That waked each new idolatry—
> Their cause, aim, source, from whence they sprung,
> Their inmost powers, as though for me
> Existence on that knowledge hung.'

Of this knowledge Satan is the prince, the high priest, the archangel. As such he makes his first appearance to man,—his friend, his counsellor,—an angel of light, offering to lead him into light and freedom, and taking a profound and affectionate interest in his welfare. But as Judas betrayed the second Adam, so he the first, with a kiss. He is permitted to succeed; man becomes his victim; there is a holiday in hell at creation's ruin.

The next glimpse we have of Satan's history is when we see him standing, along with the man and woman, to receive his sentence. He is silent now. His flatteries have ceased. His lies have been laid bare. 'The Lord God said unto the serpent, Because thou hast done this, thou art cursed above all cattle,' etc.; 'and I will put enmity between thee and the woman, and between thy seed and her seed; it shall bruise thy head, and thou shalt bruise his heel.' This is his condemnation; a forewarning of the eternal curse, and of 'the fire prepared for the devil and his angels.' It is the divine intimation to heaven and earth, to angel and devil, as well as to man himself, that God has interposed between man and man's enemy, that Satan has only succeeded in part, and that his success will be his final ruin. It is the good news to man of God's free love; the good news of a coming deliverer, of one who is to bruise Satan under His feet, who is to cast out the prince of this world.

The third glimpse we have of Satan is in the history of Job, in the age of the patriarchs. Doubtless he was working in the world before this. It was he who, as the murderer, drew on Cain to murder. It was he who led on the old world in their sin, and lust, and vanity, and defiance of God, swelling the flood of evil till the flood of waters swept them away. But, in the beginning of the book of Job, God has given us a fuller insight into the doings of Satan than we had before. He is seen there, as permitted, in some mysterious way, to appear before God. He is seen as going to and fro in the earth, watching the saints, inflicting disease, and, if permitted, death; but all under restraint of God, and simply as one allowed by God, for a purpose and a season, to do on earth a little of the work of hell, specially against the Church of God.

For ages after this we hear nothing of him till, in the reign of David, we suddenly meet with him as the tempter. Indeed, it is only thus in glimpses that we see anything of him in the Bible. He unexpectedly appears at some particular juncture, then disappears for ages; then reappears, brandishing the sword or spreading the snare of hell, and showing himself as the murderer, the liar, the deceiver, the tempter; then vanishes from our sight for a season to carry on his work in secret. We read (1 Chron. xxi. 1), 'And Satan stood up against Israel, and provoked David to number Israel.' It was in God's anger that he was permitted to do so (2 Sam. xxiv. 1), yet none the less was it truly Satan's work; his work as the murderer, his work as the enemy of Israel and of the Church.

Again he appears before us in the remarkable scene, similar to that in Job, given us by Micaiah in the history of Ahab (2 Chron. xviii. 18–22). Jehovah is seen on His throne, and His hosts are all around Him; and the question is put, Who shall entice Ahab king of Israel, that he may go up and fall at Ramoth-Gilead? One speaks, and another, till at length one steps forward with the proposal, I will entice him. I will be a lying spirit in the mouth of all his prophets. And who can this be but Satan?—he, the liar and the murderer from the beginning. Thus he rises up again, and then disappears for a season.

Again, in the remarkable scene depicted by Zechariah, he reappears. Joshua the high priest stands before the angel of the Lord, and Satan stands at his right hand to resist him (Zech. iii. 1). Here it is Satan contending against a saint to tempt or oppose; but elsewhere it is against the traitor to destroy. Ps. cix. 6, 'Let Satan stand at his right hand.'

Perhaps the most mysterious glimpse into Satan's position and operations is that in the book of Daniel. A corner of the veil that hides the world of the invisible is drawn aside, and we see him and his angels, or 'princes,' at work, in connection with the *kingdoms* of the earth. In the passage already quoted from Ezekiel, we have seen some ground for thinking that it is Satan, or one of his 'powers,' that is referred to as the prince of Tyre. Daniel, in the following passage, uses the same word prince in connection with Persia and Greece:—'The *prince* of the kingdom of Persia withstood me one and twenty days: but, lo, Michael, one of the chief princes, came to help me; and I remained there with the kings of Persia. . . . Knowest thou wherefore I come unto thee? and now will I return to fight with the prince of Persia: and when I am gone forth, lo, the prince of Grecia shall come. But I will show thee that which is noted in the Scripture of truth; and there is none that holdeth with me in these things, but Michael your prince. . . . At that time shall Michael stand up, the great prince which standeth for the children of Thy people' (Dan. x. 13–20, xii. 1). From which passages we learn that Michael the archangel was the guardian angel of Judea and of the Jews;[1] and that another, called the prince of Persia, is the guardian or presiding angel of that country; and that another, called the prince of Greece, is the presiding angel of that kingdom. These two latter, being opposed to and fighting with Michael,

[1] That Michael is not Christ (as some say) is evident from 1 Thess. iv. 16.

must be *evil* angels, some of the principalities and powers, the rulers of the darkness of this world. This is a solemn subject, of which little is revealed, and therefore I speak cautiously and reverently; but it would appear that not only are there good angels as ministering spirits for individual heirs of salvation, but some also, such as Michael, set over kingdoms; and who knows but that now, since his ministry in Judea has ceased for a season, it may have been transferred to Britain? It would appear also, that as there are evil spirits which possess individuals, so are there some of these (the greater and higher) which preside over, nay, *possess* kingdoms. And are not the four great empires of earth depicted by Daniel specially so ruled and inspired, so 'possessed;' the reins of empire in them held by invisible hands; the power, the genius, the literature, the art, the commerce of these nations wielded by infernal energies; the laws, the morals, the religion inspired by the agents of him who was a murderer, a liar, a deceiver from the beginning, and who boasted even to the Prince of the kings of the earth Himself, that he was lord of earth's kingdoms? And may we not truly speak of the devil-possessed empires of Babylon, and Persia, and Greece, and Rome? And need we wonder at their idolatries, and blasphemies, and persecutions; hatred of the light, and resistance to the cross? Need we read with incredulity the terrific picture which, in the 1st chapter of Romans, the apostle draws of heathendom,—its true name is Satan-dom,—when we learn that the inspiration which guides it is from beneath; and that the invisible rulers and instructors of its peoples, the secret prompters and presidents of its courts and cabinets, are the princes of the blood-royal of hell?

These are the chief references to Satan in the Old Testament. The glimpses of his history and doings are brief and few; but they all bear testimony to his character as the Wicked one, the enemy of Christ and of the Church.

The notices of Satan in the New Testament are more frequent; and they grow darker and darker as the great crisis and close draw on. We meet with him, first of all, in the temptation of the Lord, where three times over he assails the Son of God, tempting Him to doubt His Father's love and His own Sonship; and three times over he is repelled by the sword of the Spirit, though with every advantage on his part, and every disadvantage on the part of this Second Adam, whom he sought to seduce in the wilderness as he had seduced the first in the garden. But what were wiles or fiery darts to One who knew so well how to wield the sword of the Spirit and the shield of Faith?

Again we meet him;—and now not alone, but with his legions;—dwelling in the bodies of men, and tormenting them with his hellish cruelty. We find him possessing some directly; we find him bowing down one with infirmity; we find him rending another; we find him with seven spirits in Mary Magdalene; we find him in the herd of swine; we find him wishing to sift Peter; we find him entering the heart of Judas. All these are proofs that the days of our Lord's ministry on earth were busy days with Satan, days of visible manifestation and more direct possession: the seed of the woman and that of the serpent being now brought face to face with each other; the armies of heaven and of hell being gathered, under their respective captains, to wage desperate battle. How frequent is the reference to Satan in the history of Christ on earth! and how striking are Christ's own words, spoken either *to* him or *concerning* him! 'Get thee hence, Satan' (Matt. iv. 10); 'If Satan cast out Satan, how shall then his kingdom stand?' (xii. 26); 'Get thee behind me, Satan' (xvi. 23); 'Then cometh Satan, and taketh away the word' (Mark iv. 15); 'I beheld Satan as lightning fall from heaven' (Luke x. 18); 'Whom Satan hath bound, lo, these eighteen years' (Luke xiii. 16); 'Simon, Simon, Satan hath desired to have thee, that he may sift thee as wheat' (Luke xxii. 31); 'The devil taketh Him up to the holy city' (Matt. iv. 5); 'The devil taketh Him up to an high mountain' (iv. 8); 'The enemy that soweth them is the devil' (xi. 39); 'Jesus rebuked the devil' (xvii. 18). From these allusions we learn how completely Satan was on the alert in the days of Christ; what large range was allowed him; and what striking opportunities he had of showing himself; what power to inflict disease; to take possession of men's bodies; to operate upon their minds; to make use of their organs of speech ; to inflame their passions ; to carry on his purposes of evil through them, and in conjunction with them; in ways which, by himself, he could not have accomplished. We may not be very decided in affirming that he was allowed access to our Lord during His last hours, and that his 'messengers' were let loose to 'buffet' Him ; but there are expressions in the psalms which seem to imply this. He surely is the roaring lion, and his legions the bulls of Bashan, of which the 22d Psalm speaks: 'Many bulls have compassed me ; strong bulls of Bashan have beset me round ; they gaped upon me with their mouths, as a ravening and a roaring lion. . . . Save me from the lion's mouth' (Ps. xxii. 12, 13, 21). If so, then it was not merely the rage of earth that surrounded His cross, but also that of hell; it was not only the shouts of the multitude that fell on His dying ear, and disturbed His dying hour ; but the voice of the roaring lion, as he sprang upon his prey, and accomplished the last piece of malignity which the restraining purpose of God permitted him,—'Thou shalt bruise his heel.'[1]

In the early Church we find Satan working. He filled the heart of Ananias to lie to the Holy Ghost; he gets power to chastise saints that are delivered by the Church to him for their sin (1 Cor. v. 5). 'Whom I have delivered unto Satan, that they may learn not to blaspheme' (1 Tim. i. 20). He tempts the saints for incontinency (1 Cor. vii. 5) ; he gets advantage over them (2 Cor. ii. 11) ; he is transformed into an angel of light (2 Cor. xi. 14) ; he sends messengers to buffet even apostles (2 Cor. xii. 7) ; he has a synagogue upon earth (Rev. ii. 9) ; he has a seat, or throne (Rev. ii. 13) ; he exercises his wiles, and shoots his fiery darts (Eph. vi. 11) ; he ensnares

[1] Perhaps it is into the life of Christ that we should fit in the scene referred to by Jude (9)—Michael contending with the devil about the body of Moses. Michael the archangel is sent to raise Moses, that he may appear with Elijah on the transfiguration hill (as it is with the voice of the archangel that the dead in Christ are to be raised at His coming). Satan, who has the power of death and the grave, disputes and contends with him. Michael overcomes with 'The Lord rebuke thee.'

and assails us (2 Tim. ii. 26; Jas. iv. 7); he casts into prison (Rev. ii. 10); he deceives the nations (Rev. xxii. 2). It is against his principalities and powers that we are to wrestle.

Such were his operations *in* and *against* the Church in apostolic times; such are his operations still. It is he who fought against the Son of God, that fights against the Church of God. Sometimes he is a persecutor and murderer; sometimes a deceiver and beguiler; sometimes a tempter into open sin; sometimes an allurer into fair-seeming vanities; sometimes a persuader into error; sometimes an angel of light; sometimes the prince of darkness;—the prince of the power of the air, the spirit that now worketh in the children of disobedience.

Our Lord speaks of Satan falling from heaven like lightning; and, in the Revelation, we have the description of the great battle between the devil and his angels and Michael and his angels. Into the details of this battle we do not enter; but there is something awfully solemn about it, and something appalling about its results; the devil being cast down to earth, and brought into closer proximity with its nations; nay, and having great wrath because he knoweth that he has but a short time.

Then comes the great event to which the Church looks forward so eagerly,—the binding of Satan, at the second coming of the Lord. For ages he had wrought his works of evil against the Church; he had inspired the false religions of earth; he had raised up at last his greatest agent and instrument, his truest representative, Antichrist; he had animated the beast and the false prophet; he had glorified himself in Babylon the great. But now, all that is over. The Mighty Angel descends with the chain, seizes, binds, casts him into the abyss or bottomless pit, for a thousand years, to deceive the nations no more till the thousand years are done.

Then the earth has rest; the old serpent is cast out; Antichrist has perished; Messiah reigns; the glory of the Lord covers the earth;—all things are made new. But earth is not done with Satan, nor Satan with earth. The thousand years roll by. Satan is loosed, and goes forth once more to deceive. He musters the nations, he brings them up as a cloud against the camp of the saints and the beloved city. But fire descends out of heaven, and devours the hosts of Satan. He himself is cast no longer into the bottomless pit, but into the more terrible place of torment, the lake of fire, where the beast and false prophet have been already a thousand years.

Thus ends the history of Satan as given in the Scripture; a history not given us for speculation or curiosity, but for warning. What watchfulness, what solemnity, what holy fear become us, with such an enemy on every side! We wrestle not against flesh and blood, but against principalities and powers, against the rulers of the darkness of this world, against spiritual wickedness in high places.

Let us mark how, in these days of ours, he works, and tempts, and rages:—

He comes as an angel of light, to mislead, yet pretending to lead; to blind, yet professing to open the eye; to obscure and bewilder, yet professing to illuminate and guide. He approaches us with fair words upon his lips: liberality, progress, culture, freedom, expansion, elevation, science, literature, benevolence,—nay, and *religion* too. He seeks to make his own out of all these; to give the world as much of these as suits his purpose, as much as will make them content without God, and without Christ, and without the Holy Ghost. Nay, he makes use of these,—even of religion itself,—to separate men from the living Jehovah. Nor is it merely images, crucifixes, pictures, statues, altars, and such like, which he substitutes for God, seducing the heart and intoxicating the senses; but the true creed, and the true theology, and the true gospel, he makes use of to gratify the intellect, soothe the conscience, while the soul remains all the while a stranger to God and His Christ. For he does not care how near a man may come to Christ, provided he is not *one* with Him and *in* Him. It matters not to him how much of truth a man possess, if he can only make that truth *a screen* to separate, not a *link* to unite him and God; a non-conductor, not a conductor of the heavenly life. He knows how to employ the dim religious light of ritualism, the cold frosty rays of rationalism, yes, and even the bright warm light of evangelical sunshine, for drawing off the eye and heart from Him who is the light of the world, the bright and morning Star.

He sets himself against God and the things of God in every way. He can deny the gospel; or he can dilute the gospel; or he can obscure the gospel; or he can neutralize the gospel; —just as suits his purpose, or the persons with whom he has to do. His object in regard to the gospel is to take out of it all that makes it glad tidings to the sinner; and oftentimes this modified or mutilated gospel, which looks so like the real, serves his end best; for it throws men off their guard, making them suppose that they have received Christ's gospel, even though they have not found in it the good news which it contains.

He rages against the true God,—sometimes openly and coarsely, at other times calmly and politely,—making men believe that he is the friend of the truth, but an enemy to its perversion. Progress, progress, progress, is his watchword now, by means of which he hopes to allure men away from the old anchorages, under the pretext of giving them wider, fuller, more genial teachings. He bids them soar above creeds, catechisms, dogmas, as the dregs of an inferior age, and a lower mental status. He distinguishes, too, between theology and religion, warmly advocating the latter in order to induce men to abandon the former. He rages against the divine accuracy of the Bible, and cunningly subverts its inspiration by elevating every true poet and philosopher to the same inspired position. So successfully has he wrought in disintegrating and undermining the truth, that there is hardly a portion of it left firm. The ground underneath us is hollow; and the crust on which we tread ready to give way, and precipitate us into the abyss of unbelief.

He rages against the Cross of Christ, yet with exceeding subtlety and persuasiveness, seeking to blind men to its true meaning and use. In his enmity against it he instigates some to cut it down, others so to bedaub it with such superstitious ornament that it is the genuine cross no longer. He assails the gospel too, mixing up grace and merit; adding to it or taking from it; persuading some that it is not free, and others that it is so free that none will be lost. He attacks propitiation and sacrifice, propagating the lie that sacrifice is merely self-denial, and that the death of Christ is a sacrifice solely because the highest example of self-abnegation ever exhibited. Thus we find him everywhere assailing truth and vitalizing error, working against the true religion, and inspiring and energizing the false. He is the very life and soul of all anti-Christian unbelief and lawlessness, raising up the many antichrists, and ripening the world for the last great Antichrist about to be revealed in the height of rebellion and pride; as if he would make good to man his promise to the first Adam, 'Ye shall be as God,' and to the second Adam, 'All these things will I give Thee if Thou wilt fall down and worship me;' for the Antichrist accepts what the Christ refused, and is crowned as Satan's king and vicegerent upon earth.

But his time approaches and his day is short. The nations shall muster on Armageddon; the kings of the earth shall combine; all shall worship the beast. But the triumphing of the wicked is short. His doom is sealed; first, in the bottomless pit, and then in the lake of fire.

And what a history! what a career! He comes to his end, and none shall help him. He passes away into captivity, and there is none to sympathize with the captive, mighty and majestic though he be in his chains.

> 'When Nero perish'd by the justest doom
> That ever the destroyer yet destroyed,
> Amid the roar of liberated Rome,
> Of nations freed and of a world o'erjoyed;
> Some hands unseen strew'd flowers upon his tomb;
> Perhaps the weakness of a heart not void
> Of feeling, for some kindness done when power
> Had left the wretch one uncorrupted hour.'

But over the downfall of this mightiest of princes,—the prince of the power of the air, the god of this world,—not a note of lamentation shall be heard. The heavens shall rejoice and the earth be glad. The saints shall sing Allelujah, as the smoke riseth up for ever and ever.

And yet there is something unspeakably solemn in his downfall. For what history has been like his, so stupendous, so triumphant, so terrible?

Nor can we deem him devoid of feeling. A being of such mighty intellect and power cannot be insensible. He is no stock nor stone. His capacities for joy and sorrow are vast; but it is only with the latter that he has aught to do. We picture him to ourselves as a being all pride, malignity, revenge, and cunning; so much so, that we forget that he was made with capacity of feeling. But the heart that is capable of these things must be capable of being *profoundly wretched.* He has not, indeed, human tears to weep. Our sorrows, our burdens, our fears, our anguish, are not his. But he has something of his own, no less bitter than ours. Ours are human, his are superhuman; for no intelligent being can be passive; he must be happy or miserable according to the capacities of his being. As truly as the unfallen angels are happy, so truly are the fallen wretched. 'The fire prepared for the devil and his angels' is something terrible beyond conception. What it amounts to I know not; but in the case of Satan it must be pre-eminent torment, unutterable woe; such as groans cannot express, and to which tears would afford no relief; and it may not be without use; it may help to solemnize us,—to reflect on the great and eternal misery of this great enemy of God and man. It is the misery of an unholy but majestic nature; the torment that springs from hellish hatred of all good. And, in addition to this, it is the misery of disappointment, failure, mortification, misfortune, remorse; the misery of reflection on 6000 years of constant, persevering malignity against God and His Christ, relieved by not one deed of goodness; yet at last his plans all ruined, his work undone; his Babels and Romes all in the dust; his Nimrods, his Sennacheribs, his Herods, his Neros, his Napoleons, his Antichrists, his false prophets, his forgers of lies, all passed away; every fragment of his laborious handiwork broken in pieces, and earth, in spite of all his efforts, a happy, holy, glorious paradise, with the seed of the woman, the last Adam, for its King. All this will be to him the bitterness of bitterness, the torment of torment.

Yet in all this misery, vast though it be, one source of anguish can never be his,—a rejected Christ. Certainly, not to have loved the most lovable of all beings must of itself be wretchedness, especially to an intellect like his, that can understand worth; but still there is no stinging remembrance of a *rejected* Saviour. This, the very woe of woes, the gall and wormwood of the eternal cup, is the portion of the lost sons of Adam, who had salvation within their reach, but madly flung it away. Terrible as is the doom of the fallen Archangel, this, at least, will form no part of his awful hell.

III.

THE SONS OF GOD.

ELSEWHERE we have given our interpretation of the passage in Genesis where the expression is found.[1] But there is room for some investigation both into the words themselves, and also into the history of the expositions which have been given of them. It may be worth our while to make a little further inquiry into this passage, as Dr. Maitland in his *Eruvin*, and Dr. Kitto in his *Daily Bible Illustrations*, have revived the patristic exposition, and affirmed that sons of God must mean angels. The latter writes diffidently, but the former abates nothing of his usual dogmatism, even in treating of a passage confessedly peculiar.[2]

Dr. Maitland asks, How could the intermarriage of the seed of Seth and the seed of Cain produce giants? We might as

[1] Gen. vi. 2.

[2] What would Dr. Maitland say to Hävernick, who denounces the 'angelic' theory as one of the silliest whims of the Alexandrian Gnostics and cabalistic Rabbins?

well ask, How could the intermarriage of angels and men produce giants? When angels have taken man's form (as to Abraham, etc.), they have not indicated any superior stature. If Dr. Maitland will tell us how the one class of marriages produces giants, we will satisfy him as to the other. Nor can we think it an unsupported affirmation in us to say, that from all that God has made known to us in His word regarding angels, good or bad, their nature, their history, their doings, etc., such intermarriages are impossible. Or, arguing physiologically, might we not say that in all the various parts of animal and vegetable nature, the intermixture of *genera* is impossible; so, *à fortiori*, the intermixture of two races who differ more from each other than genus does from species is impossible.[1]

But the intermixture of the Sethites and the Cainites was very likely to produce a race of superior bodily constitution. For these two races, continuing separate, and intermarrying themselves with very near kindred, must have greatly degenerated; and the intermixture of the two was very likely to generate a stronger race. Nor is it at all unlikely that such was the result also in after years, when Israel intermarried with the Moabites. About this time we read of giants again. And this is one of the things in which Dr. Maitland's theory halts. If intermarriage with angels was required to produce giants in the time of Noah, it must have been needed again afterwards to produce them in the time of Israel. It is not a little curious that the same word, 'Nepheelim,' is used in both cases (Num. xiii. 33), 'There we saw the Nepheelim, the sons of Anak, who come of the Nepheelim.'[2] As all the antediluvian 'Nepheelim' must have been swept off at the flood, there must have been in after ages the recurrence of the same scenes as before (intermarriages with angels). If Dr. Mait-

[1] Besides, as Hengstenberg remarks, 'the standing designation of angels as holy ones, includes in it the neither marrying nor being given in marriage' (Matt. xx. 30).

[2] The word 'Nepheelim' occurs only in these two places, Genesis and Numbers.

land's theory be tenable, Anak must have married an angel, and his sons Ahiman, Sheshai, and Talmai, who are called 'Nepheelim,' must have been semi-angels. Nay, some of Anak's ancestors must have also married angels, seeing it is not only said that the 'Nepheelim' were sons of Anak, but he himself came of the same race, being half an angel and half a man. Anak's wife must have been a *female* angel, whereas in former times the angels that came down must have been all *male*. To use the language of patristic demonology, the antediluvian angels must have been *incubi*, and the postdiluvian angels *succubi*.[1]

We are told more than once, in the 6th of Genesis, that it was *man's* sin that was so great in the earth; that it was on account of *man's* sin that the deluge came. But if the old Jewish and patristic theory, revived by Drs. Kitto and Maitland, be true, then it was not *man's* sin that wrought the evil, but the sin of angels. For it is clear that they were the guilty parties in this transaction, if they were parties at all. It is against the 'sons of God' that the accusations are manifestly pointed. It was their superior guiltiness that brought the world's criminality to its crisis.[2] If they were not men, what does the judgment that fell upon the world so specially for their sin, mean? Is earth to be punished for the sin of angels? Is man to be swept away because angels have corrupted themselves? On the other hand, how natural the whole scene, if the sons of God were the Sethites, the representatives of the patriarchal Church! They were the salt of the earth; and the moment that the salt lost its savour, corruption shot through the mass, and earth ripened for the wrath of God.

Nor can anything be more natural and likely in another way. For ages the two great sections of the race had kept

[1] Pope Innocent VIII., in a decretal against witches, gives warning to all who abuse themselves in such ways,—'dæmonibus incubis et succubis abuti.' Tostatus states the two kinds, and relates the history of Merlin, 'vatem in Anglia celebrem,' who was produced by means of a *succubus*.

[2] 'The genesis of human corruption, and its ascent to the highest point, are designed to be represented.'—HENGSTENBERG.

separate. Adam, Seth, and their posterity, retained the primeval seat of man. They still dwelt in Eden, though outside of paradise, and worshipped at the well-known altar, within sight of the flaming sword and the symbolic cherubim. Eden was to them what Canaan was to Israel. There they dwelt alone, and were not mingled with the nations. There these sons of God, headed by the patriarchs (for Seth must have lived to the days of Noah), maintained the true faith and the honoured name. But as ages went on, the population increased, and the two races, spreading out, approached each other. From the statement of Moses, it would appear that the Cainites had been specially fruitful in daughters. These, by reason of proximity of place, had at length come into contact with the sons of God. Like the Moabitish women in the case of Israel, like the 'outlandish women' in the case of Solomon, they tempted the Sethites by their beauty. The races mingled, and a new and peculiar progeny was the result. But more than this, the boundary between the seed of the woman and the seed of the serpent was now broken down, defection became general, wickedness increased, and the world was ripe for judgment.

Against all this Noah and his fellows (for he was the eighth preacher of righteousness) protested, 'condemning the world;' but in vain. They went on intermingling. They went on 'eating and drinking, *marrying and giving in marriage*, till the day that Noah entered the ark.' The seed of the woman, called here the sons of God, dwindled down into two or three; the seed of the serpent covered the whole peopled earth.

Whilst, however, it is stated that the intermarriages of the sons of God and the daughters of men produced 'Nepheelim,' it seems also implied that there were Nepheelim on the earth before, which completely upsets one of Dr. Maitland's arguments. 'The Nepheelim were in the earth in those days, and also after that,' etc. Hävernick goes further, and maintains that the Nepheelim are not said at any time to be the fruit of the intermixture. 'There is nothing in vi. 4 of a race of giants springing from this union. "In those days were the well-known Nepheelim in the earth" cannot without violence receive such a reference, specially when what follows is taken into connection—"also after that, the sons of God went in unto the daughters of men," *i.e.* at that time there were men of that kind, and they continued even till a later period.' Calvin, also, though he does not go so far, yet puts the matter thus: 'The giants had a prior origin, but afterwards those who were born of the promiscuous marriages imitated their example.' He confirms this by the expression '*and also*,' as if it were implied that not only were these Nepheelim found previously in the race of Cain, but also afterwards in that race which resulted from the mixture of the two races.

An old writer has well asked, 'What sort of creatures could the offspring of men and angels be?' Would they be men, or would they be angels? How far would they partake of the one nature, and how far of the other? And could these semi-angels semi-men produce offspring? In Genesis and Numbers it is implied that this was done, whereas we know that, according to physical laws, intermixtures of genera can go no further than the first generation. But granting that the intermixture goes on from one generation to another, what sort of race is it that is produced? And in what relation do they stand to Adam as a head? If they are either semi-angels or semi-demons, as the theory of Dr. Maitland and Dr. Kitto must concede, then they are but half-descended from Adam, and so cannot be represented by him, or partake of the corruption that flows from him. Nay, further, in what relation can these semi-angels stand in reference to salvation? Are they capable of salvation by Christ? Could they believe on Him who took not on Him the nature of angels, but who took on Him the seed of Abraham? Could they be washed in His blood, or made one with Him who is *not* bone of their bone, nor flesh of their flesh? And for what shall they be condemned? For rejecting Christ? For refusing Noah's message about the promised seed of the woman? Yet what was the seed of the woman to those who did not belong to the human race?

The Jewish rabbis were the originators of the fable. From them the Fathers took it, as they did many other Jewish traditions, preserving and decorating them, as they would the relics or bones of an old saint. These doctors find no difficulty in telling us what became of the angels themselves who thus sinned with the daughters of men, as well as what became of the children. 'After they had begotten children,' says one rabbi, 'the holy and blessed God took them to the mountain o darkness and bound them in iron chains.'[1] The children of these angels, the rabbis have, like the heathen poets, buried beneath the mountains.[2] Nay, more, some of them maintained that the sin of these angels and the sin of Eve was the same, so that, just as Sammael ensnared Eve, so did Aza and Azail the daughters of Eve in Noah's days.[3] Others of them, such as Aben Ezra, have taken the more sober view.

It might be curious, but certainly not profitable, to go over at length the expositions of the Fathers upon this passage,—both on the words 'sons of God,' and also on the word 'giants.' We had noted a good many portions as specimens; but, on second thoughts, we leave them in their folios. They are all very much of the same cast. Jerome does not tell us what he thinks; he simply says, 'Non angeli;' Ambrose contradicts himself, but leans to the angelic theory; Augustine and Chrysostom are the chief Fathers that set themselves to refute the fabulous comment, and to establish the true one. Augustine's remarks are so good, that we are inclined to give a sentence or two. 'The human race advancing and increasing, there was produced, by this freedom of will, an intermixture and confusion of both cities (Church and world, Jerusalem and Babylon), each sharing the other's sin. Which evil, again, found its origin in the female sex—not, indeed, in the same way as from the beginning; for it was not these women who, seduced then by the guile of any one, persuaded men to sin, but those who from the beginning were of depraved habits in the earthly city, were beloved by the sons of God, the citizens of another city sojourning in this world, on account of their beauty of person. Which blessing is indeed a gift of God;

[1] Schottgenii *Horæ Hebraicæ et Talmudicæ*, p. 1050.
[2] See Bush on *Genesis;* Doughtei *Analecta Sacra*, p. 9.
[3] Hackspanii *Cabbala Judaica*, p. 357.

but seeing it is given to the bad, the good ought not to reckon it a great blessing. . . . Thus the sons of God were taken with the love of the daughters of men; and as they enjoyed these wives, they declined into the habits of the earthly society, forsaking the piety which they had retained in the holy community. And thus was beauty of person, made no doubt by God, but a temporal and carnal thing, the lowest good of all, evilly loved, and God slighted,—God the eternal, the internal, the sempiternal good. . . . Of this love the order being confounded, these sons of God neglected God, and loved the daughters of men.'[1]

Bishop Patrick says: 'The plain sense is, that they who had hitherto kept themselves unmingled with the posterity of Cain, according to a solemn charge which their godly forefathers had given them, were now joined with them in marriage, and made one people with them. Which was the greater crime, if we can give any credit to what an Arabic writer saith, mentioned first by Mr. Seldon in his book *De Diis Syriis*, that the children of Seth had sworn by the blood of Abel they would never leave the mountainous country which they inhabited to go down unto the valley where the children of Cain lived. The same author (Patricides, with Elmacinus also) says that they were inveigled to break this oath by the beauty of Naamah (Gen. iv. 22), and the music of her brother Jubal. For the Cainites spent their time in feasting, music-dancing, and sports, which allured the children of Seth to come down and marry with them, whereby all manner of impurity, impiety, idolatry, rapine, and violence filled the whole earth. This Moses here takes notice of, that he might give the reason why the whole posterity of Seth, even those that sprang from that holy man Enoch, were overwhelmed with the deluge, as well as the race of Cain.'

It seems evidently to these scenes that our Lord refers when, speaking of the days of Noah, He says they were eating

[1] *De Civ. Dei*, book xv. chap. 22. Though he cites the passage as 'the angels of God,' he proceeds to show the meaning of the term, chap. 23

and drinking, marrying and giving in marriage; and just as it was the apostasy of the godly, and the intermixture between the seed of the woman and the seed of the serpent, with the accompanying violence and lasciviousness, that hastened the flood, so shall it be the defections of the last days, the incontinency and ungodliness of the last generation, that shall consummate the world's guilt, and prepare for its judgment.[1] Thus shall the salt lose its savour, corruption strike through the whole mass like leaven, and the fiery deluge sweep away another world of the ungodly; only, however, to deliver creation from the bondage of corruption into the glorious liberty of the SONS OF GOD.[2]

[1] May there not be a reference to these scenes in Rev. xiv. 4, 'These are they who were not defiled with women,' *i.e.* these are the sons of God who kept themselves undefiled with the daughters of men?

[2] The *literature* of this passage is curiously extensive, beginning with the rabbis, and coming down to Dr. Kitto. The fullest discussion of all the points connected with or suggested by the passage is in the Jesuit Pererius Valentinus, who had devoted upwards of forty of his small folio pages to the subject (vol. ii.). He omits, however, the rabbinical views; indeed, his work, learned as it is in the Fathers, gives no indication of rabbinical or oriental lore. See Dr. Well's *Critical Notes*, p. 9; Patrick's *Commentary;* the 5th Excursus of Doughteus in his *Analecta Sacra;* Pfeiffer's *Dubia Vexata Scriptura*, locus xxii.; L. Vives' Note on Augustine's *City of God*, book xv. chap. 23; Suicer's *Thesaurus* under ἄγγελος and υἱός; Suidas' *Lexicon* under 'Seth;' Lord Barrington's *Theological Works*, vol. ii. p. 462; Calvin's *Commentaries.* But the best statement on the subject is to be found in Hengstenberg on *The Pentateuch*, vol. i. p. 325. Hävernick is also good—*Introduction to the Pentateuch*, p. 111.

MURRAY AND GIBB, EDINBURGH,
PRINTERS TO HER MAJESTY'S STATIONERY OFFICE.

www.ingramcontent.com/pod-product-compliance
Lightning Source LLC
LaVergne TN
LVHW020122110826
845151LV00001B/246

* 9 7 8 1 4 2 5 5 4 1 4 2 2 *